An
Introduction
to
MODERN
JEWISH
Philosophy

SUNY Series in Jewish Philosophy
Kenneth Seeskin, Editor

AN INTRODUCTION TO

MODERN JEWISH

PHILOSOPHY

NORBERT M.
SAMUELSON

STATE UNIVERSITY OF NEW YORK PRESS

Published by
State University of New York Press, Albany

© 1989 State University of New York

For information, address State University of New York
Press, State University Plaza, Albany, N.Y., 12246

Library of Congress Cataloging-in-Publication Data

Samuelson, Norbert Max, 1936-
    An introduction to modern Jewish philosophy/Norbert M. Samuelson.
    p. cm.—(SUNY series in Jewish philosophy)
Includes bibliographies and index.
ISBN 0-88706-959-2. ISBN 0-88706-960-6 (pbk.)
1. Philosophy, Jewish—History—19th century. 2. Philosophy, Jewish
—History—20th century. 3. Judaism—History—Modern period, 1750-
4. Rosenzweig, Franz, 1886-1929. I. Title. II. Series. B 159.S25 1989
296'. 01—dc19   88-15379
                                                           CIP

To all my students at Temple University (1975-1987), in appreciation of their enthusiasm, constructive criticism, and devotion in studying earlier drafts of this text.

CONTENTS

INTRODUCTION

This text is intended for readers with minimal or no background in Judaism. It introduces them to a mature study of different kinds of thought categories of the Jewish people from the time of their expulsion from Spain in 1492 C.E. (Common Era) up to the 1980's. The text consists of summaries followed by a selected bibliography of primary and secondary sources for the summaries.

In presenting a general summary of any period of thought, authors necessarily make several selections. First, they decide that certain conceptual topics and certain thinkers are more important than others. The general criteria for such selection are based on the inherent value, the originality, and the historical importance for the subsequent development of Jewish thought, as judged by these authors. While these judgements attempt to be objective, not all scholars would agree with any particular selection. Second, the authors decide that certain interpretations of the concepts chosen to be summarized are more correct than others. Again, not all scholars would agree with any particular set of interpretations.

The general method followed in this work is to present standard scholarly interpretations except in cases where this author is convinced that they were not correct. Where the standard interpretation is presented, no arguments are given in support of it. However, where a non-standard interpretation is used, the standard view is mentioned and a brief argument is given for why this author prefers his interpretation to the usual one. Readers should note that no statement of an interpretation of thought is a statement of fact. Ultimately readers should not rely on any secondary source for their understanding of any thinker. Rather, they should make up their own minds about what an author intended to say by reading of the primary sources, but they cannot and should not dictate any student's final judgment about what those sources in fact say.

The selected bibliography contains books that support the interpretations given in this text as well as books that present alternative interpretations, The more of these boks that readers read in addition to this text, the better will be their basis to pass judgement on any interpretations of modern Jewish thought. However, readers also should note that this bibliography is not intended to be complete in any way. This author assumes that the readers are not likely to be able to handle anything but English texts on their own. Generally only English translations of primary sources in foreign languages are mentioned. Original texts in foreign languages are listed only if no reasonably reliable translation is available. Rarely is a secondary source mentioned in a language other than English.

The text is divided into thirteen chapters which in turn are classified under three section heads. In general, each chapter is intended to be a basic reading assignment for one class session in a standard semester undergraduate college course. Depending on the available time, a session could be spent on any subsection of a chapter. For example, three sessions could be given to chapter 8 (Mendelssohn and Modern Jewish Thought), or four to chapter 9 (Hermann Cohen). Chapter 11 (Franz Rosenzweig) is the longest and most difficult chapter. It is designed to require a minimum of three sessions.

The first main section provides a general historical overview for the Jewish thought that follows. The second section summarizes the variety of basic kinds of popular positive Jewish commitment existent in the twentieth century. The Jewish movements covered in this section are not technically the best Jewish thought, but they are the most widely believed and the most influential expressions of contemporary Judaism. The third section summarizes the basic thought of those modern Jewish philosophers whose thought is technically the best and/or the most influential in Jewish intellectual circles.

Past experience has shown me that students without any background in Judaism desire guidance to know what to emphasize. To meet that request I conclude each chapter with a list of key names, terms, and questions, Because this text merely summarizes at the most general level the history behind and the thought of only the most important modern Jewish philosophers, I am inclined to want the students to know everything. However, since I expect them to prepare one chapter for every class session and I realize that there are limits on how much even the best students can absorb in a short period of time, I have restricted each list to a maximum of twenty entries.

Part I

Historical Background

MIGRATIONS FROM SPAIN AND THE POPULARIZATION OF KABBALAH

PRE-SEVENTEENTH CENTURY JEWISH MYSTICISM

1492 C.E. was a monumental year in Spanish and Jewish history. Christopher Columbus landed in the West Indies and claimed the "New World" for Spain. Christian forces had conquered the kingdom of Granada, the last vestige of Muslim power in Spain, at the beginning of the year, and Ferdinand of Aragon together with Isabella of Castile expelled the Jews from the now-united Roman Catholic kingdom. Five years later, Emanuel I also expelled the Jews from Portugal. From this major settlement of Jewish life and culture west of the Pyrenees, some Jews migrated westward to the New World, but most Jews reestablished their communities to the East.

In the sixteenth century, centers of Jewish life arose in Holland. In the seventeenth century, Dutch Jews prevailed upon Oliver Cromwell to readmit their people into England. However, the major migration of Spanish Jews in the sixteenth century in Christian Europe was back to the Germanic lands and further eastward into a territory that later would become known as the "Pale of Settlement," encompassing eastern territories in nineteenth-century Prussia, Austria, Poland and western territories in Russia. Furthermore, in the sixteen century many Jews moved from Spain to Italy and from Italy into the Turkish Empire. Jewish communities were established there in the Turkish-Ottoman controlled Egypt and Palestine. The most notable settlement for the growth of Jewish religious thought was the city of Safed in Palestine.

Those Jews who settled communities in Italy, Greece, Turkey, Palestine, Egypt and other places bordering the Mediterranean Sea became known as Sephardic Jews, the Hebrew term *Sephardi* meaning Spanish. Those Jews who settled throughout Central and Eastern Europe further to the North became known as Ashkenazic Jews, the Hebrew term *Ashkenazi* meaning German. Sephardic and Ashkenazic Jewish communities became quite distinct and developed significantly different Jewish cultural-religious patterns. Still it should be noted that their common heritage through the fifteenth century and their continued commitment to rabbinic Judaism, at least until the middle of the nineteenth century, formed a bond far stronger than their differences. Furthermore, there was considerable travel between Sephardic and Ashkenazic communities, and cultural-religious ties between the two Jewish sub-civilizations remained close. Similarly, while Ashkenazic communities in Central Europe differed from those in Eastern Europe,—particularly during the past one hundred years—economic, cultural, and religious ties between these regions remained close.

The birth of the sixteenth century also marked the end of the six-hundred-year tradition of Muslim-influenced Jewish philosophy. However, while Jewish philosophy lay relatively dormant for the next three hundred and fifty years, Jews did not cease to involve themselves in new forms of creative thought about religious questions. The forms by which Jews sought to understand God and God's relationship to the Jewish people ceased to be philosophic, but the seeking itself continued. For the next three hundred years the primary form through which this quest was pursued was the tradition of *Kabbalah* or Jewish mysticism. In fact, this tradition is contiguous with and almost as old as the tradition of rabbinic Judaism itself. Furthermore, many of the medieval Jewish philosophers taught an approach to life which, if not itself necessarily kabbalistic, at least provided a thought framework consistent with 'mystical' communal and individual life styles.

The major influences that tended towards a mystical interpretation of Judaism were neo-Platonism* and Sufism.** However, according to one interpretation of Maimonides' *Guide of the Perplexed,* the "secrets (SODOT) of the Torah" that he sought to communicate to those prepared to receive them were kabbalistic. Whether or not this is a correct interpretation of Maimonides' intentions, such as interpretation is consistent with much that Maimonides presented in the *Guide.* This interpretation testifies to the fact that medieval Jewish philosophy in general and Maimonides' religious thought in particular need not be inconsistent with a commitment to *Kabbalah.* In fact, Maimonides' son became a kabbalist, and the subsequent generations of Jewish mystics in Christian Europe and the Ottoman Empire treated the *Guide* as an important theoretical text in Jewish mysticism.

What is meant in this context by 'mysticism' can be explained in the following way. Normative rabbinic Judaism claimed that by accepting and following rabbinic tradition, the individual Jew would come to know the true views of God; and he would be related to God by doing what God wanted. With respect to knowledge, the best of this or any other normative Western religious tradition could offer was that by accepting the theoretical teachings of the tradition, the 'believer' would have true views. But these true beliefs could not be called knowledge. In the Greek and medieval senses of the terms, the normative believer could claim 'true opinion' but he could not be said to 'know' what he correctly affirmed. Simply to affirm that something is the case is not knowledge. Knowledge consists of both affirming what is the case and knowing the reasons why (the *logos*) what is affirmed is the case.

For the normative believer, true opinion or belief about God and God's will through the mediation of his religious tradition was satisfactory. However, for some believers this was not enough. They were not satisfied merely with correct belief. They also wanted to know why what they believed to be true was in fact true. Such people became religious philosophers. The difference between normative Jews and Jewish philosophers can be illustrated as follows: Consider a book of math problems where the answers to the problems are given in the back of the book. Most students would be satisfied with accepting the answers in the book without working out the problems themselves. Better students would not be satisfied until they solved the problems on their own, even if they had no doubt that the answers given were correct. In this metaphor the answers in the book are rab-

---

* I.e., the tradition of Christian mysticism rooted in the writings of Plato.
** I.e., the tradition of Muslim mysticism.

binic tradition, and the students who must work out the problems themselves are religious philosophers.

Similarly, with respect to practice, the best that this or any other normative religious tradition could offer was that by accepting the practice or concrete discipline that the tradition dictated, the 'believer' would be doing what God command that he do; and by doing the divine will, the believer would be related to God. This relationship with God is indirect and remote. God has directly related himself to and communicated with the religious geniuses, i.e., prophets and teachers of the believer's tradition, but the believers themselves have no such direct relationship. Instead they are related to God only secondarily—through the community that embodies the tradition of direct relationship with the Lord.

For normative believers such indirect relationship through the mediation of the religious tradition was satisfactory. However, for some believers it was not enough merely to receive divine directives without also having a personal, direct relationship with God. Such people became religious mystics. The difference between normative Jews and Jewish mystics can be distinguished in this way. Imagine a large office which contains at one end a separate office for the manager beyond which is another office in which the president resides. At regular intervals the manager enters the president's office where the manager receives instructions for the employees. The manager then withdraws from the president's office, passes through his own office to the large main room where the workers have their desks, and tells the staff what their president wants them to do. Most of the employees would be satisfied accepting the instructions from the manager without ever meeting the president of the company. The more ambitious employees would not be content until they personally met the president, even if they had no doubt that the instructions from the manager were correct. In this metaphor God is the president, the prophets and the rabbis are the manager, the people of Israel are the company, and the Jewish mystics are those employees who are seeking personally to meet the president.

While some Jewish philosophers were mystics and some Jewish mystics were philosophers, it is not the case that all Jewish philosophers are mystics and all Jewish mystics are philosophers. For example, Bahya ibn Pakuda was both a mystic and a philosopher; Gersonides was a philosopher but not a mystic; and Isaac Luria was a mystic but not a philosopher. However, what all three shared in common was that although they did not question the veracity of the theoretical and practical teachings of rabbinic Judaism, in certain respects these teachings were not personally satisfying. In the case of the philosophers, these believing Jews were not content to accept the tradition's gift of true belief. In the case of the mystics, these equally believing Jews were not content to accept the tradition's gift of true practice. Both categories of Jews wanted personal confirmation of the truths of the tradition—the former by seeking rational grounds or justifications of their beliefs, and the latter by seeking a direct, personal relationship with the God of Israel.

The ultimate concern of all Jewish mysticism was practical, enabling the individual Jew who had developed the proper character to achieve a direct, personal relationship with God. Still, Jewish mystical traditions can generally be distinguished as either theoretical or practical mysticism. What is called "theoretical mysticism" are those teachings in mystical communities which deal with topics generally associated with religious philosophy—the nature of man, the universe, God, and the relationship between the three. What is called "practical mysticism" are those teachings in mystical communities which deal with concrete means or training by which the initiate into the mystical community may go beyond the rabbinic community to a direct relationship with God. Most Jewish mystical associations tended to be pantheistic, so the direct relationship sought with God was described in terms of a union with or an absorption into the essence of God. 'Pantheism' refers to that view which claims that everything that exists ultimately exists as part of God. Hence, direct relationship with God consisted in achieving that mental or spiritual state in which the individual would overcome his consciousness of apparent difference or separation from God and sense the reality of his participation or unity in God. The desired consciousness had often been called "ecstasy". The term for this state used by the Jewish mystics was DEVEKUT, which literally means the abstract state of cleaving. By DEVEKUT the kabbalists intended a state of cleaving to or being one with God.

Merkabah Mysticism

There are four major communities or traditions of Jewish mysticism, henceforth simply called Kabbalah, which can be noted prior to the seventeenth century. The first tradition, known as merkabah mysticism, arose in the first century B.C.E. under the influence of Gnosticism, and continued through the tenth century in the Muslim Empire. The term MERKABAH literally means 'chariot' and is associated with the purported ecstatic vision described in the first chapter of the Book of Ezekiel. In the terminology of medieval Jewish philos-

opher, the expression MA'ASE MERKABAH, the events of the chariot, refers to the study of metaphysics, cosmology, and cosmogony,
while the expression MA'ASE BᵉRESHIT, the events of creation, refers
to the study of the physical sciences. As the mystics used these words,
both MA'ASE MERKABAH and MA'ASE BᵉRESHIT refer to theoretical mystical traditions of cosmology and cosmogony, accounts of the
nature and origin of the universe in which casual categories are reified,
i.e., projected as existing entities in their own right.

Often these theoretical structures are called mythologies. The
problem with the term *mythology* is that it often carries the connota-
tion that the accounts given are intended to be stories that are less
true than other kinds of accounts. If this is what is meant by the word
mythology, then it is probably not appropriate to term Jewish mystics' explanations of the relation between God and His created universe mythologies.

On one hand, the earliest mystics spoke about a universe beyond
our material world which consisted of seven halls or palaces
(HECHALOT) populated by angels (called ḤAYOT or beasts, following the terminology of Ezekiel's chariot vision), structured in a hierar-
chy below the eighth, most perfect palace in which resided the 'throne
of God' or God as He is in Himself. On the other hand, they spoke
of the measurements of God's body (SHI'UR KOMAH). In what
sense either the description of the purported divine body or the seven
heavens was to be understood cannot easily be determined. Both
accounts were purportedly true, but neither account could have been
thought of in the same terms as a description of the color and shape
of physical objects such as tables or trees. However, in what way these
varying types of accounts were seen to be different and in what way,
if any, they were related is most difficult to say. It is not even clear
if the explanations of the divine body and the seven heavens themselves are accounts in the same or different ways.

Similarly these same merkabah mystics described what they
called SᵉFIROT, which means 'spheres' (as the terms was used by
medieval Jewish philosophers) or 'regions' or the twenty-two letters
of the Hebrew alphabet. How the SᵉFIROT are related to the
HECHALOT is not always clear, and the relationship of categories
need not be the same in the thought of every Jewish mystic. According to some mystics, the SᵉFIROT were independent of the
HECHALOT in that they were thirty-two paths to wisdom. According to other mystics, the SᵉFIROT were identical with the number of
deities of the Pythagorian cults. As such, the SᵉFIROT are living
numerical beings identical with the ḤAYOT or angels that occupy the

seven heavenly palaces. Generally, the term SᵉFIROT referred to ten overflows or emanations from God, which served as links between the all-perfect, one God, called the "Infinite" (EYN SOF), and the material world. In other words the SᵉFIROT are similar to the intelligences of medieval Jewish philosophy. However, the relationship between the mystical SᵉFIROT and the philosophical intelligences is only a similarity and not an identity. The two sets of purported entities are both emanations of God, but the two sets are characterized in quite different ways. Generally, the ten SᵉFIROT from God came to be characterized as follows: The first emanation from God was called (1) the Supreme Crown (KETER 'ELYON) of God. This is God, but less perfectly than God in himself as the EYN SOF. Each subsequent emanation is also God, in correspondingly less perfect ways. The remaining nine SᵉFIROT are named: (2) wisdom (HACHMAH), or the primordial idea of God; (3) the intelligence (BINAH) of God; (4) the love or mercy (HESED) of God; (5) the power (GeVURAH or DIN) of God, usually with reference to divine punishment and stern judgment; (6) the compassion (RAHAMIN) of God, by which He mediates between his mercy and power; (7) the eternity (NEZAH) of God; (8) the majesty (HOD) of God; (9) the foundation (YeSOD) of God; and (10) the kingdom (MALCHUT) of God. In the Zohar* this tenth emanation from God is called "the community of Israel," which means the mystical archetype of Israel's community rather than the Jewish people as they are found in the material world. As God's tenth sphere, the community of Israel is identical with God's presence or the SHeCHINAH in rabbinic tradition.

Thirteenth Century Spanish Hasidism

Subsequent to the classical merkabah mysticism, a new theoretical mysticism arose in Spain and Southern France in the beginning of the thirteenth century. These old Spanish mystics called themselves HASIDIM, which means either saints or pious men. Rather than representing a rejection of anything taught in merkabah mysticism, the Hasidim went beyond their description of the MERKEBAH or the world of the seven heavens and the divine throne, to what these Hasidim called *inner merkabah*, which was the world of the EYN SOF itself. Whereas the merkabah mystics concerned themselves with describing the emanations or primary instruments of God's self-revelation, the old Spanish mystics concentrated on the theory of achieving

* (The Book of Splendor.) It first appeared in Castile in the late thirteenth century.

direct relationship with God beyond the SᵉFIROT.

This Spanish Ḥasidism was centered in Gerona in Catalonia for six generations (about 1200 C.E. to 1350 C.E.). Its leading theoreticians were Abraham Abulafia and the anonymous author of the *Zohar.*

Abulafia was born in Saragossa in 1240. He moved from Saragossa to Tudela in Navarre; and from there, in 1274, he became a vagrant, wandering and teaching his doctrines in Italy and Greece. After 1291, nothing more is known of him. Although he wrote several works, the only one that has survived his his *Book of the Sign* (SEFER HA-OT). He taught a kind of mysticism known as "ecstatic kabbalah." This type of system is generally called "theosophy," i.e., the attempt both to perceive and then describe divine mysteries, in the belief that it is possible to become absorbed into God through this contemplation. The object of the contemplation was God's unity (YIHUD) with His SHᵉCHINAH, which underlies the differences of the multiple SᵉFIROT of the merkabah mystics. By means of this contemplation the Kabbalist sought both to "untie the knots" of his soul, thereby achieving higher forms of perception, and to bring about the perfection (TIKKUN) of the world. The sources of this conception are Greek.

The Ḥasid combined Aristotle's notion of *Aporia* with Plato's "myth of the cave" in *The Republic.* Aporia are knots which block thought from flowing freely. These knots to rational speculation, in Aristotelian philosophy, became knots that hinder one's seeing beyond the physical world of sense perception into the higher orders of the universe. As one untied these knots to mystical perception, he/she uplifted himself/herself to a higher order of reality, while bringing his/her physical universe into closer and higher relationship with God.

Of the products of the Spanish Ḥasidim in ecstatic kabbalah, the most influential work in terms of the history of Jewish mysticism was the Zohar. The work was originally attributed to Simeon Ben Yoḥai (second century C.E.). It first appeared in Castile after 1268, and was circulated by Moses Ben Shemtob de Leon of Quadelajara in Castile (died 1305) in the last two decades of the thirteenth century. Whether Moses Ben Shemtob or someone else at this time was the real author of the book is a matter of speculation.[1]

Thirteenth Century German Ḥasidim

Almost contemporaneous with the old Spanish Kabbalah was a mystical tradition in the Germanic lands. In contrast to the theoretical emphasis of Spanish Ḥasidim, the Ḥasidism of Germany was practical. In other words, there the concern was with concrete training for the kabbalist to achieve DEVEKUT, the mystical union with

God. The leading figures in German Ḥasidism were all members of the Kalonymus family. They were Samuel, the son of Kalonymus of Speyer, who lived at the end of the twelfth century; his son Jehudah of Worms who died in 1217; and Jehudah's disciple, Eleazar Ben Jehudah of Worms, who died between 1223 and 1232. Their combined teachings are preserved in SEFER ḤASIDIM.

The Kabbalah of Safed

Finally, in Safed, about 1532, a new kabbalist tradition arose among Spanish emigrants. The dominant influences of the Safed school of Kabbalah were the theoretical mystic Moses Ben Jacob Cordovera and the practical mystic Isaac Luria (1534-1574). Luria's practical Kabbalah proved the most influential as it was spread to Italy and throughout Europe at the end of the sixteenth century by Israel Sarug and Ḥayim Vital Calabrese (1543-1620), who wrote *The Gates of Holiness* (SHA'ARE KᵉDUSHAH).

Insofar as this Kabbalah was theoretical, its most unique addition to the account of the universe was the explanation of how evil came to exist in God's universe. At first, only God as the *EYN SOF*, or the Infinite, existed. But He existed only as spirit or thought. From God's love of perfection—i.e., from His love of Himself—God sought to objectify Himself. The process by which God made Himself an object for contemplation was called ZIMZUM, which literally means "concentration" or "contraction." In other words, the Infinite contracted Himself, and by so doing, enabled Himself to be limited or objectified. In this way He brought about the creation of the world, which is His self-objectification. This objectification manifested itself as light. The first divine light is known as the primordial man (ADAM KADMON). In this context, *ADAM* refers not to the man mentioned in the first chapters of the Book of Genesis, but to primordial divine light. This light poured into KELIM or vessels, which are the instruments by which God performs His actions. However, the light was too powerful for the vessel. The vessel shattered, thereby dispersing the divine, pure light into a pure darkness.

In our world, there is neither pure darkness nor pure light. Rather, all of our universe is a mixture of darkness lightened by fragments of divine light, called "sparks." The darkness is the evil here accounted for by this doctrine of the shattering of the vessels (SHᵉVIRAT HA-KELIM). As a consequence of this explanation, the kabbalist strives to remove from the divine sparks the KELIPOT. These KELIPOT (sparks) had to be cleansed out of the light in order for the vessels to contain the pure divine light. By means of this cleansing, the vessel and that unified light which is God will be restored. According to the kabbalist, this restoration will be achieved in the time of the coming of the Messiah. By this means, the kabbalist strives to bring the Messiah and the Messianic Age.

SEVENTEENTH-CENTURY JEWISH MYSTICISM

European rabbis raised accusations of heresy against the exponents of an Aristotelian approach to Jewish philosophy. While it is possible that some of these philosophers had serious questions about aspects of rabbinic Judaism, still there is no reason to suspect any of the major medieval Jewish philosophers of being disaffected from rabbinic Judaism. While the most rationalist of them sought to know why the traditional dogmas of rabbinic Judaism were true, they did not in fact doubt their veracity. Many normative rabbis viewed kabbalism with suspicion. Possibly some Jewish mystics were inclined to violate willfully some laws and practices of rabbinic tradition. However, no evidence leads to the suspicion that any of the major kabbalists, prior to the seventeenth-century C.E., either advocated or practiced disciplines that were prohibited by Jewish law. In other words, both the philosophers and the mystics were committed rabbinic Jews.

At the same time, it is not altogether unreasonable to believe that the European rabbinic communal leaders were suspicious of both the Jewish philosophers and mystics. It has already been noted that insofar as a Jew became either a philosopher of Judaism or a kabbalist, he was saying in fact that in some respect the normative tradition was not enough for him. To the extent that this tradition was not satisfying, this Jew was implicitly, if not explicitly, criticizing the established mode of Jewish life.

There were grounds for the Jewish establishment to regard its philosophers and mystics with suspicion. So long as the structure of traditional rabbinic Judaism enabled most Jews to live their lives fully and satisfactorily in their relations with each other, their neighbors, and their God, there was no real reason to fear the implicit criticism in either philosophy or mysticism. So long as the classical structure of rabbinic Judaism was adequate to the needs of the world in which the Jewish people lived, both philosophy and mysticism remained the activity of an elite few that had minimal, if any, impact on the thought of the Jewish masses. Most of the prayers added to the daily rabbinic prayerbook were the work of medieval philosophers and/or mystics. Still it is questionable to what extent the average Jew reciting these traditional prayers recognized in their content something beyond the popular theology of the early rabbis of Judea and Sassanian empire.*

After the expulsion from Spain it became increasingly difficult for individual Jews and the Jewish community as a whole to live peacefully in medieval Europe. Periods of prosperity and peace were increasingly brief. Jewish life became more and more dominated by poverty and physical violence. The Jewish community continued to be generally faithful to the authority of its rabbis, upholding the rabbinic ideals of non-violent resistances.[2] Particularly in Eastern Europe, these techniques of survival proved increasingly ineffective against foreign attacks or *pogroms*. At no time before the second half of the seventeenth century could it be said that many Jews became disaffected from rabbinic Judaism. Their thoughts and aspirations turned away from the application of God's law for the Jews in this world, to a longing for the coming of the Messiah and the Messianic Age, which would bring this world of pain and evil to a close.

The longing for the Messiah is itself a rabbinic theological doctrine, representing the fulfillment of the aspirations of the Jewish people under the Torah. As 'fulfillment,' it also means practically the end of rabbinic Judaism. The law, as it is understood in the tradition of HALACHAH, is intended and designed to function in this world. In the world to come, this law at least will be greatly modified and at most will cease to operate altogether. Implicit in the rabbinic Jewish community's greater concentration on the coming of the Messiah was many Jews' unconscious judgment that the classical structure of rabbinic Judaism could no longer enable the Jewish people to function adequately in the existing world. They rejected the existing world, affirming a not-too-distant better world. This rejection carried with it an implicit denial of classical rabbinic Judaism as well. What was otherwise only implicit became explicit with the mass Jewish acceptance of the mystical messianic pretender, Shabbatai Zevi (1626-1676).

Shabbatai Zevi

In kabbalist circles the year 1648 had long been predicted as the year in which the Messiah would appear. In that year Shabbatai Zevi in the rabbinical school of Joseph Escapa in Smyrna (in modern Turkey) pronounced God's name (*YHWH*), thereby implicitly proclaiming himself to be the Messiah Then this young kabbalist went to Saloniki[3] and was married to the Torah, thereby purportedly fulfilling the expected marriage of the Messiah to the personified "daughter of

---

* The ruling Zoroastrian empire of Persia from 225 to 641 C.E.

heaven." The rabbinate of Smyrna excommunicated him, and the rabbinate of Saloniki banned him from their city. Still, the expected and accepted news of the coming of the Messiah spread throughout the Ottoman Jewish World. In Cairo, Shabbatai Zevi found his first communal acceptance with the support and financial backing of Raphael Joseph Chelebi, the Egyptian master of the mint and tax farmer. In Gaza, Shabbatai gained the support of Nathan Benjamin Levi (1644-1680), the son of an immigrant from the Germanic lands. From Gaza, the messianic pretender, with his prophet Nathan, travelled to Jerusalem where, in 1665, he was proclaimed the Messiah. After his "coronation," popular support for Shabbatai spread throughout the Ottoman Empire as well as Central and Eastern Europe. Communities of followers of the new Messiah could be found in such disparate cities as Venice, Amsterdam, Hamburg, London and Avignon. Finally, Shabbatai set sail for Constantinople, where he expected to be received by Mohammed IV with the honors to which he was then accustomed. Instead he was arrested as a threat to the sovereignty of the Empire. On September 16, 1666, he was given the choice of conversion to Islam or death; he chose conversion. The converted Messiah spent the rest of his life under a comfortable house arrest and is said to have died in Dulcigno (in modern Yugoslavia) on Yom Kippur, 1676.

Before his conversion a great mass, if not the majority, of Jews in the European and Ottoman worlds had accepted the authenticity of this one claimant to the status of Messiah. Stories are told of thousands of families selling their property and preparing to return to the holy land. After his conversion the groups of Shabbatians lost most of their support. Nevertheless, the claim continued to be made by the faithful that Shabbatai Zevi was in fact the Messiah. His conversion was explained in a number of ways. Some claimed that the man who converted was not really Shabbatai Zevi. Others granted that it was Shabbatai who had "accepted the turban," but that his conversion was a necessary step toward bringing about the fulfillment of the Messianic Age. According to some Shabbatians the act of conversion was simply a mystery that the faithful and true servants of God would accept. Still others said that, in order to purify his people to enable them to enter the Messianic Age, the Messiah had taken upon himself a degradation worse than death. In the subsequent century several kabbalists appeared who claimed to be reincarnations of Shabbatai. Among these claimants were Abraham Michael Cardoso (died 1706) in a town near Smyrna; Jacob Querido (died about 1700) in Saloniki; Nehemiah Hiya Hayun (died after 1726) at Serajevo; and, most notably, Jacob Leibovicz of Podolia (died 1791), who was known in the Turkish Empire as Jacob Frank ("Frank" being the term used in the East for all Europeans).

All of these post-conversion Shabbatai groups firmly believed that they lived at the end of this world and the beginning of the world to come. They dedicated their lives to effecting this transition of possible worlds. However, they did not agree either among communities or among the members of a given community what they should do in order so speed the transition. Underlying their disagreements was the ambiguity of the accepted principle of the imitation of God (*Imitatio Dei*) which in this case meant the principle of the imitation of the Messiah. All of them agreed that their duty was to imitate the HASIDUT or piety of the Messiah, but in what way should they imitate him? Some contented that they should imitate his traditional religious virtues, and these kabbalists remained overtly strict practicing halachic Jews. Others claimed that the fulfillment of the messianic ideal could be achieved not only by the pious "gathering of the sparks"—by the mystical geniuses through perfect virtue—but also through perfect vice; and Shabbatai himself, as his conversion testifies, had chosen this latter alternative. In imitation of Shabbatai, they sought perfect depravity for the sake of salvation of the world. This tendency most notably meant going beyond simple violations of the *HALACHAH* and even beyond cruelty and sexual depravity to what they regarded to be the greatest sin of all in this world, conversion, either to Islam or to Christianity. The most notable Shabbatian groups to take this path of maximum depravity were the Frankists or the followers of Jacob Frank.

What made it conceptually possible for these pursuers of the messianic to struggle to do what they considered loathsome was the view that what this world calls good and evil, most perfectly specified in the Torah, is applicable only to this world. In the world to come, good and evil may be the opposite of what is virtue and vice here. This ethical judgment about the range of moral values, a judgment that normative rabbis themselves also tended to accept, made them particularly suspicious of any Jewish groups claiming that the Messiah had come or was about to come. Since in most cases the Kabbalah was intimately linked to messianic expectations, Kabbalah itself was considered suspect by the rabbis. When the Messiah appears, the Torah will come to an end in fulfillment. If the Jews turn to a would-be redeemer who is not in fact the Messiah, then, as happened in the case of the Shabbatians, the Torah will be destroyed and not fulfilled. While always suspicious of Kabbalah, the rabbinic establishment had not strongly attacked its proponents, since Jewish mysticism was the activity of only the few. However, after Shabbatai Zevi, when kabbalism captured the imagination of the masses, rabbinic authorities fell heavily on the kabbalists in order to squash this now major threat to the survival of rabbinic Judaism.

Eastern European Hasidism

It was this fear, that Kabbalah is intimately tied to a messianism threatening the very survival of a Torah-centered Judaism, that lay behind the Jewish establishment's attack in Eastern Europe upon a new kabbalist community that grew up around Israel Baal Shem Tov (called "the Besht"), who founded his Hasidism in Poland in 1760. The new Hasidism was unique. Unlike the Shabbatians, it was not primarily a messianic movement. Unlike the earlier Hasidim, it was primarily a practical and mass movement rather than a movement that strongly emphasized theory among a small group of the spiritual elite. In general, the goal of Eastern European Hasidism was to enable the average Jew to find joy rather than hardship in observing the Torah. In this way Hasidism attempted to reestablish rabbinic Judaism for the masses of Eastern European Jewry, so that it could continue to function as a living, satisfying force in an otherwise bleak world. In time, the Jewish religious establishment realized that this Hasidism was a force among the people to strengthen rather than weaken rabbinic Judaism. By the nineteenth century the terms "pious," "traditional," or "orthodox" Jews and "Ḥasidim" became synonymns in the vocabulary of Ashkenazic Jews.

NOTES

1. See Gershom Scholem, *Major Trends in Jewish Mysticism*, New York: Schocken, 1954. Lecture Five, pp. 156-204.

2. In the face of attacks against them the Jewish community usually prayed and either bribed or fled from its enemies.

3. Saloniki is located in what is now Greece, but at that time it was part of the Ottoman Empire.

KEY NAMES

Abraham Abulafia, Ḥayim Vital Calabrese, ḤASIDIM, Isaac Luria, Israel Baal Shem Tov (the Besht), Israel Sarug, Jacob Leibovicz

(= Jacob Frank) Kalonymus family, Moses Ben Jacob Cordovera, Merkabah Mysticism, Moses Ben Shemtob de Leon of Quadelarjara, Nathan Benjamin Levi, The Pale of Settlement, SEFER HA-OT, SEFER HASIDIM, Shabbatai Zevi, Safed, SHA'ARE KEDUSHAH, Simeon Ben Yohai, *Zohar.*

KEY TERMS

Ashkenazic, DEVEKUT, EYN SOF, HALACHAH, HASIDUT, HECHALOT, ecstatic Kabbalah, inner merkabah, Kabbalah, KELIPOT, MERKABAH, Pantheism, Practical Mysticism, Sephardic, SeFIROT, SHeVIRAT HA-KELIM, SHI'UR KOMAH, theoretical Mysticism, TIKKUN, ZIMZUM.

KEY QUESTIONS

1. What directions did Jewish life take after the expulsion from Spain?

2. Compare and contrast Jewish philosophers, kabbalists, and normative traditional Jews.

3. Describe the five major traditions of pre-seventeenth century Kabbalah. What is unique about each? Where was each located? At what time? Who were the major spokesmen of each?

4. In general, how did the kabbalists characterize the ten emanations from God?

5. What did the thirteenth-century Spanish Hasidism add to Merkabah Kabbalah?

6. How did the kabbalists of Safed explain the existence of evil in this world? How and when will evil be overcome?

7. What were the factors that led to mass Jewish belief that the Messiah would come in the seventeenth-century?

8. What reasons did people give for continuing to follow Shabbatai Zevi after his conversion to Islam?

9. Who were the Frankists, and why did they behave in the way that they behaved?

10. When did the rabbinic establishment cease to tolerate Kabbalah, and why did the rabbinate begin actively to oppose the

Hasidism of the followers of the Besht?

11. In what ways was the new Hasidism of Eastern Europe unique?

RECOMMENDED READINGS

General

Barry W. Holtz, *Back to the Sources: Reading the Classic Jewish Texts.* New York: Summit Books, 1984. Chpts. 6 and 7, pp. 305-401.

Robert M. Seltzer, *Jewish People, Jewish Though: The Jewish Experience in History.* New York: Macmillan, 1980, Chpts. 9 and 10, pp. 419-305.

Specific

Milton Aron, *Ideas and Ideals of the Hassidim.* New York: The Citadel Press, 1969.

Don Ben-Amos, *In Praise of the Ba'al Shem Tov.* Bloomington: Indiana University Press, 1970.

David Biale, *Gershom Scholem: Kabbalah and Counter History.* Cambridge, Mass.: Harvard University Press, 1979.

Martin Buber, *The Legend of the Baal-Shem.* Translated into English by Maurice Friedman. New York: Harper & Brothers, 1955.

———Tales of the Hasidim: The Early Masters. New York: Schocken, 1947.

Samuel Dresner, *Levi Yizhak of Berditchev.* New York: Hartmore House, 1974.

———*The Zaddik.* New York, Schocken, 1974.

Arthur Green, *Tormented Master: A Life of Rabbi Nahman of Bratslav.* University, Ala.: University of Alabama Press, 1979.

Louis Jacobs, *Hasidic Thought.* New York: Behrman, 1977.

Gershom G. Scholem, *Major Trends in Jewish Mysticism.* New York: Schocken, 1961.

———*The Messianic Idea in Judaism and Other Essays on Jewish Spirituality.* New York, Schocken, 1971.

———*On the Kabbalah and Its Symbolism.* Translated into English by Ralph Manheim. New York: Schocken Books, 1965.

———*Sabbatai Sevi: The Mystical Messiah, 1626-1676.* Translated in English by R. J. Zwi Werblowsky. Princeton: Princeton University Press, 1973.

R. J. Zwi Werblowsky, *Joseph Karo: Lawyer and Mystic*. Philadelphia: The Jewish Publication Society of America, 1977.

Elie Wiesel, *Souls on Fire: Portraits and Legends of Hasidic Leaders*. Translated into English by Marion Wiesel. New York: Random House, 1973.

2

EMANCIPATION AND ITS CONSEQUENCES

From the beginning of the history of Jewish thought, the question, "what is a Jew?" had not been raised. There was no problem about what it meant to say that someone is a Jew. Simply stated, a Jew was any person who was part of a particular people or nation called at one time "Israel," at another "Judea," and then again "Israel." This nation was defined in terms of its covenant with a deity named "YHWH," who at one point in Jewish history happened to be characterized as the God of the world. Historically, there were disputes over what this definition entailed in terms of what specific legislation God demanded of this people, how this religious state was to be administered, and who had the authority to decide these questions. There were no disputes over the definition itself. Changes in the external or foreign environment in which the Jewish people lived at different times brought about changes in the structure of Judaism. Rule by monarchs gave way to government by priests, and rule by priests was replaced by the dynasty of the rabbis. Throughout all of these external pressures, the children of Israel were able to preserve their communal, national, and religious identity. However, in the seventeenth century, particularly in Central Europe, new changes began to affect Jewish life, forcing the Jewish people to rethink and even reconstruct the very idea of what they thought it meant to be a Jew. The new historical factor was the rise of the secular national state, which happened to entail the political emancipation of the Jews.

Corresponding to the rise of Protestant religions in Western Europe, a new economic and political system of government arose that gradually deposed the feudal and Roman Catholic Holy Roman Empire. Conceptually underlying the new economy of capitalism and the new politics, labeled either "republicanism" or "democracy," was a distinction between two categories of individual and communal affairs, the one called "secular" and the other called "religious." A new political-religious ideology arose in Europe affirming that the state or nation ought to have dominion over secular affairs; religion ought to have dominion over religious affairs; the state ought to have no authority in matters of religion; and religion ought to have no authority in matters of the state. Religious affairs had to do with matters affecting relations between people and God, whereas secular affairs had to do with matters affecting relations between people, While this distinction rarely was carried out with complete consistency—an impossibility since there is a large area of affairs that concern both relations between people and relations between people and God—after the sixteenth century the doctrine of the separation of religion and state functioned as an ideal for the modern Western nation. To the extent that any state "modernized," at least in principle it separated membership in a religious polity from citizenship in the nation and prohibited the state from having any right to restrict religious freedom within the nation.

The first modern European states to extend this principle to the Jews were France and Holland. France granted full citizenship to the Jews in 1791 and Holland followed in 1796. By the beginning of the nineteenth century, every European state that France conquered under Napoleon emancipated the Jews. In 1813, the allied monarchies of Europe successfully stopped Napoleon from making all of their continent part of the French Republic, but they did not stop the spread of the new kind of state that the French Republic embodied. Through the course of the next one hundred years, almost every European state became a secular nation, politically independent of its related church, with its monarchs either eliminated altogether or their powers so limited that they ceased to be politically significant. Tangentially, as a nation became more or less secular, the Jews within that nation were to a greater or lesser extent emancipated. Even in those states that Napoleon had tried but failed to conquer—most notably the states that encompassed the "Pale of Settlement" in Eastern Europe, where comparatively little modernization took place—the ideal of emancipation dominated the strongly French-influenced thought of both gentile and Jewish intellectuals.

The movement of the children of Israel from a nomadic to a land-owning, agrarian people in Canaan had forced Judaism to change its political and legal structure. The defeat of Judea in its wars for independence against Rome and the subsequent dispersion of Judeans into the Middle East, where Jews became merchants again, demanded a reconstruction of the political structure of Judaism. The introduction of Greek thought into the intellectual Jewish life of the Western Muslim Empire drove the intellectual elite of the Jewish people to rethink their views of God and the universe. With mass expulsion from Spain, this long developed internal structure of Jewish life called "rabbinic Judaism" began to show signs of strain. The mass movement of messianic kabbalism was symptomatic of this stress. Now the Jewish people faced a new threat from their external environment—emancipation. Emancipation might lead to a total loss of identity for each individual Jew as part of a collective Jewry. If the Jew now was welcome to become a citizen of France or Holland or England or Germany, subject to the governments of these states, then the Jew was no longer a citizen of a territorially-dispersed Jewish state, subject to the governments of the rabbis. In effect, Jews' acceptance of the ideal of becoming modern carried with it the rejection of rabbinic Judaism as it had functioned, with relatively little change, since at least the first century C.E.

Emancipation in Western Europe, most notably in Germany, produced three kinds of Jews. First, most Jews simply remained within the Jewish world and were not overtly affected by the Christian world at all. Second, there were Jews who readily abandoned Judaism to move into the general society, because they saw participation in that society to be an improvement over life in the Jewish world. These were not self-hating Jews. Rather, they were people who, given an option, chose what they believed to be a better alternative. They did not primarily abandon Judaism; rather, they primarily chose to become western, believing that to become Western required leaving Judaism. The German Jewish poet Heinrich Heine was such a Jew. Heine converted to Christianity in order to enter law school. He did not particularly like Christianity, and he did not particularly dislike Judaism. Neither were very important to him; and because of this fact, he could convert to gain something that was important to him, namely, entrance into law school. These Jews in fact converted; or, if they did not, their not converting made little difference because their Judaism made no difference to them. Most Jews who entered western civilization did not convert. They did not deny their Jewish identity, but that heritage played no active role in their lives. Their Jewishness was very important to anti-Semites and anti-Semites were very important to these Jews, but that they were Jewish was not important to these Jews. Consequently, combating anti-Semitism often was their most important expression of Jewish identity.

Third, there was a small group of Jews who decided to enter Western civilization and to remain Jewish. This last group sought to make sense out becoming westernized and remaining Jewish. They were the smallest group, but for our purposes they were the only Jews who mattered.

The attempted reconciliation often was carried out in the name of rabbinic Judaism, particularly in Germany and among German Jews who settled in the United States. Still, all of these Jews were forced to restructure Judaism to fit into their new world. Where the Jews were emancipated, rabbinic Judaism survived only in the way that monarchy continued in some modern European states; namely, the former rulers were preserved with largely ceremonial but no longer any real political power. In fact, all of the dynasties of the past had come to an end. Only enough of their physical presence remained to enable those who cared about it to feel some continuity with their religious, cultural, and political past.

The reason rabbinic Judaism could not survive the movement into the modern world unscathed has to do with the inherent conceptual separation of the religious and the secular in the so-called enlightened world. Classical rabbinic Judaism, like all other pre-Reformation religions in the western and mediterranean worlds, was in its very conception antithetical to such a separation The Jewish people, insofar as they were a people governed by law, were a nation; but they were not simply a state. They were a nation called into existence and given a law by God. Insofar as they were a people committed to the rule of a particular God, the Jewish people advocated a particular religion. In fact there was no way to distinguish what, in the communal and private lives of the Jewish people, was religious and what was national.

The rabbi governed his people in all matters by a process of common law whose ultimate authority was God's revelation at Sinai. Hence, laws dealing with sanitation were as much religious—i.e., responses to God's will—as they were secular; and, laws dealing with the time at which the Sabbath is to begin were as much secular—i.e., communal, civil legislation—as they were religious. The same point can be made about Church law in the Holy Roman Empire and the laws of the Caliphs is the Muslim Empire.

Before the end of the seventeenth century, there was no question of Jews becoming citizens of the gentile state where they resided. To be a citizen of the Muslim Empire meant to become a Muslim. Similarly, to be a citizen of the Holy Roman Empire meant to be a Roman Catholic. At most what the Jews sought from their neighbors was to live in peace with them, with maximal trade and some social-cultural intercourse; but there was no question of common citizenship. The Jew was different from his neighbor in language and/or dress and/or culture and/or political identity and religion. While Jews sought their neighbors' tolerance of these differences, they did not desire to have them obliterated. However, at least by the nineteenth century, many Jews fought to have these distinctions removed; and most Jews, affirming both their modernity and their Jewishness, desired the disappearance of most differences. Which differences should be preserved is the issue around which the modern question of what is a Jew revolved. In general, Eastern European Jewish intellectuals sought to preserve cultural and/or political and/or linguistic separateness while Central European Jewish intellectuals sought to maintain religious differences. In other words, admission to the modern world entailed that the Jews must redefine themselves as Jews in a way that would be consistent with the principle of the separation of the secular and the religious. Whereas Eastern European Jews tended to redefine themselves in secular or culturally-political terms as members of a distinct people, Jews further to the west more often saw themselves as advocates of a distinct religion. The Eastern European tendency gave rise to Zionism while the Central European tendency brought about Reform Judaism.

Several factors contributed to these differences in sectional choices of redefinition within the Ashkenazic communities. First, the Jews in Eastern Europe lived under the territorial control of several nations, most notably Russia, Lithuania, Poland, and Rumania. All of these Jews resided in a single continuous geographical territory, and from the sixteenth until the twentieth century they preserved some form of united self-rule. In contrast, the Jewish communities of Central Europe were largely autonomous, island Jewish states, located in ghettos in the midst of major cities and separated from each other by a sea of gentile states, most notably Germany, Austria and Hungary. Hence, the very territories occupied by Jews prior to their emancipation contributed to the fact that Eastern European Jews affirmed a nationalist identity and Central European Jews did not.

Second, a modernist clergy who promoted the progression from feudalism to republicanism developed in the Germanic lands. No such counterpart could be found in any of the orthodox churches of the East since these religious polities identified their own well-being with the preservation of feudalism. The modernist of Central Europe could find religious support for his progressivism, but the modernist of Eastern Europe could not. This tendency to identify established religious authority with the old world that modernists sought to overthrow was reinforced by the cultural impact of the French encyclopedists and other literary figures (mostly Moliere, Voltaire and Flaubert) of the new French culture, all of whom generalized their hostility toward the French Catholic Church to religion in general. For the most part, the normative, establishment rabbinate of all of Europe feared and usually fought the new politics. Given the intellectual inheritance of Eastern European Jewish intelligentsia, it was understandable that they saw this opposition as representative of religion in general; and they in no way desired to find their new, modern identity as Jews on religious grounds. The cultural experience of Germany in particular enabled emancipated Jews to the West to distinguish between a "revolutionary" and an "old guard" clergy, Jewish as well as Christian.

Third, in both Ashkenazic subcultures the demand to be both modern and Jewish required that the Jew find some way in which he was like his gentile neighbors and some way in which he was different. Eastern Europeans, Russians in particular, tended to share in different territories a common religion upon which their new political unities could be based, while they came from diverse ethnic or cultural backgrounds. Conversely, the Christians of Central Europe had grave religious differences and found their unity in a common culture and language. Hence, it was reasonable that German Jews would affirm their unity with their fellow gentile citizens on the grounds of a common Germanic culture and language while affirming their uniqueness as Jews in terms of religion. It was also understandable that Russian Jews would affirm their unity with fellow enlightened gentiles in a common commitment to some version of French secular enlightenment, while finding Jewish uniqueness on ethnic, nationalist grounds.

Two qualifications of this picture are necessary. First, the different choices between Judaism as a nation and Judaism as a religion rarely were drawn rigorously. Most Jews inclined to define Judaism on religious grounds sought to deemphasize the nationalist-cultural inheritance of their people, but they did not totally deny it. With the exception of only the most radical fringe of the Reform movement, reformers continued to have a special place in their religious outlook for the Hebrew language and the land of Israel. Similarly, excluding only the most radical fringe of the Zionist movement, Zionists continued to affirm their identity with all Jews whether or not they migrated to the state of Israel. For the Judaism continued to occupy a special place in the formation of a secular Jewish state.

Second, in drawing this overview of the transition of the Jewish people into the modern world, it can be said that the feeling of many Jews in their seventeenth-century rabbinic world that the new world of the *Messiah* was at hand was translated in the eighteenth, nineteenth, and early twentieth centuries into a feeling that the new world of the *messianic* was at hand. However, this new messianic conception, under the impact of European Humanism, contained no vision of a supernatural or superhuman Messiah who would personally bring about the new age. Rather, human beings themselves would establish the new world that would universally supplant this old world. What feudal Jews called HA'OLAM HABA, the world to come, modern Jews called "The Age of Enlightenment."

The form this enlightenment was to take depended on the individual modern Jew's analysis of what it meant to be a Jew and what was wrong with this world. Zionists identified the messianic age with the establishment of an autonomous, secular, Jewish state. Nineteenth-century German Reform Jews identified it with an age of universally-accepted ethical monotheism, when religions would differ solely in their external practices, but not in the content that those practices are intended to embody. Jews such as Freud, Marx, and Trotsky prophesied that the new science of their day would enable rational men to institute the kind of psychological or social and economic therapy on individuals and communities to enable all people, Jews and gentiles alike, to live as brothers without distinction in an inherently good society. Similarly, many more Jews identified the "world to come" with the "new world" of the United States. There the evils that had entered all past human societies would be abandoned, because the americas were not hindered by the traditions of the past.

While all of these visionaries promoted and acted out quite different programs, they shared greatly in their hopes for the immediate future. Like the messianists before them, they believed that human beings are inherently good; that they can free themselves from the accumulated evils of the past, which are tied to ancient traditions, and can be cleansed by new institutions and beliefs; that the time for this change was at hand; and that the world was steadily getting better. In this sense, the mass of Jews continued to be messianists even after the conversion of Shabbatai Zevi.

This second, post-medieval messianic dream called "Enlightenment" would last longer than the first messianic movement of Shabbatai Zevi. In this case, there would be no mass recognition that the Jews had not passed from this world into the world to come until Hitler reawakened them in the mid-twentieth century.

KEY TERMS

emancipation, enlightenment, HA'OLAM HABA, Humanism, Jew, modern, Pale of Settlement, Progressivism, rabbinic Judaism, religious, secular

KEY QUESTIONS

1. Why is the question, "Who is a Jew?" a modern problem?

2. Why did emancipation threaten the survival of rabbinic Judaism?

3. What were the two basic strategies that Jews developed for remaining Jewish in the modern world? In what way does this generalization have to be qualified?

4. Why did it tend to be the case that Reform Judaism developed in Central Europe and Zionism developed in Eastern Europe? Give three reasons for the tendency and two qualifications of this generalization.

5. How did the Jewish messianic aspirations of the seventeenth century express themselves in the nineteenth century? How did this modern Messianism differ from classical rabbinic Messianism? How did these modern Jewish Messianisms differ from each other? How were they alike?

RECOMMENDED READINGS

General

Robert M. Seltzer, *Jewish People, Jewish Thought: The Jewish Experience in History.* New York: Macmillan, 1980. Chpt. 11, pp. 513-546.

Specific

Arthur Hertzberg, *The French Enlightenment and the Jews.* New York: Columbia University Press, 1968.

Jacob Rader Marcus, *The Rise and Destiny of the German Jew.* Westport, Conn.: Greenwood Press, 1974.

Milton Meltzer, *The World of Our Fathers: The Jews of Eastern Europe.* New York: Dell, 1974.

Paul R. Mendes-Flohr and Jehuda Reinharz, *The Jew in the Modern World: A Documentary History.* New York: Oxford University Press, 1980.

Michael Meyer, *The Origins of the Modern Jew: Jewish Identity and European Culture in Germany, 1749-1824.* Detroit: Wayne State University Press, 1967.

Moses A. Shulvass, *Jewish Culture in Eastern Europe: The Classical Period.* New York: Ktav, 1975.

Mark Zborowski and Elizabeth Herzog, *Life is with People: The Culture of the Shtetl.* New York: Schocken, 1952.

3

SETTLEMENT IN AMERICA

Three distinct periods of Jewish emigration from different Jewish subcultural centers define the history of the Jewish people in the United States. The first migration of Jews, between 1654 and 1825, originally came to the New World as a consequence of their expulsion from Spain. The families of many of these Spanish Jews originally settled in Spanish and Portuguese territories in the Caribbean and in South America, where they could preserve much of their former European cultural life without any personal threat from the Roman Catholic Church. Eventually however, the Inquisition was established in the Spanish colonies, and life in the New World became almost as precarious as it was in Spain and Portugal. When the Dutch conquered the Eastern Coast of Brazil in 1630, its capital city, Recife, became the major center of Jewish life in the Americas. However, the Portuguese recaptured Recife in 1654, and the Jews were forced to leave their city. Among these Jews was a group that intended to sail to Amsterdam but instead landed in New Amsterdam, which was taken from the Dutch by the British in 1664 and renamed New York. In this way New York became the first settlement of Jews in the United States. During the subsequent 250 years, Sephardic Jewish communities arose in all of the American port cities. Charleston,

S.C., with a community of 500 Jews, was the largest Jewish settlement. The next largest Jewish communities were in New York, N.Y.; Newport, R.I.; Philadelphia, Pa.; Savannah, Ga.; and Richmond, Va.

The major occupations of the Sephardic Jews in the New World, ranging from jewel trade to slave trade and banking, were all related to shipping, which is the main reason why the major settlements of these Jews were in the Eastern port cities. The origins of this kind of occupation for Spanish Jews went back to the Muslim conquest of the Syrian Christian world in the middle of the seventh century C.E. At that time and place Christians were involved in commerce and Jews were farmers. Since the Muslims were interested primarily in agriculture, the Jews eventually found themselves forced out of their then traditional occupation by special taxes levied against non-Muslims in agriculture. At the same time the Jews received incentives from the Muslims to replace the Syrian Christians in commerce. The new rulers recognized the power and importance of sea trade, and they felt more comfortable with Jews in these positions than Syrian Christians.[1] Hence, mercantilism and the related profession of banking became Jewish occupations in which the Jews continued even after the collapse of the Muslim Empire.

There are still some Sephardic synagogues and communities in the United States today. However, they have had little impact on the development of American Jewish life since the middle of the nineteenth century. The more important factor was that 1,500,000 Ashkenazic Jews subsequently settled in the United States. In comparison, the Sephardic community consisted of a mere 15,000 Jews. Also, their low birth rate and eventual assimilation into American gentile life further reduced their numbers.

The major importance of Sephardic Jewry in America was their initiation of a struggle for full civil equality in the United States. The first of a long series of such battles began shortly after the first shipload of Jews from Recife landed in New Amsterdam. The governor of this Dutch colony was opposed to the settlement of Jews in his domain. However, his employer, the West India Company in Amsterdam whose governing board contained a number of Jews, forced him to be more tolerant. Still, Peter Stuyvesant would not trust Jews to stand guard duty on the walls of the city, a responsibility shared equally by every citizen of the colony. Instead, the Jews were required to pay a special tax in order to enlist non-Jews to fulfill this duty for them. The first "civil rights" battle that Jews fought in the New World was for the right to be treated equally in the performance of military duties.

In general, equality of obligation and rights in the military services was one of the major civil rights issues for Jews in the United States. Other battles included the right to vote and the right to hold public office. The major restriction to Jews holding public office was that usually the oath of office involved some form of Christian pledge. Unless an alternate oath was instituted, there was no way for a Jew to accept an elected office without committing perjury. With respect to Jewish thought, underlying this struggle for civil equality was the desire of Jews to live normally and equally in the gentile world. This theme of the pursuit of normalcy was perpetuated by the Ashkenazic Jewish settlers who followed.

The second major migration of Jews to the New World consisted primarily of German Jews who, together with other Germans, were escaping the economic depression of their former homeland. Between 1825 and 1880, 250,000 Jews emigrated to the New World, establishing 270 synagogues and communities throughout the cities of the East Coast and the villages of the Midwestern regions of the United States. Their Sephardic predecessors had been primarily upper-class merchants with international shipping connections. This first wave of Ashkenazic settlers were mainly lower middle class merchants, traders, or peddlers with few connections and little property except for second-hand items, primarily clothing, that they brought over with them.

The following is a paradigm nineteenth-century German-Jewish success story in America: Mr. Morganstern (a mythological Jew in this mythological tale) arrived at the port of New York with nothing but a sack of used clothes. He acquired a push cart and proceeded to move with his only possessions into the wilderness that lay west of the Appalachian Mountains in order to seek his fortune. For many years he traveled from one frontier village to another, trading his original possessions for many other kinds of items. After some time he had acquired a sufficient number of goods to settle in one Western village and open a general store. The village grew into a town and later into a large city, where Mr. Morganstern's enterprise became a large and economically powerful department store chain. In more or less this way, department store chains such as Marshall Fields or Mandel Brothers arose in new midwestern cities such as Cincinnati, Detroit, or Chicago.

During this time of economic growth, Mr. Morganstern raised a family and brought one of his wife's cousins from the "Old Country" to work for him. Since Mr. Morganstern now was selling new items rather than used ones and since his major trade remained clothing, our mythological hero decided that it would be desirable to establish his cousin in a major Eastern city such as New York or Boston or Baltimore. There he would have easy access to cloth and could manufacture clothes for Mr. Morganstern would be able to do business with someone he could trust better than a stranger. He could buy the clothes cheaper than he probably could otherwise. He would have helped a member of his family go into business for himself. Finally and possibly best of all, he would have put a thousand miles of wilderness between him and one of his wife's relatives. In time, given the bonus of a guaranteed market for his product, Mr. Morganstern's cousin became the head of a large factory or series of factories that manufactured clothing. More or less in this way, companies such as Hart Shaffner and Marx were born.

Beyond the personal wealth and economic power that the Jewish-originated clothing business in America brought to the German Jews, this new industry made a major contribution to the developing American society. The European states consisted of centuries-old, rigid class systems. These classes were separated not only by wealth and language, but by clothing as well. The clothes of the wealthy were of good quality and expensive; whereas, the clothes of the less fortunate were poor in price and workmanship, with the consequence that one could tell to what class a man belonged by the clothes that he wore. In America, the hope was to eliminate such traditional class distinctions. In this new capitalist world the idea was that all people would belong to the middle class. In fact, until the twentieth century, most Americans, no matter how rich or how poor, considered themselves to be members of the middle class. Although this vision of a single class society was never real, at least the mythology functioned to permit a great deal of flexibility in American class structure. Here it was not impossible for the children of any family, no matter how poor, to rise to a higher economic and social level. By producing clothes that were relatively inexpensive and of relatively good quality by European standards, the German Jewish community made a major contribution to the equality of classes in the United States. For example, although an American artisan might own only one suit and Andrew Carnegie would own many, and although the artisan's suit would wear out in less than a year and Carnegie's suits could last for years; nevertheless, the social-economic class of a steel magnate could not so easily be distinguished from the class of a skilled worker in American as it could in Europe. In general, Jewish retailers in the United States developed medium-priced goods of medium quality.

These products contributed to blending American classes in a way that was not possible in nineteenth-century Europe, where most products were either worse or better than their American counterparts. Jews remained owners of small clothing stores rather than large department stores, or they had small shops rather than large manufacturing centers, both of which contributed to early America's efforts to approximate its "messianic" ideal of equality.

How these German Jews came to be clothing merchants is distantly linked to the banking activities of their Sephardic brethren. With the decline of the Muslim Empire and its fleet, Jews with capital were invited into the Germanic lands to sell money at interest to the social and political elite of these feudal states, who gave land as collateral on their loans. In other words, the Jews became bankers. When these lords and bishops could not pay their debts and could find Christians (primarily Italians) from whom they could negotiate new loans, they excluded the Jews from the banking business. However, since the conditions under which the Jews were admitted to the Germanic lands were such that no other occupation was open to them, the Germanic Jews continued their activities in banking; only now their customers were poorer people who had little for collateral on their loans except their clothes. In other words, Jewish bankers became pawn brokers for the poor. When economic conditions became particularly bad in Germany and loans could no longer be repaid, these Jews could not make a living. Many of them took their collateral, namely used clothing, and emigrated to the United States.

The reason there was no rabbinic leadership in the New World must be noted. Most people do not move to a new land; rather, they leave their old one. The positive attractions of a new society tend to overcome the enormous disadvantages of leaving the place where one has always lived only when there are enormous disadvantages in remaining where one has been. It is no easy matter to move to a place where language and customs, taken for granted in the old home, must be entirely relearned. Rarely did anyone in a prominent position in the old world move to the new one. Rabbis, being the political leaders of their European Jewish communities, were unlikely to chose to begin life anew in an unknown world. Furthermore, as had already been noted,[2] America promised to be a new world which was a threat to their old world of rabbinic Judaism. Hence, few Sephardic rabbis came to the United States. For example, in 1773, there were only three rabbis in the entire New World: in Jamaica, Curacao, and Surinam.[3] However, many rabbis came with the German immigrants.

They were predominantly reformers who were looking to establish an enlightened Judaism that the German governments and the normative rabbinate had suppressed in the old world. Among these early American Reform rabbis were Leo Marzbacher, Max Lilienthal, Samuel Adler, Isaac Mayer Wise, and David Einhorn. Among their first congregations or temples were Har Sinai in Baltimore (established in 1842), Emanuel in New York (established in 1845), and Sinai in Chicago (established in 1858). By 1881, there were approximately 270 synagogues in the United States, the overwhelming majority of which were Reform. Consequently, whereas the German-born Reform movement could barely survive in the land of its birth; in nineteenth-century America, Reform Judaism became normative, establishment Judaism.

The third major migration of Jews to the New World consisted primarily of Eastern Europeans from the Pale of Settlement. Between 1880 and 1924, 1,750,000 of these Jews settled in the United States, while others emigrated to Canada, Mexico, and various countries in South America. By 1915, there were 1,901 synagogues in the United States. By 1938, 72 percent of all Jews in American synagogues belonged to orthodox SCHULS, whose membership was almost entirely of Eastern European descent. Only 18 percent affiliated with the German-Jewish Reform temples.

A third rabbinic-oriented form of American religious Judaism, namely Conservative Judaism, evolved from this migration of Eastern European Jews to the United States. Actually the Conservative movement was founded by American-German Jews. Within nineteenth-century American Reform Judaism, there was a major ideological conflict between what were called "radical" and "conservative" reformers. On one hand, there were those Reform Jews, predominantly located in western or midwestern states, who wanted the Reform movement to develop as a representative body for all variations of American-Jewish religion. One of these leaders was Isaac Mayer Wise. He was hostile to the new forms of biblical criticism that had developed in German scholarship and that raised doubts as to the authenticity of the Jewish-claimed revelation of the Torah at Sinai. Wise's commitment to a total communal expression of Judaism, as opposed to a parochial Reform movement, is represented in the names of the institutions that he founded. He names his organization of rabbis the "Central Conference of American Rabbis," called his rabbinical seminary in Cincinnati, Ohio the "Hebrew Union College," and titled his organization of American synagogues the "Union of American Hebrew Congregations." The word *Reform* appears in none of these titles, while the term *American* is used in two of them. Opposing him were Reform Jews, such as David Einhorn, predominantly located in the East Coast. Their commitment was primarily to the ideology of Reform. They were not prepared, in any way, to compromise this enlightenment ideology for the sake of union with all Jews.

A compromise was reached between these two factions. The more conservative, mid-western Reformers were granted the institutional structures of the movement. Isaac Mayer Wise's seminary, rabbinical organization and synagogue body became Reform's official organizations, and Wise was president of all three. However, the official Reform ideology adopted in both its prayer book and its statement of principles, the 1885 Pittsburgh Platform, was the radical ideology of Einhorn. While Reform Judaism was clearly committed to the preservation of 'Judaism,' the ideological emphasis on 'Reform' was equally strong. Among the more extreme of the radicals were some more committed to the Reform, i.e., enlightenment religion, than to Judaism, which led to Felix Adler (1851-1933)—the son of Samuel Adler, who was the rabbi of New York's Temple Emanuel—founding the Ethical Culture Society in 1876. Conversely, among the more traditional of the Conservatives, were some more committed to Judaism than to Reform. It was these reformers—most notably Sabato Morais (1823-1897), the rabbi of the old Sephardic synagogue Mikveh Israel in Philadelphia; Henry Pereira Mendes (1852-1937), the rabbi of Congregation Shearith Israel in New York; and Marcus Jastrow (1829-1903)—who founded the Conservative movement.

A single auspicious event precipitated the Conservative break-off from the Reform movement: The convention of the Union of American Hebrew Congregations at Highland House resort in Cincinnati in 1883 was supposed to be kosher; the first dish served at the main banquet however was shrimp, and the most traditional of the assembled rabbis left the conference and eventually founded Conservative Judaism. However, as was noted above, if it were not for the movement's appeal to many Eastern European Jews, it is most likely that the movement would have died or at best had no greater appeal among the predominantly German-Jewish American community than did Adler's Ethical Cultural Society.

By 1938, 27,000 or 10 percent of all synagogue-affiliated Jews belonged to Conservative synagogues. The great majority of Jews in America, most of whom were Eastern European, did not belong to any religious institution. Only 32 percent of the American Jewish community at that time could be identified as members of any kind of congregation. Only 1,000,000 to 1,500,000 Jews in the United States were synagogue members, out of 4,600,000. In fact, the Jewish identity of the Eastern Europeans lay in new form of secular Jewish institutions that this third wave of Jewish migration promoted.

If you had picked up a copy of an American-Jewish newspaper, like the *Baltimore Jewish Chronicle* in the 1910s, you might have found the following kind of information: The lead article on the front page might report a strike in a local garment factory with Mr. Stern quoted on behalf of management and Mr. Levinsky representing the labor union. In the section devoted to social news, you might discover that our fictitious Mr. Stern was also the president of the largest Reform temple in Baltimore, while Mr. Levinsky was president of the Vilna *Landsmannschaft*. The *Landsmannschaften* were organizations of Jews from the same area in the Old World. American Jews formed these organizations for a variety of secular reasons: Jews bore primary responsibility for taking care of "their own kind of people"; it was best to associate with "one's own"; Jews were more their "own kind of people" than other people; than other Jews. Minimally, the *Landsmannschaften* functioned as social clubs in which Jews from a given town or area could find out personal news from the old country. Beyond these functions, the *Landsmannschaften* became organs for social welfare that assisted immigrants in finding jobs and becoming settled in the New World. Furthermore, they perpetuated the Old World synagogue membership functions of visiting the sick and burying the dead. What was unique about the *Landsmannschaft* was that it was the first primary institution of Jewish communal life in two thousand years that was not ruled by rabbis. In time these functions were taken over from the *Landsmannschaften* by other non-rabbinic Jewish welfare organizations, such as B'nai B'rith, the American Jewish Committee, and the Jewish Welfare Federations. Until the 1950s, they were the primary power organizations in the American Jewish community.

Most of the Eastern European Jews remained either on the East Coast or the West Coast. Where they settled depended on how they left Eastern Europe. Those travelling eastward ended up on Pacific ships that brought them to the West Coast. Most traveled westward; they took Atlantic ships and disembarked on East Coast cities, most notably New York. Upon arrival most found employment as laborers in the factories of their upper class German-Jewish cousins. Their working conditions were no worse and possibly even better than those of non-Jews in gentile factories. The condition of all American workers at the turn of the century was desparate. Their *Landsmannschaften* provided the kind of internal organization necessary to form effective labor unions, such as the International Ladies' Garment Worker's Union in New York. From these secular Jewish societies arose effective union leaders such as Samuel Gompers of the Cigar Makers Union, who founded the American Federation of Labor. The labor movement in America was not the creation of Eastern European Jewry. Still, these Jews, with their moderate, socialist politics and their traditional commitment to non-violent tactics, turned the earlier unions into an effective force for the benefit and welfare of the American working class.

A very different but equally important contribution of Eastern European Jews to the United States came through the development of the Yiddish theatre and the motion picture industry. Among the German Jews in America, dominated by the cultural influences of Germany, a number of enlightened theologians, most notably Kaufmann Kohler (1843-1926), arose. For reasons noted above,[4] religious theology was not the means by which Eastern European Jews expressed their creative abilities as Jews. Enlightened Russia was not noted for its philosophers and theologians in the German model, but it was noted for its novelists, poets, and playwrights. Eastern European Jewry in the nineteenth century had produced such poets as Haim Nahman Bialik, and novelists such as Mendele Moher Sforim (Sholom Abramovich) and Sholom Aleichem (Sholom Rabinowitz). Under the influence of these writers, the first high quality, original American theatre was established. By the 1930s largely in order to receive United States Federal Government grants during the Great Depression and to reach a broader audience—since most of their children could no longer speak Yiddish—these artists worked in English and thereby made a major contribution to the birth of quality American drama. Trained as artists in the Yiddish theatre were such well-known American Jewish playwrights as Clifford Odets and Arthur Miller. Also there were non-Jews, such as Eugene O'Neill, who applied their experience of the American-Jewish theatre to develop American-Irish theatre.

The German-Jewish skills at middle class business and the Eastern European talents in drama combined to create the American motion picture industry. Until the end of World War II, movies were synonymous with nine studios, eight of which were Jewish family businesses. The Jewish studios were Paramount (Barney Balaban, Jesse Lasky, B.P. Schulberg, and Adolph Zukor); M.G.M. (Marcus Loew, Louis Mayer, and Irving Thalberg); Warner Brothers; Selznick

International; Goldwyn Pictures; Harry Cohn's Columbia Pictures; Carl Laemmle's Universal Studios; and Fox Pictures. The one non-Jewish company was Darryl Zanuck's 20th Century Fox. All of the producers were immigrants who barely spoke English.[5] Nor did they have any background in theatre. Jesse Lasky was a newspaper boy; Adolph Zukor, Marcus Loew, and Carl Laemmle were furriers; Louis Mayer was in scrap metal; Samuel Goldwyn was a glove salesman; and William Fox was a dress maker. The only one who had anything even close to acting experience was Harry Cohn, who had been a pool hustler and a song plugger. None of them started out making movies. They all began by owning movie theatres. Then they moved from owning movie theatres to making movies, for the same reason that their counterparts who started out selling dresses decided to manufacture them. If you manufacture the product you sell, all of the profit is yours, and there is one less person who can cheat you.

The founders of the American motion picture industry were simply businessmen interested in profit. They were not artists, and they had no education. In no case were they idealists. Perhaps it would be more accurate to say that with respect to political and social ethics they were primitives. To the extent that they ever thought about values (and it is doubtful that they did), it would be to desire a world in which everyone would be free to buy their product—entertainment.

Nor were the producers interested in the values of the people who worked for them. All that mattered about the employees was that they be skilled craftsmen Hence, without interest in anything but their technical skill, the producers hired for their entertainment industry the best artists in America, which meant the writers, directors, and actors of the Yiddish theatre in New York.[6] These people too were immigrants, but they were intellectuals with social concerns. They were Jews, but they were secular Jews, who considered all religion (and Judaism in particular) to be unworthy of adherence. As "modern men"[7] they advocated the advancement of a set of values which ranged, depending on whom we are discussing, from the universalist humanitarian, secular values of the liberal French Enlightenment on the right to the socialist values of Tolstoy on the left. In most cases, the Jewish artists were not given the freedom by the studios that virtually owned them[8] to use their craft to express only their values.

Again, the studio moguls were interested in neither promoting nor frustrating the aspirations of their employees; the moguls were only interested in making money. If propaganda films would make money, then they would make such pictures. If these would not be profitable, then they would oppose the films. In spite of the employers, both consciously and unconsciously, the values of the artisan employees of Hollywood can be found in their films.

Judaism speaks of *HA'OLAM HAZEH* (this ordinary world to which the Torah applies) and *HA'OLAM HABA* (the coming world of the Messiah, at which time the Torah will be transcended). Americans spoke about "the old world" (the non-democratic, nonprogressive, traditional world of Europe), and "the new world" (the universe of the democratic, progressive, free-from-old-world-superstitions-prejudices-and-anti-Semitism America). For most Jewish immigrants "the old world" was the English translation of *HA'OLAM HAZEH* and "the new world" was the messianic *HA'OLAM HABA*. Most Jewish immigrants believed America to be the messianic realm. Their first task after arriving was to free themselves and their children from the profane, ordinary ideas and mannerisms of traditional Judaism and Europe in order to make themselves worthy to enter the world of the angels ("Yenkees").

Symbolic of their success and their failure were the new names they adopted. Moishe (Moses) became Milton, Yitzchak (Isaac) became Irving, and Shloimi (Solomon) became Sheldon. Now Milton, Irving, and Sheldon are all good Anglo-Saxon names, totally unknown in Jewish tradition; and as such these should be good "Yenkee" names. But for the most part, the only "Americans" who had these names as first names were Jews. Adopting these names was an attempt to become "American-in-general" and no longer specifically Jewish. As such the names were a failure. While Jews succeeded in losing their old identity, they failed to become Americans. Rather, as these names indicate, they became a distinctive breed of American and Jew, i.e. one who wanted to be only an American and no longer a Jew.

A major cause of their failure was their urban environment. "Yenkees" were white, Anglo-Saxon, and liberal Protestants who lived in houses on streets named after trees in towns like Kokomo, Indiana. But the Jews lived with Italian or Polish or other immigrants. The irony is that after the World War II, when the second-generation Americans ran to the country trying to become "real" Americans, they were no more successful than their parents. Another irony makes their flight from the fantasy of film to the fantasy of the suburbs more successful. Hollywood's films played in Kokomo and Bloombsurg as well as in Chicago and New York. The films probably had a similar impact in big city and small. The real Yankees watched the screen and said, "Oh, so that's what we are like." The Jewish fantasy of what the gentile American was—the film makers did not know it was fantasy—probably changed what these "Yankees" themselves really were. As these Jews tried to transform Jews into gentiles, quite unintentionally, they contributed to changing both gentiles and Jews into contemporary Americans.

The Jewish filmmakers consciously avoided dealing with themes of anti-Semitism. They did not do so because they were escapist Jews. Rather, they made this decision because they believed that no movie would ever change the mind of an anti-Semite. They believed the opposite might be the case: as a result of what they saw on the screen, latent Jew-haters might become active ones.[9] Yet sensitivity to Jewish images is evident in most films. For example:

(1) While the poverty of the immigrant ghettos produced both Italian and Jewish criminals, in Hollywood's movies gangsters are Italian and not Jewish.

(2) Good Jews are secular and seek assimilation; only the bad Jews want to remain religious and separate. The classic example of a "bad Jew" is the two-minute appearance of the "Pharisee" at the beginning of W.D. Griffith's "Intolerance" (1916). That short scene, combined with his racist glorification of the Ku Klux Klan in "Birth of a Nation," guaranteed that Jews would boycott subsequent Griffith films. Both films were produced independently by Griffith, because no Hollywood Studio would touch them; and both contributed to his financial ruin.

The eight Jewish studios and 20th Century Fox only presented what they considered to be positive Jewish types, i.e., secular, humanist Jews. In the world of Hollywood there were virtually no rabbis. There were some cantors, like the father in "The Jazz Singer" (1927). These characters are portrayed unsympathetically as well-meaning, good-hearted people who failed to overcome their immigrant ways. They appear to be unable to adopt the true values of love and brotherhood, i.e., assimilation, that are the American way of life.

It is worth mentioning that until recently mixed-marriage (marriage between a Jew and a Christian) was almost universally a positive movie value associated with being a good American. The prototype of all stories on this theme was the play, "Abie's Irish Rose." In fact the original "Jazz Singer" was written by Samuel Raphaelson as a rebuttal to "Abie's Irish Rose." In the original version, Jakie Rabinowitz/Jack Robins at the end chooses his people and being a cantor over Mary Dale and Broadway. The Warner brothers produced the story, because they wanted to make a talking film with Al Jolson.

The "Jazz Singer" was his choice. Jolson and sound guaranteed that the film would be a financial success, so the film makers were given considerable freedom. What they produced is one of the most Jewish films ever made in Hollywood. Nevertheless, the producers could not tolerate an ending in which the Jewish hero chooses being Jewish over the secular values of America. Hence, the film contains two, quite contradictory endings. First Rabinowitz (Jolson) sings Kol Nidre (Raphaelson's ending), and then he performs on Broadway (Hollywood's ending).

(3) After Hitler came to power in Germany, Hollywood cautiously produced a few anti-Nazi films. The experiment failed because theatres were burned down in some German neighborhoods, and fuel was added to the European anti-Semitic charge that the media was controlled by Jews.

The Hollywood moguls made every effort to make their industry appear to be gentile, because of American anti-Semitism and Hollywood's sensitivity to it. This is the major reason why an entertainer of Danny Kaye's stature was told that unless he had nose surgery, he had no future in Hollywood; and other actors had to change their names.[10] In 1941, Hollywood's fear of its "Jewish" appearance intensified when Gerald P. Nye of North Dakota and Bennett C. Clark of Missouri began a senate investigation of how the Jewish-controlled media was drawing the American people into a "Jewish" war, in which good Christian Americans would have to die to save Jewish lives.[11]

A major consequence of this anti-Semitic accusation was that Hollywood disassociated Nazi Germany from anti-Semitism. The motion picture world in no way revealed that Hitler had anything special to do with Jews. One of the only films which explicitly suggested that the Nazis were anti-Semitic was Charlie Chaplin's "The Great Dictator," which he had to produce himself, since the Hollywood studios considered it to be too controversial. Even after Pearl Harbor, when Hollywood produced a constant flow of patriotic war films, Nazi Germany was accused of being against freedom, democracy and the American way, but no suggestion was made that it was anti-Semitic.

Another consequence was that in the World War II movies of the 1940s, Jewish soldiers usually fought in the Pacific against the Japanese, lest it be suggested that American Jews were fighting to save Jews and not because they are loyal Americans. A paradigmatic Jew of the films of this period is Dave Goldman (John Garfield) in "Gentleman's Agreement." On two separate occasions he declares that he is not opposed to anti-Semitism because of the "poor, poor

Jews" (who presumably at some level must deserve to suffer, for why else would they always be made victims), but because such prejudice is contrary to "everything America stands for." In these cases the expression of values in film is totally intentional. Here Hollywood's Jews are countering the attempt of government and the American public to impose its anti-Semitic values on the film industry. The movies would like to have nothing to do with values of any kind, except as they vaguely define the American (and not the Jewish) way of life.

Until the late 1940s, hostilities between German and Eastern European Jews were strong. Often this conflict expressed itself as a division between Reform and Orthodox Judaism; but this expression is misleading, since most Eastern European Jews were for all practical purposes secularists. More than religion, the conflict had to do with culture and economics. Culturally, Germans and Eastern Europeans always shared a mutual contempt for each other; and, when not united against gentiles, German and Eastern European Jews displayed this mutual contempt. Economically the conflict was between employers and employees in the same factories. Since the Reform movement became closely associated with the German manufacturers, Reform temples met with a great deal of hostility from Polish and Russian Jewish laborers. Most of the religious reforms were condemned as "gentile," but what in this case appeared "gentile" had more to do with German atmosphere—for example the use of German-Romantic hymns added a German kind of decorum to the service—than it did with religious reforms as such. The changes instituted by the Eastern European Conservative movement were based on the same kind of religious principles to which the reformers were committed. These changes met with none of the hostilities expressed against the Reform temples. Not only were they less extreme, but also these revisions were made by and for American Jews whose cultural background was in the Pale of Settlement.

By 1956, only one-third of the American Jewish community held synagogue membership, but both the Reform and the Conservative movements had grown rapidly at the expense of Orthodoxy. Whereas in 1938, 72 percent of all synagogue members were Orthodox; by 1956, only 700 out of 1,728 congregations in the United States were Orthodox. Most of these were considerably smaller in membership than either Reform or Conservative congregations. At this time, 250,000 families were members of some 520 Reform congregations while 200,000 families belonged to 508 Conservative synagogues. While the lines between Reform, Conservative, and Orthodox rabbis continued to be on ideological grounds, the same could not be said for the vast majority of their congregants. Neither was their division based any longer on ethnic background. By this period of the third generation of many Eastern European Jews, most American Jews largely had lost their Old World cultural identity. Consequently, Eastern-European-in-origin Jews could be found as readily in new Reform temples as in Conservative synagogues. As theologically distinct Protestant churches were distinguished by the social economic class of their members, so Reform temples tended to be the Jewish "churches" of upper class Jews, while Conservative synagogues seemed to attract the middle class Jewish merchants. As the cultural distinctions between Central and Eastern European Jews disappeared in the United States, so the economic and social difference between these Jews also tended to decline. The late comers to the United States rose socially and economically as their children became professionals rather than laborers. Corresponding to these changes, the Conservative synagogues tended to become more liberal and the Reform temples tended to become more traditional. By the 1950s, both kinds of synagogues had reestablished themselves in suburban villages where most prosperous Jews had moved after World War II, and all but institutional differences disappeared between these two movements. Then it became possible to speak of both as liberal Judaism.

In the 1930s, Mordecai Kaplan[12] attempted to establish a unified liberal religious expression of American Judaism called "Reconstructionism." However, while this movement appealed to many intellectual, rationalistic, and religiously-oriented American Jews, many of whom became Reform or Conservative rabbis, the attempted union did not succeed. The Reconstructionist movement itself became a third, institutionally-distinct branch of American liberal Judaism. The Reconstructionist movement played a major role in determining both the ideology and the communal political structures of post-World War II, American suburban Jewish life, because of the impact of Kaplan's thought on the young liberal rabbis who became the spiritual leaders of the new synagogues that arose in America's suburbs.[13]

The settled waves of Jewish immigrants to America not only changed their own forms of life, but they radically altered the structure of rabbinic Judaism as well. In Europe the synagogue played a minor role as a house of public prayer and study, whereas the rabbi played a major role as the virtual judge, legislator and executive of the Jewish community. In America the role of the synagogue expanded while the role of the rabbi declined. In a nation where all Jews could be accepted as citizens and most Jews sought this secular status, the liberal rabbi had a small political role at best. The rabbi continued to be the community's expert on Jewish law, but few legal issues beyond *KASHRUT** and marriage were left in their domain. More and more the rabbi became that member of the community whose prime responsibility was to preach sermons, conduct worship services, and fulfill pastoral functions. As the synagogue was transformed into the Jewish equivalent of an American Protestant church, so the rabbi, who in a former age had been transformed into the Jewish "Caliph," now became the Jewish "Protestant minister." Many rabbis still held political power in the American Jewish community, and most of its important leaders have been rabbis. However, the secular welfare organization took over the predominant role in the American Jewish community The rabbi's influence was no longer based on his spiritual calling. but rather on his role as an active Jew in secular Jewish affairs.

Throughout the nineteenth and early twentieth century, there had also been a Zionist movement in America;[14] but it had little appeal to most communities of American Jews. In the 1920s, this situation changed. Until then those who saw the need for a Jewish state could be refuted by the fact that all Jews could come to the "promised land" of the United States. The Johnson-Lodge immigration acts of 1921 and 1924 prohibited mass immigration to the United States. Hence, Zionism became a live option in America. American Jewry's failure to open American immigration to at least 1,000,000 of the 6,000,000 Jews slaughtered by the Nazis, ensured that most positively-identified American Jews became in some sense of the word Zionists.

NOTES

1. Presumably the reason why the Muslim conquerors felt this way was that the Christians who had formerly ruled themselves might not be loyal to their new rulers. There was no reason to assume that Jews would be less loyal to Muslims than they had been to Christians.

2. See chapter 2.

3. See David and Tamar de Sola Pool, *An Old Faith in the New World*. New York: Columbia University Press, 1955. p. 227

4. See chapter 2.

---

* In the rabbinic dietary laws by which food substances are judged to be permitted (Kosher) or not permitted for consumption.

5. For example, consider the following statements of Samuel Goldwyn: "I can answer you in two words: im possible"; "You can include me out"; and "I read part of it all the way through."

6. Those who mastered English became the stars of film; those who did not played Indians.

7. I.e., as universal man, i.e., as intellectuals who had transcended what they believed to be the narrow superstitions of organized traditional Jewish religion.

8. Harry Cohen said, "I kiss the feet of talent"; but he also said, "He who eats my bread sings my song."

9. For example, the only studio willing to produce "Gentleman's Agreement" (1947), was the gentile studio, 20th Century Fox.

10. Let a few examples suffice. Julius Garfinkel became John Garfield, Emmanuel Goldberg became Edward G. Robinson, Leo Jacobi became Lee J. Cobb, Muni Weisenfreund became Paul Muni, Melvyn Hesselberg became Melvyn Douglas and Marion Levy became Paulette Goddard.

11. Hollywood would face a similar trauma again in the 1950s when the charge would be made that Hollywood was "Communist." The anti-semitism hidden in this accusation was played down because of the antipathy Americans had at that time to Nazi ideals. The response in the 1950s matched that of the 1940s. Hollywood gave in without a fight. Again, they did so not because of ideology, but because of what a fight might mean at the box office. In fact, the Hollywood blacklist ended only because Otto Preminger listed Dalton Trumbo's name as the screenwriter for "Exodus" (1960), and the film was financially successful.

12. See chapter 12.

13. See chapter 5.

14. The women's Zionist organization Hadassah became one of the major Jewish institutions in the United States.

KEY NAMES

Sholom Aleichem (Sholom Rabinowitz), American Jewish Committee, Ḥaim Naḥman Bialik, B'nai B'rith, Central Conference of American Rabbis, David Einhorn, Ethical Cultural Society, Samuel Gompers, Hebrew Union College, Marcus Jastrow, Kaufmann Kohler,

Mendele Moḥer Sforim (Shelom Abramovich), Henry Pereira Mendes, Arthur Miller, Sabato Morais, Clifford Odets, Pittsburgh Platform, Recife Brazil, Union of American Hebrew Congregations, Isaac Mayer Wise.

KEY TERMS

Assimilation, *HA'OLAM HABA*, *HA'OLAM HAZEH*, *Landsmannschaft*, New world, normalcy, Old world, Reform Judaism, *Schul*, Temple, *Yenkee*, Zionism.

KEY QUESTIONS

1. Describe the three major immigrations of Jews to the United States. Where did they settle? How many came? Why did they come? What were their occupations?

2. How did Jews come to be involved in shipping and commerce?

3. What is the major importance for Jewish and American history of each of the Jewish migrations to the United States?

4. Why was Reform Judaism so successful in nineteenth-century America? Why was the Conservative movement successful in the early twentieth century?

5. Why were Eastern European Jews not attracted to the American Reform temples?

6. How did the conservative and radical reformers in Reform Judaism differ?

7. What factors led to the rise of the Conservative movement in America?

8. How did Jews become involved in theatre and the motion picture industry? What were the eight Jewish studios and who were their moguls? What values can be found in their movies?

9. Why did many Jews want to assimilate in America? Why were they unsuccessful?

10. Why at first was there little interest in Zionism in American Jewry? When and why did Zionism begin to have success?

RECOMMENDED READINGS

General

Robert M. Seltzer, *Jewish People, Jewish Thought: The Jewish Experience in History.* New York: Macmillan, 1980. Chpt. 14, "Jewish Migration and the Expansion of the American Diaspora," pp. 642-647.

Specific

Stephen Birmingham, *The Grandees*, New York: Dell, 1971.
————*Our Crowd*, New York: Dell, 1967.
Joseph L. Blau, *Judaism in America: From Curiosity to Third Faith.* Chicago: University of Chicago Press, 1976.
Sarah Blacher Cohen (ed.), *From Hester Street to Hollywood: The Jewish-American Stage and Screen.* Bloomington: Indiana University Press, 1983.
Lester D. Friedman, *Hollywood's Image of the Jews.* New York: Ungar, 1982.
Allon Gal, *Brandeis of Boston.* Cambridge, Mass.: Harvard University Press, 1980.
Nathan Glazer, *American Judaism.* Chicago: University of Chicago Press, 1972.
Irving Howe, *World of Our Fathers: The Journey of Eastern European Jews to America and the Life They Found and Made.* New York: Simon and Schuster, 1976.
Oscar I. Janowsky (ed). *The American Jew: A Reappraisal.* Philadelphia: Jewish Publication Society of America, 1964.
Jacob R. Marcus, *The Colonial American Jews, 1492-1776.* Detroit: Wayne State University Press, 1970.
————*Studies in American Jewish History.* Cincinnati: Hebrew Union College Press, 1969.
Jacob Neusner (ed.). *Understanding American Judaism: Toward the Description of a Modern Religion.* New York: Ktav, 1975.
Marshall Sklare, *America's Jews.* New York: Random House, 1971.

4

THE HOLOCAUST AND THE STATE OF ISRAEL

The German Kaiser abdicated at the end of World War I. Germany adopted a new democratic constitution at Weimar and transformed Germany into a liberal, democratic republic. In 1922, Germany entered an inflation spiral that led to a depression between 1930 and 1932 which destroyed its economy. The economic collapse brought on a political collapse that resulted in Adolf Hitler becoming the chancellor of Germany in 1933.

THE HOLOCAUST

Hitler's National Socialist German Worker's Party, otherwise called the "Nazi Party," advocated the total destruction of all Jews. Its leaders argued that Jews are creatures that appear to be human but really are not. In some respects they have superior talents to most humans; namely, their intelligence and cunning surpasses that of humanity. But they are below the level of human beings in physical strength, virtue, and morality. Jews are in essence evil creatures who use their talents to destroy mankind. These creatures have used their talents to destroy mankind. These creatures have used their intelligence to indoctrinate the civilized world with beliefs such as Communism and racial equality, whose purpose is to destroy humanity. Hence, these Jews represent a threat to human survival which cannot be overcome until all of the Jews of the world are eliminated.

The Nazi party never hid its intent to free the world from Jews. Still, most people did not believe they would attempt to realize their fantasy. At first, Nazi Germany seemed no worse than many medieval European states in its treatment of Jews. From 1933 to 1935, Jews were officially labeled "non-Aryans," and were barred from certain occupations where they could exert political influence—the civil service, education, law, and medicine. From 1935 to 1938, a series of laws, which began with the Nuremburg Laws, stripped Jews of both political and social equality; and marriages between gentiles (Aryans) and Jews (non-Aryans or Semites) became criminal offenses. Beginning in 1938, Jews were put under the control of the Gestapo, who were commanded to eliminate first German Jews and then the rest of the world's Jews. The first major event to mark this program was a systematic destruction of Jewish property on November 9-10, 1938, known as *Kristallnacht* ("night of glass").

Hitler created a state within the German state known as the SS (the *Schutzstaffeln*, which means "guard troops"). The SS created camps into which all of the enemies of the Nazi state were concentrated in order to annihilate them. Some, such as the Communists, were enemies because of what they believed. Others, such as the homosexuals, were enemies because of what they did. And yet others, such as Jews and gypsies, were enemies simply because they existed. All of them were doomed to extinction. If the Germans had won World War II, they all would have been annihilated.

The most important death camps were Auschwitz, Belzec, Chelmno, Majdanek, Sobibor, and Treblinka, all located in Poland. In Chelmno, from December 1941 through early 1943, between 150,000 and 340,000 Polish Jews, gypsies, and Russian prisoners of war were executed, using truck fumes. In Belzec, carbon monoxide was used to murder 600,000 Jews between March 1942 and spring 1943. In Sobibor, many prisoners of war and 250,000 Jews were killed between May 1942 and October 1943. In Majdanek, at least 125,000 Jews were killed in 1942 and 1943. In Treblinka, about 800,000 Jews were gassed between July 1942 and October 1943. And finally, in Auschwitz between one and two million Jews were eliminated with hydrogen cyanide gas (Zyklon B) between January 1942 and November 1944. Before World War II, 9.2 million Jews lived in Europe. At the end of the war, only 3.1 million remained.

There were many acts of resistance by Jews against the Nazis the most famous of which was the uprising in the Warsaw ghetto that began on April 19, 1943, and lasted for six weeks. This uprising became the Jewish people's symbol that *never again* would they allow themselves to be victimized anywhere without offering physical resistance. This motive contributed significantly to the creation of the new secular State of Israel in 1948.

THE STATE OF ISRAEL

On August 29, 1897, the first Zionist Congress, organized by Theodor Herzl, met in Basel, Switzerland. This organization became the leading policy body for many world Zionist organizations formed in the late nineteenth century, among them the World Zionist Organization, the Jewish Colonial Trust, and the National Assembly. Of particular importance were the Jewish Agency and the Jewish National Fund (J.N.F.). The Jewish Agency used the funds the J.N.F. raised from world Jewry to settle Jewish communities in Palestine.

Under Herzl's leadership, attempts to establish a national Jewish homeland in Palestine were conducted through diplomatic contacts that he had developed with the governments and/or monarchs of Germany, England, and Turkey. At this time the territory of Palestine was under Turkish control. The Ottoman Turkish sultan was open to the principle of Jewish settlement in Palestine or in any other part of his empire. Still, Herzl could find no way to persuade him to permit the establishment of a distinct Jewish polity in any Turkish territory. In contrast, the British first offered Herzl the possibility of establishing a Jewish state in British-controlled Egypt. Herzl rejected this offer. He knew the Jewish people desired a Jewish homeland established in the territory tradition decreed to be their own. In his mind, the desire to return to the land of Israel could be separated from the aspiration to establish an independent Jewish political entity. For him the political entity took precedence over the return to a given land. As the conditions of the Jews in Eastern Europe deteriorated, most notably with the Kishinev Pogrom, Herzl became less insistent on pursuing the creation of a Jewish polity only within Palestine. He began to feel that there was an immediate need to create a political refuge for unfortunate Eastern European brethren, no matter where it was located. Hence, when the British representative Joseph Chamberlain offered the possibility of a Jewish nation in the

British-held African territory of Uganda, Herzl was receptive. The proposal to establish a Jewish homeland in Uganda was raised on Herzl's behalf by his friend Max Nordau at the sixth Zionist congress in Basel in 1903. The Uganda proposal was accepted by a majority of the world delegates at the congress, most of whom had no intention of settling in this "Jewish homeland." The representatives of the one territory for whom a Jewish state was being created—the Jews of Eastern Europe, especially Russia—rejected the decision, walked out of the Basel congress en bloc, and held their won meeting in Kharkov. There they affirmed that there could be no Jewish state in any place other than Palestine.

The two parties to the Uganda dispute usually are referred to as the "politicals," namely, Herzl, Nordau, and their followers; and the "practicals," namely the Eastern European delegates, the most prominent of whom were Haim Weizmann and Menahem Ussisschkin. These labels are misnomers. The term *practicals* gives the impression that Herzl's proposal was reflected primarily because it was not a realistic solution to the Jewish problem.[1] However, this was not why the proposal was rejected. The reasoning behind the practicals was entirely idealistic. They argued that in light of the historical, cultural traditions of the Jewish people, Palestine and only Palestine could be their homeland. Herzl and his followers retorted from their turn-of-the-century perspective that it was utterly unrealistic to expect to establish a Jewish state in Palestine. Palestine had belonged to the Turks for several hundred years. The Ottoman regime was corrupt, but there was no reason to expect that it would fall or lose territory; and every diplomatic channel for dealing with them already had been explored in vain. From the perspective of 1903, the Eastern European Zionists seemed to have doomed the Zionist movement by insisting on the establishment of a Jewish homeland only in Palestine. However, events occurred within the subsequent years which could not have been predicted in 1903, and which made the idealistic stance of the Russian Jews the most practical one.

A war broke out in 1914 between the Allies (England, France and Czarist Russia) and the Axis (Germany and Austria). This war eventually involved almost all the Westernized nations. Turkey was one of the secondary participants in World War I. The Ottoman interest was merely to ally with the side most likely to win and thereby share in the territorial booty that the victors undoubtedly would take from the losers. Unfortunately, the Turks chose the wrong side. Consequently, instead of expanding their empire, they lost their territories in North Africa and the Middle East, which were divided between the victorious English and French. As a result, Palestine ceased to belong to the Turks, who were hostile to political autonomy in their colonies; instead it belonged to the British, who, in principle, favored political autonomy for all of the inhabitants of their new possessions, including Jews. With the influence on the Lloyd George government by a Russian-born Jew named Haim Weizmann,[2] the British foreign secretary, Lord Arthur James Balfour, issued a declaration on November 2, 1917. the statement was reaffirmed in a White Paper in May 1921 by the then colonial secretary, Winston Churchill. They both stated that the British "view with favor the establishment in Palestine of a national home for the Jewish people." In this way, the position of the Russian idealists, who after 1903 controlled to world Zionist movement, became politically practical.

However, until 1936, the World Zionist Organization remained in the hands of Jews who were residents of Europe and America. While the Zionist leaders debated their respective strategies, Jewish immigration to Palestine was occurring. Ideological-political parties formed which eventually took over the Zionist movement and, more importantly, became in 1948 the government of the state of Israel.

There were three major periods of immigration of European Jews, primarily form Eastern Europe, to Palestine before 1948. The first migration to Palestine ('ALIYAH) began in 1882. It consisted largely of Russian Jews who subsequently lived in settlements created and paid for by wealthy European Jews and Jewish organizations. Most notable among these were the settlements of the Palestine Colonial Association (P.I.C.A.), financed by Baron Edmund de Rothschild, and the children's schools of the Alliance Israelite Universelle.

The second 'ALIYAH began in 1904. By 1907, there were approximately 70,000 Jews in Israel. By the end of this migration, 15,000-20,000 new Jews had settled in the "Holy Land." These people were, for the most part, and entirely different breed from the first wave of settlers. Since the nineteenth century, most of the Jews who came were religiously traditional old people who had come to be buried in consecrated soil. Local Arabs called the Jews "people of death," because the ones that they saw came neither to work nor to settle, but to die. Most of the Jews of the first 'ALIYAH had neither the inclination or the ability to fight the harsh conditions that they found in their promised land. They preferred to live on poor settlements run by Arab labor, protected from theft by Arab guards, and financed by European Jews.

For the Jews of the second 'ALIYAH, these conditions were

unacceptable. They had come to create a homeland of their own. As long as their settlement was run by "foreigners" and financed from abroad, there could be no autonomous Jewish state. Among these new immigrants were disciples of Aaron David Gordon, who preached that only after the Jews left their 'unnatural" occupations that exile (*GALUT*) had forced upon them and returned to agriculture would the Jewish people again become "natural," free, and independent. Among the new, young, and radical immigrants was David Ben Gurion, who arrived in 1906, and Isaac Ben Zvi. Like other secular Jews committed to socialism and influenced by the teachings of A.D. Gordon, they worked with the help of J.N.F. funds to establish self-sufficient agricultural collectives called *kibbutzim*, most notably Daganiah Aleph and Deganiah Bet. On these settlements the Jews themselves worked the fields. There they learned to handle both the horses and weapons needed to defend themselves. No longer would they rely on the labor and military prowess of their gentile, Arab neighbors. In this way these so-called young militants transformed what otherwise would have been a typical European colonial settlement into an essentially independent Jewish polity, integral to the land that it occupied. In so doing, Jews placed themselves in direct competition with Arabs for jobs, which marked the beginning of overt hostility between the two aspiring Middle Eastern nationalisms with mutually-opposing self-interest, hostility that has not yet been resolved.

With the outbreak of World War I, immigration ended. In December 1917, the British army under Viscount Edmund Henry Hynman Allenby took Palestine from Turkey. The third '*ALIYAH* began in 1919 and brought more of the young, militant, Eastern European, secular, socialist Zionists to the Holy Land. By 1925, the Jewish settlement in Palestine had grown to 429,000 inhabitants. The Arab nationalist leaders viewed this large scale immigration with fear, because this increase in population—of persons most Arabs indiscriminately regarded as "foreign Europeans"—seemed to mean there would be less jobs for native Arabs. Also, this large presence threatened Arab aspirations for the autonomous political states the British had promised them. Consequently, in 1921 riots broke out between Arabs and Jews in the area of the new Jewish city of Tel Aviv, riots in which the writer Haim Brenner died. The conflict spread throughout all conjoined settlements of Arabs and Jews in Palestine and sporadically continued until the outbreak of World War II in 1939. Then the Arabs allied themselves with the Germans for basically the same reason that they joined the British under Thomas Edward Lawrence in World War I against the Turks. In principle, the enemy of their enemy was their friend, and anyone who made a colony out of their lands was an enemy. Hence the Nazis, by virtue of being the enemies of the English, were the friends of the Arabs. The Jews had no such choice. The Jewish army division in Palestine, organized in 1936 by Captain Orde Wingate, joined the British in the North African campaign. In 1948, this British-Jewish brigade, known during the War for Israeli Independence as the *HAGANAH*, became the Israeli Army.

A number of political parties were formed in colonial Palestine based on Zionist ideological grounds that laid the framework for the political structure of the State of Israel. The following were the more notable of these parties:

(1) Much of Orthodox Judaism remained hostile to Zionism. They believed only the Messiah could establish a Jewish state. For men to do the work divinely destined for the Messiah was sacrilege, and no state could properly call itself Jewish if it was not based on *HALACHAH*. Clearly the predominantly secular Zionist leadership had no intention of creating a halachic political entity. There were many Orthodox Jews, including rabbis, who, while favoring the establishment of a halachic state created by the Messiah, were willing to work with other Jews in the creation of a Jewish political entity. By so doing, they hoped to bring about a state which, if not uncompromisingly rabbinic, would be what they considered to be "Torah-true" Judaism. The original Zionist party of these Jews was called *MIZRAHI* which subsequent to 1948 united into a "religious block" with the equally Orthodox *HA-POEL HA-MIZRAHI* and *AGUDAT YISRAEL*. In the 1950s this block represented no more that 10 percent of the Israeli population. Nevertheless, approximately one-third of the State's population could be said to be in a religious sense Orthodox. The religious block has had significant influence in areas that infringe upon Jewish law, most dramatically in considerations of what it means to be a Jew.[3]

Most of the young settlers in Palestine were secular, enlightened Jews who, like Ben Gurion and Ben Zvi, were strongly influenced by the writing of A.D. Gordon and were, to varying degrees, socialists.

(2) At the most extreme end of this secular spectrum was *HA-POEL HA-ṢA'IR*, which was formed by the Marxist Ber Borochov. In 1949, out of this party, which for a time joined with its less extreme counterpart, was formed the communist *MAPAM* party. While larger than the religious block and perhaps more influential in the normal political life of the Jewish state, *MAPAM* did not win the support of most of Israel's Jews.

(3) The largest and most influential of Israel's many political parties was the socialist *MAPAI* party, which in 1930 grew out of the older Labor Zionist Party (*POALEY ZION*) founded by Naḥman Syrkin (1867-1924). In 1936, *MAPAI* gained control of the Zionist Congress. Subsequently, all of Israel's heads of state through the 1960s were *MAPAI* leaders.

Of far less political importance but of considerable intellectual stature were two totally different kinds of political groupings.* They were not political parties in the sense that *MIZHRAḤI*, *MAPAI*, and *MAPAM* are. They had some influence on Israeli politics, but they neither advocated a total program for the operation of the Jewish state, nor ever had an actual share in the official government of the state. They formed in response to the eventually-recognized presence of a large body of Arab nationalists in Palestine who were hostile to and often violent against the emerging Jewish political entity.

(4) The *IRGUN ZVAI LEUMI* and the more extreme "gang" of Abraham Stern advocated the use of terror and violence to secure their state from Arab threats. Out of the Irgun and the Stern Gang arose a number of small, vehemently anti-Arab parties which eventually formed a coalition—*GAḤAL*. It functioned through the 1960s as the main minority party in the State of Israel. In the 1970s GAḤAL evolved into a new coalition, called LIKKUD. Under the leadership of Menaḥem Begin, LIKKUD became the majority party. Their major support came from the new state majority of Sephardic Jews who emigrated to Israel from Arab countries.

Both original terrorist groups were opposed by the HAGANAH, which objected to any illegal use of physical force or violence in attaining their political, nationalist aims. However, the terrorists and the HAGANAH agreed that their political situation was such that there could be no Jewish state without the use of physical force.

(5) Opposing all of these Jewish military bodies arose a small group of Jewish intellectuals who were totally opposed to any use of violence in achieving the desired Jewish state. Its most famous representatives were the theologian Martin Buber and the first president of the Hebrew University, Judah Magnes. This group said that if bloodshed must be the price of a Jewish state, such a Jewish entity should not be created. Instead, they proposed the formation of a joint Arab-Jewish polity in Palestine. In working towards this end, they established the IḤUD (unity) movement. The events of the war for Israeli independence in 1948 resulted in a Jewish territorial state in

---

* Viz., the groupings listed as (4) and (5) below.

which relatively few Arabs resided. Most Arabs outside of the Jewish state were increasingly committed to the destruction of any Jewish polity in the Middle East. Consequently, the issues of the IHUD remained mute until after the 1967 Arab-Israeli War, when a large number of Arabs again resided in Jewish-held territory. Although the IHUD party itself no longer exists, a number of small Israeli parties, such as SHELI, still reflect the political ideology of the IHUD.

NOTES

1. In fact, the proposal was not practical. The mass of Jews could not be drawn to settle in Africa. Also, public pressure in England forced Chamberlain to withdraw his offer to give Jews such valuable British territory.

2. Weizmann was a reader in chemistry at the University of Manchester. He helped the British during the First World War to improve their explosives.

3. See chapter 6.

KEY NAMES

Arthur J. Balfour, Menahem Begin, David Ben Gurion, Isaac Ben Zvi, Ber Borochov, Aaron David Gordon, Theodor Herzl, Jewish Agency, Kishinev, Jewish National Fund, Judah Magnes, Max Nordau, Edmund de Rothschild, Abraham Stern, Nahman Syrkin, Uganda, Menahem Ussischkin, Warsaw Ghetto Uprising, Haim Weizmann, Orde Wingate

KEY TERMS

'ALIYAH, Balfour Declaration, concentration camp, GALUT, Gestapo, GAHAL, HAGANAH, IHUD, KIBBUTZIM, IRGUN ZVAI LEUMI, Kristallnacht, LIKKUD, MAPAI, MAPAM, MIZRAHI, Nazi, Nuremburg Laws, politicals, practicals, Schutzstaffeln (S.S.)

KEY QUESTIONS

1. How did Hitler rise to power in Germany? Why did he want to destroy the Jewish people? What were the three stages through

which Hitler carried out his program against the Jews?

2. What were the six most important Nazi concentration camps? How many Jews were exterminated? How were they murdered?

3. Why did the Sixth Zionist Congress accept the Uganda proposal and why did the proposal fail?

4. What were the reasons of the Eastern European Zionists for rejecting the Uganda proposal? Were their reasons practical? Why did their position turn out to be the practical one?

5. Describe the three major Jewish migrations to Palestine before 1948. How many Jews were involved in each? How did the first differ from the last two?

6. How and why did the Arab-Jewish conflict begin?

7. What factors motivated the first Arab-Jewish riots in 1921?

8. What were five of the major political groups formed after the creation of the state of Israel? How much influence has each had on the political life of Israel?

9. Why did some Orthodox Jews oppose the modern State of Israel and why did others support it? How many Jews in the state were Orthodox?

10. What events occurred in the 1960s to revive the issues about a Jewish state that Buber and Magnes raised in the 1940s?

11. How was the former GAHAL coalition under the leadership of Menahem Begin able to become a majority political party in the nineteen seventies?

RECOMMENDED READINGS

General

Robert M. Seltzer, *Jewish People, Jewish Thought: The Jewish Experience in History.* New York: Macmillan, 1980. Chapt. 14. pp. 626-642, 647-683.

European Jewry

Salo W. Baron, *The Russian Jews Under Tsar and Soviets.* New York: Macmillan, 1975.
William J. Fishman, *Jewish Radicals: From Czarist Shtetl to London*

Ghetto. New York: Random House, 1974.

Michael Marrus, *The Politics of Assimilation: A Study of the French Jewish Community at the Time of the Dreyfus Affair.* London: Oxford University Press, 1971.

George L. Mosse, *Germans and Jews.* New York: Grosser and Dunlap, 1970.

Ismar Schorsch, *Jewish Reactions to German Anti-Semitism, 1870-1914.* New York: Columbia University Press, 1972.

The Holocaust

Lucy S. Dawidowicz, *The War Against the Jews, 1933-1945.* New York: Holt, Rinehart and Winston, 1975.

Terrence Des Pres, *The Survivor: An Anatomy of Life in the Death Camps.* Oxford: Oxford University Press, 1976.

Alexander Donat, *The Holocaust Kingdom: A Memoir.* New York: Holt, Rinehart and Winston, 1965.

Yaffa Eliach, *Hasidic Tales of the Holocaust.* New York: Avon Books, 1982.

Eva Fleischner, (ed.). *Auschwitz: Beginning of a New Era?* New York: Ktav, 1977.

Albert H. Friedlander, (ed.). *Out of the Whirlwind.* New York: Union of American Hebrew Congregations, 1968.

Gerald Green, *Holocaust.* New York: Bantam, 1978.

Raul Hilberg, *The Destruction of the European Jews.* New York: Quadrangle, 1961.

Janusz Korczak, *Ghetto Diary,* New York: Schocken, 1978.

Primo Levi, *Survival in Auschwitz: the Nazi Assault on Humanity.* New York: Collier, 1961.

Nora Levin, *The Holocaust: The Destruction of European Jewry, 1933-1945.* New York: Schocken, 1968.

———*While Messiah Tarried: Jewish Social Movements, 1871-1917.* New York: Schocken, 1977.

Ber Mark, *Uprising in the Warsaw Ghetto.* New York: Schocken, 1975.

Milton Meltzer, *Never to Forget: The Jews of the Holocaust.* New York: Harper and Row, 1976.

Jacob Robinson and Philip Friedman, *Guide to Jewish History Under Nazi Impact.* New York: Ktav, 1968.

I.J. Rosenbaum, *The Holocaust and Halakhah.* New York: Ktav 1976.

Sylvia Rothchild, *Voices from the Holocaust.* New York: Meridian, 1981.

Yuri Suhl, *They Fought Back: The Story of Jewish Resistance in Nazi Europe*. New York: Schocken 1975.

Zosa Szajkowski, *An Illustrated Sourcebook of the Holocaust*. New York: Ktav, 1977.

The State of Israel

Menachem Begin, *White Nights: The Story of a Prisoner in Russia*. Jerusalem: Steimatzky's Agency, 1977.

Marver H. Bernstein, *The Politics of Israel*. Princeton: Princeton University Press, 1957.

Yehuda Bauer, *Flight and Rescue*. New York: Random House, 1970.

Michael Curtis and Mordecai Chertoff, *Israel: Social Structure and Change*. New Brunswick, NJ: Transaction Books, 1973.

Moshe Davis (ed.), *Patterns of Jewish Identification in World Jewry and the State of Israel*. New York: Arno, 1977.

Abba Eban, *My People*. New York: Behrman. 1979.

Amos Elon, *The Israelis: Founders and Sons*. New York: Holt, Rinehart and Winston, 1971.

Leonard Fine, *Israel, Politics and People*. New York: Little, Brown and Co., 1968.

Walter Laqueur, *A History of Zionism*. New York: Schocken, 1976.

Howard M. Sachar, *A History of Israel*. New York: Alfred A. Knopf, 1976.

Chaim Weizmann, *Trial and Error: The Autobiography of Chaim Weizmann*. New York: Harper and Brothers, 1940.

Part II

Popular Expressions of Modern Judaism

Introduction to Part II

The closer one comes to the contemporary period in a study of Jewish thought the greater the diversity of kinds and schools of thought to be considered. This reality is by no means unique to the history of Jewish thought. At most periods in history, there are a number of competing ideologies in any human community's life. From the perspective of the period itself, it is difficult to say which ideologies will make a significant contribution to the future life of that community. Generally, the greater the time lapse the easier it is to say that one ideology is more important than another. In looking at twentieth century Jewish thought, there are a far greater number of approaches to note than in any previous period. In subsequent ages most of the ideologies outlined here will be disregarded simply because they will have failed to endure as relevant to any significant community of Jewish people.

In writing any general history of a community's thought, authors necessarily choose to consider trends based on two very different, often incompatible criteria of selection. One one hand, they tend to select thought that influenced a large segment of the community, especially ideas that had political consequences. On the other hand, they prefer thought that is historically original and/or intellectually sound. Unfortunately, often the thinkers who were most influential were the least original and technically profound, while those who were most original and clear were the least influential. A number of technically profound Jewish thinkers have emerged whose skill is comparable to the Jewish masters of the Middle Ages. These thinkers are not directly involved in the popular changes in Jewish life instituted with European emancipation, the rise of liberal Judaism, and the reestablishment of the State of Israel. Note that the most influential and the most profound modern Jewish thought are not the same.

Consequently, this author has divided his discussion of modern Jewish thought into two distinct sections. The first deals with popular expressions of contemporary Judaism[1] and the second, with more technical modern Jewish thought.[2]

The schools of popular thought being considered here can be divided into those Jewish thinkers who see Judaism primarily in secular, cultural (or ethnic or nationalistic) terms and those who view it primarily in religious terms. The category of secular Jewish thought is further divided into thought indigenous to either Zionism or the State of Israel and a view of Jewish identity within a society where Jews, at least numerically, are a minority. The category of secular Jewish thought can be further divided between tendencies that lent themselves to the development of specific communal institutions and tendencies that would affect the quality of life in a Jewish religious institution but would not be in themselves a basis for developing a distinct communal institution. Finally, the emphasis is on directions or categories of Jewish thought rather than on the thought of single individuals or groups of individuals. Consequently, several of the Jewish thinkers to be considered here are representatives of more than one of the thought categories that will be outlined.

NOTES

1. Part II, Chapters 5 and 6.

2. Part III, Chapters 7 through 13.

5

JEWISH RELIGION

The first category to be considered is the thought underlying the development of the various normative institutions or movements of contemporary mass Jewish religion. All of the forms of institutional thought minimally share the following characteristics:

(1) Although the movements have both influence and exponents in all of the major centers of twentieth-century Jewish life, they are primarily expressions of Jewish life in the United States.

(2) All of the movements can be called "rabbinic" in the following terms:

(a) They consider themselves to be rabbinic and, to a great extent, they legitimize their existence as the continuation of rabbinic Judaism.

(b) They promote Jewish communal structures in which the synagogue and the rabbi play primary roles.

(c) They have their *raison d'etre* in a theology that presents an interpretation of the classical biblical and rabbinic concepts of "God," "Torah," and "Israel." They disagree about the meaning of Torah, whereas the understanding of God and Israel is, for the most part, a constant among them.

LIBERAL RELIGION

Georg Wilhelm Friedrich Hegel and the German Romantic disciples of Immanuel Kant believed that they were living when and where God as spirit, embodied in the Christian church, and God as ethical ideal were about to become actual or fulfilled in the secular, physical world. The instrument for this purported fulfillment was "enlightened" Christianity. Corresponding to this new rational Christianity was a strong faith in the new so-called empirical science, exemplified by the physics of Newton. The scientific, critical method of the physical sciences was applied to the human and moral sciences, and for our purposes to biblical studies. Sharing in this conjoined religious and scientific belief, several enlightened German Jews dedicated themselves to the development of what they called a *Wissenschaft des Judentums*, i.e., a science of Judaism, with primary emphasis on Bible and Jewish history. The pioneers of the new, non-traditional rabbinic studies of Judaism were Moses Mendelssohn (1729-1786), Leopold Zunz (1794-1886), and Abraham Geiger (1810-1874). As Jews shared the German intelligensia's optimism about the new science, often simply labeled *Reason*, so they shared the judgment that enlightened religion was bringing about the realization of Spirit in matter. They advocated a form of rational Jewish religion to join in the battle and the victory of rational Christianity. This intellectual climate underlay the early theology of Reform Judaism.

CLASSICAL AND MODERN REFORM JUDAISM

Although any number of German gentile philosophers influenced the early classical Reformers, the roots of their thinking were also Jewish. Moses Maimonides (1135-1204) and Baruch Spinoza (1634-1677) stand out as the intellectual forefathers of classical Reform. Maimonides taught the highest level of ethical and religious life a man could achieve was that of a prophet. He defined a prophet to be someone who through the human perfection of his imagination and his intellect could envision God.[1] When combined with Cartesian Rationalism as a substitute for Aristotelianism and joined with the theory of the KABBALAH,[2] Maimonides' notion of the perfect life became Spinoza's ideal of the "intellectual love of God."[3] Spinoza taught that the noblest form of human activity is a life dedicated to abstract, unemotional, and mathematical speculation, the highest form of which had God as its object. Furthermore, Spinoza posited that perfect rational thought of God enabled the thinker to achieve unity with God. Consequently, whatever legitimacy the performance of traditional religious rituals might have, perfect relationship with God was a matter of how a man thought, rather than how a man performed. A pious Jew or Christian, who had no knowledge of "true" philosophy or science but faithfully practiced all the rites of his religious community, was spiritually inferior to the "true" philosopher or scientist who followed none of these practices. While this consequence had been implicit in Maimonides' doctrine of prophecy, he never stated it explicitly. What was, in this case, implicit in the *Guide* was stated explicitly as a central theological theme in classical Reform Judaism.

Spinoza probably considered ritual to contain little that was of ethical or religious value while Maimonides taught that Jewish ritual was on final analysis rational.[4] Basing themselves on the way in which Maimonides accounted for the rationality of Jewish practice, the classical theologians of Reform Judaism, such as Kaufmann Kohler (1843-1926) in his *Jewish Theology*, reasoned as follows: Judaism is that religion or spiritual community that first taught the world the doctrine of ethical monotheism, i.e., there exists one perfect God of the world who demands right conduct from all people. By right conduct, the reformers meant that people should live their lives virtuously. This imperative entailed treating other human beings with compassion rather than cruelty, having objective and critical intellectual curiosity rather than blind acceptance of past traditions, approaching all of life on rational, unemotional terms, and being more concerned with Divine Truths than with the mundane affairs of this world. While these Truths were revealed originally to the Jewish people, they are Truths intended for all mankind. The purpose of every ritual in Judaism is to teach these universal dogmas through the employment of existing, local, temporal mores and customs. Only the Eternal Truth of ethical monotheism is essential to and constant within Judaism. Everything else is accidental and temporal. Judaism can in no sense compromise its mission to teach ethical monotheism to the world, but everything else in Jewish tradition is subject to change.

The principle underlying judgments concerning ritual change are the following: Does any practice embody any undesirable moral and/or theological teaching? Does a given practice have positive value (promote a desirable end) or no negative value (neither negates nor discourages a desirable end)? If the answer to both questions is yes, then the practice should be either continued or instituted, as the case may be. Conversely, if a given practice has negative value and no positive value, then it should be discontinued. If a given practice has neither positive, nor negative value, then it may be practised by individual Jews; but there is no reason either to require or encourage its observance.

The fuzzy area of judgment, in the above religious model involved those practices seen to have both negative and positive values. These theologians did not state how to rate values so that the individual Jew could judge which ones, in the case of value conflicts, were more important. Similarly, it was not altogether clear what it meant for a practice to have value. For example, one practice by being unique to Jews could simultaneously enhance the practitioner's sense of identity with the Jewish people while separating him from community with non-Jews. The most notable example of this kind of practice is *KASHRUT* (the set of rabbinic dietary laws). Clearly all of the reformers considered it undesirable to be more separated than necessary from gentile relations. It is not altogether clear that all of the reformers considered a practice that enhanced identity with the Jewish people on no other grounds than the fact that they are Jewish to have any kind of value at all. Even if it were granted that for Jews to associate with Jews was desirable, it was far from clear just how good this association was. Furthermore, given that a practice was value-neutral in all other respects, they might have claimed that it had positive value simply by virtue of the fact that this act was traditional. It is far from clear whether or not the classical reformers would agree with this judgment.

Their ambiguity in stating criteria for judging communal practice combined with ambiguity in important theoretical areas. Under the influence of both Humanism and the new biblical criticism, the classical reformers rejected any literal acceptance of rabbinic dogma of the oral and written law. These religious thinkers affirmed that the prophets had reported and recorded Divine Truth and that Moses was the greatest of the prophets, but they denied that the words of Scripture literally were dictated by God to Moses at Sinai. Rather, Moses and the other prophets were themselves the authors of their teachings, which authentically reflected the Divine Mind. They did not claim that the written Torah was simply the product of human genius, but neither did they assert that it was God's product. Rather, the written Torah came about from an interaction between God and men called "divine inspiration," in opposition to "revelation" in which God influenced men to know and teach his truths.

The written Torah was said to hold greater religious truth than any other human product. Yet, it was not clear what in these texts was so valuable and what was not. In general, a distinction was drawn between the ethical and the ritual teachings of Scripture. Whereas the ethical teachings, embodied in the Ten Commandments, were divinely inspired and truly prophetic, the ritual teachings were said to be merely the human products of a given age.

The doctrine of the oral law was given no positive consideration in classical Reform theology. Although not called uninspired, the oral tradition did not have the same high status as the written law. It rarely received any comment. Nothing in particular was said about the relative place of rabbinic law and literature, on a scale of divine value, in relation to gentile writings.

What lay behind all of these ambiguities was the question, how was Reform an expression of Judaism and not simply enlightenment religion? In fairness to the classical reformers, these Jews had no problem about being Jewish. Rather they asked, how could they live as Jews and remain an integral part of the new gentile civilization they affirmed? This problem dominated their thinking. Jews in the United States by the 1940s had successfully become integrated into gentile society. Then the converse question arose, as Americans were they in any significant sense Jewish? The program of classical Reform gave them little help in solving this problem.

The modern Reform Jewish thinkers, the most famous of whom are Leo Baeck, Solomon Freehof, Stephen S. Wise, and Abba Hillel Silver, often were highly critical of their Reform intellectual forefathers. Still, they shared far more in common with classical Reform Judaism than they did with any other modern expression of Judaism. Like the classical reformers and in contrast to the secularists, they argued that Judaism is primarily a religion committed to the mission of teaching ethical monotheism. In contrast to Orthodox Jews, they taught that the Torah was a product of divine inspiration rather than revelation. Therefore, they were far freer than their Orthodox or Conservative counterparts in sanctioning abstention from traditions and instituting new practices.

The difference between the doctrines of divine revelation and divine inspiration can be illustrated in the following way. Consider a student named Morris who attends a lecture in physics by Albert Einstein. Even though Morris studies physics in school, he is not a physicist. The contrast between the text of Einstein's lecture and Morris' notes from that lecture illustrates the difference between divine revelation and divine inspiration. In this analogy, Einstein is God and Morris is Moses. Depending on whose judgement is involved, the Torah is either Einstein's text or Morris' notes. To compare the Torah to Morris' notes is to claim that the Torah was divinely inspired, whereas to compare the Torah to Einstein's text is to claim that the Torah was divinely revealed. As Einstein's text was written by Einstein, it correctly states the purported truth he asserted on this occasion. In like manner, given the claim of divine revelation, the Torah was written by God and correctly states the truth as God asserted it at Sinai. In contrast, as Morris' notes were written by Morris, so, given the claim of divine inspiration, the Torah was written by Moses. Morris recorded what he heard Einstein say rather than what he thought about physics himself. Morris could only record what he in some sense could understand. Consequently, his notes reflect an understanding of physics beyond what Morris could do on his own, but inferior to what Einstein actually did. In this same way the Torah, which expresses the result of Moses' understanding of what God communicated, states truths beyond those Moses could discover himself, but inferior to what God would think. In this way, the intellectual status of the Torah remains sufficiently high through the doctrine of divine inspiration that it occupies a place in the scale of truths higher than that of any other human creation. At the same time, its position is not so high that everything that it asserts must be affirmed to be true.

What differentiated the modern Reformers from their classical forefathers was that the Reformers placed greater positive emphasis on the role of traditional practices or rituals as an essential aspect of Judaism than did the classicists. Having said that the essence of Judaism is ethical monotheism, the classical reformers had to face the consequence that there was no essential difference among true Judaism, true Christianity and true Islam. The only clear way to distinguish all three major Western religions is not abstractly, in terms of the theological doctrines, but concretely, in terms of each religious body's ritual demands. However, if all ritual is accidental to a religion and if the real distinctions among Western religions are ultimately only ritual, then there is no important difference in belonging to one enlightened religious group or another. If the value of ritual lies only in the ideals that it embodies, and an individual is aware that this is the purpose of ritual, then rationally he will see himself in one of two situations with regard to any specific practice. Either he already acknowledges the particular embodied ideal, in which case he does not need to observe the ritual; or he rejects it, and he does not observe the practice since he judges it to be perverse. There seem to be no grounds which would justify, let alone encourage, an individual who accepted the classical Reform conception of worship willingly to perform any ritual. Reform Jews and even Reform congregations continued to acknowledge that to be Jewish is not in itself essential to Judaism and to observe ritual has no real rationale. However, for most Reform Jews after the 1930s, these consequences would have been considered to be *reductio ad absurdum* arguments against Reform if they could not find some way out by reconstructing their theological principles.

Several post-World War II Reform theologians have attempted to formulate a new theology of Reform in uniting three affirmations: First, Reform Judaism is committed to ritual or halachic change in the light of historical context. Second, Jewish traditional practices remain central in Judaism. Third, a sense of primary identity as part of the Jewish people remains essential. Most notable among these thinkers is Eugene Borowitz (born 1924). However, for the most part, the mass of Reform congregants have paid little attention to this literature. Their members are content to institute in their synagogues the changes that modern Reform theologians advocate without theological considerations.

CONSERVATIVE AND RECONSTRUCTIONIST JUDAISM

The Conservative movement may be characterized as nontheological in comparison with the other religious approaches to modern Judaism. Insofar as its distinctiveness can be stated in theoretical terms, Conservative Judaism adopted the Reform principle that Jewish practice is subject to change in different times and places. However, the Conservative movement expressed a far greater concern than did Reform Judaism for preserving as great a link as possible with Orthodoxy. A widespread popular conception of Conservative Judaism as that branch of American religious Judaism that changes more than Orthodoxy but less than Reform is not entirely without justification. Nevertheless, underlying this emphasis on practice is some explicit and much implicit theology.

Insofar as an explicit theology of Conservative Judaism has been stated, its spokesman was Solomon Schechter (1847-1915). Like his theological predecessors in the Reform movement, Schechter was committed to change in Judaism beyond the degree of flexibility possible in twentieth-century Orthodoxy. Also, like the modernist reformers, Schechter did not want change to be so radical that by becoming modern the Jews would cease to be Jewish. As both Schechter and the Reform modernists approached these seemingly conflicting goals, the problem was to determine some set of principles by which certain features of historical rabbinic Judaism might remain inviolate while others would be carefully modified. The proposed methodology for drawing this distinction lay in determining what classical reformers called the "essence of Judaism."

It was thought that if something belongs to the essence of Judaism, when it ceases to be characteristic of the community, the group ceases to be Jewish. What is thought to be part of the essence is considered inviolable, but what is judged nonessential can be changed without endangering the community's identity. The problem was to discover the essential properties of Judaism. The methodology by which this question was answered consisted in exploring Jewish history to determine those characteristics which are universally, as well as uniquely, true of Judaism. It would then be possible to state what in Judaism is to inviolable or essential. For this reason, Jewish religious thought centered around the modern approaches to Jewish history of the *Wissenschaft des Judentums*. Consequently, Jewish history at this time was inherently theological, while Jewish theology was more historical than philosophical.

The classical reformers, whose orientation had been theological rather than historical, had claimed the essence of Judaism to be ethical monotheism. It was apparent to most Jewish thinkers of the mid-twentieth century that even if the dogma of ethical monotheism was universally true of all historical expressions of Judaism, it was not uniquely true of Judaism, since both Christianity and Islam were committed in principle to this same abstract ideal.

Schechter never denied that dogma could be found that are universally true of Jewish communal experience, but he insisted that such truths by themselves did not state a satisfactory essence of Judaism. Such an approach incorrectly excluded a necessary ingredient of Jewish essence, namely, the Jewish people themselves. Schechter asserted that in judging which ritual could change and which should remain the same, attention must be paid to both the universal ideals of Judaism and to the preservation of historical continuity with the Jewish people. No matter how reasonable on conceptual grounds it might seem to institute any given revision, if it is unacceptable to the Jewish people themselves or if it is so drastic that it offers no communal ties to the Jewish past, then the change in question is unacceptable.

In order to legitimize his judgment of the centrality of what Jews have done and continue to do in considering proposed Jewish practice, Schechter employed the classical rabbinic expression, 'the chain of tradition,' as a technical term for his proposed criteria. In classical rabbinic usage, 'chain of tradition' meant the specific procedure of common law in rabbinic courts by which halachic judgments were both passed and legitimized as proper interpretations of the Torah as Moses had received it at Sinai. As Schechter used this expression, chain of tradition meant that in forming new modes of Jewish communal life rabbis must preserve a link to the past ways of life of the Jewish people. Whereas in classical rabbinic Judaism the link was divinely ordained law, in Schechter's Conservative Judaism the link became the *de facto* practices of Jewish people. In Reform Judaism the essence of Judaism consisted primarily of what were thought to be Divine Truths. In Schechter's Conservative Judaism the essence consisted of the admittedly fallible forms of behavior of a finite, temporal community in relationship with its deity.

By distinctly emphasizing human behavior over any form of divine truths and by advancing a historical rather than a theological orientation to Jewish life, Schechter's Conservative Jewish theology was more reflective of American life and thought than any other expression of contemporary Jewish religion. However, in virtue of the fact that its principles for change lay ultimately in the behavior of the masses, or in what might be called a democratic principle of judgment in Jewish communal legislation, it was difficult both in theory and in practice for Conservative Judaism to innovate new expressions of Jewish religious life. In principle, Schechter's Judaism was committed to the source of change residing in the Jewish people, but there seemed to be no way for Conservative leaders to innovate until the change already was practiced and adopted by a significant sample of Jewish people. In fact, most innovations in the Conservative movement (such as mixed seating, the bat mitzvah, confirmation, and the employment of modern music in worship) were adaptions of practices originated in the Reform movement and proven inoffensive to most affirmatively identified liberal religious Jews. For many, if not most, Conservative Jews this limitation on originality was not a problem. Some liberal Jews believed that the threat of assimilation was sufficiently great that without innovation the Jewish community could not be preserved in the Western world. Such a liberal Jew was Mordecai Kaplan (1881-1934).[5]

In the 1930s Kaplan wrote two books, *The Future of the American Jew* and *Judaism as a Civilization*, which attempted to solve the following problem. Since he was a liberal and not an Orthodox Jew, Kaplan affirmed participation in Western European and American civilization and shared the modern secular optimism about empirical science and humanism. At the same time, Kaplan was a Jew and not merely a liberal, so he affirmed participation in what he understood, from the influence of liberal Jews such as Schechter, to be a distinct Jewish civilization. Kaplan rejected both the extreme secular judgment of the Jewish nationalists[6] and the extreme religious judgement of the reformers as naive. Kaplan recognized that to call Judaism simply a nation or a religion was in the light of Jewish history far too simplistic. Incorporating the partial truths of both extremes, Kaplan posited that Judaism is a "civilization," an organized community of people with a distinct culture and religion.

Kaplan considered it to be of ultimate value for a Jew, insofar as he was a Jew, to preserve his civilization, whose existence was threatened by American emancipation. He recognized that citizenship in modern secular states meant the end of the old rabbinic Jewish community and the demise of those cultural and religious aspects of Jewish civilization promoting distinct Jewish identity. From Kaplan's perspective, the ultimate goal of all aspects of Jewish life—political and social organization as well as culture, ideology and religion—was the preservation of Jews in an identifiable collective as Jews. Toward this end Kaplan proposed an organized structure for distinct Jewish communities in America with cultural, religious, and social autonomy, reinforced by universal links with other Jewish communities without political autonomy. In addition, he proposed the establishment of an autonomous political Jewish state in Palestine, which, because of its historical position and its political autonomy, would eventually become a cultural, religious center for his loosely connected world Jewish community.

In this way Kaplan attempted to incorporate into Jewish thought what he judged valuable in a century of enlightenment. From Reform Judaism he took the recognition of the importance in Jewish life of intellectual pursuits, most notably Jewish science, art, theology, and ethics. From the spiritual or cultural Zionism of Aḥad Ha-'Am, he accepted the desirability of establishing an autonomous political state which could serve as a cultural and spiritual center for world Jewry. From the Conservative movement, he inherited the principle that the preservation of the Jewish people is more central than questions of ideology in determining what is of primary importance in Jewish existence. From American Pragmatism, he absorbed the attitude that the value of thought lies in dictating concretely productive forms of behavior rather than asserting abstractly true statements.

The strength and importance of Kaplan's theology lay in its ability to blend innumerable different values of early twentieth-century

American life into a coherent approach to Judaism and to prophesy, with far greater accuracy than any other Jewish thinker of his time, the course of Jewish life in America. The very elements that gave Kaplan's writings their value were attacked in the 1950s and 60s by conservative-oriented, liberal religious Jewish thinkers.

In terms of philosophy, as Pragmatism became suspect as intellectually dishonest, Kaplan's Reconstructionism became suspect as spiritually dishonest. What it basically means to say that a statement is true is that the statement asserts a state of affairs that, in fact, is the case. Truth is not primarily a question of workability, in any sense of the term. No matter how useful a statement may be, it may be false. Also, there are many true statements that are of little or no use. What was intellectually suspicious about Pragmatism was that it seemed to discount truth in making truth judgements. Similarly reconstructionists seemed to discount God in their religious judgements. Religious practice or behavior in the Western world usually had to do with human behavior in relationship with God, and not simply with human behavior. Religious Jews practise what they do because they believe that this kind of activity has something to do with what God wants of them and their fellow Jews. They do not perform what they call *MITZVOT* only because they think that the actions are good for the Jewish people independent of any consideration of God. If the existence of the Jewish people as such is a value, then, presumably, in principle one could speak of a Godless Judaism.[7] For most religious Jews such a position would be untenable. For them the primary purpose of Jewish ritual must in some sense be related to an existing God. In Kaplan's thought ritual has to do with an existing Jewish people. God is reduced to the status of one among many concepts useful in promoting Jewish identity among Jewish intellectuals.

In fairness to Kaplan, his discussion of a Jewish religion presupposed a commitment to the values of Western secular civilization as well as a positive faith in the constructive powers of empirical science. The above criticisms indicate a certain skepticism among many young Jewish intellectuals in the fifties that underlay their criticism of Reconstructionism. The spiritual fathers of the new theology that arose in opposition to Kaplan's Humanism were the early twentieth-century German-Jewish existentialists, Martin Buber and Franz Rosenzweig.[8] Their most important American voices were Abraham Heschel, a professor at the Conservative movement's Jewish Theological Seminary, and Eugene Borowitz, a professor at the Reform movement's Hebrew Union College–Jewish Institute of Religion.

ORTHODOX JUDAISM

Orthodoxy is that contemporary religious interpretation of Judaism, which claims not to be contemporary, because it understands itself to be a continuation of classical, rabbinic Judaism. In several respects Orthodoxy is what it claims to be. Theologically, its understanding of God, Torah, and the people of Israel is unchanged from the main themes of rabbinic thought in classical and medieval rabbinic Judaism. Contemporary Orthodoxy continues to use classical rabbinic methods for deciding Jewish practice. They are constituted in regional rabbinic bodies known, as they were traditionally, as BᵉTEY DIN. Their courts base their judgments on rabbinic decisions recorded in rabbinically-sanctioned legal collections, ranging from the two Talmuds to the SHULḤAN ARUKH to contemporary collections of decisions by notable nineteenth and even twentieth century rabbis.

There are a number of respects in which contemporary Orthodoxy is different from past rabbinic Judaism. For example, it is not possible to speak of any universal centralized body for rabbinic decision making, after the decline of the gaonate centered in Baghdad; nonetheless, prior to the mid-nineteenth century rabbinic Judaism manifested a considerable degree of uniform authority.

While there were significant differences between the halachic judgments of the Ashkenazic and the Sephardic centers of Jewry and, to a lesser extent, between Central and Eastern European Ashkenazic rabbis, still there tended to be single rabbinic authorities who were recognized universally as ultimate appeals in questions of *HALACHAH*. Although there was no formal system for deciding that the judgments of one rabbi had authority than the judgments of another rabbi, certain rabbis emerged in each generation who were recognized as courts of final legal appeal for that generation.[9]

Even in the twentieth century, European and Israeli Orthodox communities have managed to elect "chief rabbis" who, within their respective nations, are acknowledged as ultimate authorities in communal legal matters. With the exception of some Ḥasidic communities it has never been possible in the United States, where the greatest number of Orthodox Jews reside, to designate a "chief rabbi." Various organizations have been formed, such as the Union of Orthodox Jewish Congregations and the Union of Orthodox Rabbis, which have attempted to maintain uniformity in halachic decisions among Orthodox communities. These bodies have been far less successful than even the central rabbinic and congregational bodies of the Reform and Conservative movements in gaining recognition by its membership. Whereas Reform and Conservative rabbis in some sense recognize the authority of the Central Conference of American Rabbis and the Rabbinic Assembly of America respectively, the corresponding Orthodox congregations can claim no such submission among their members. For the most part, the Orthodox rabbi is a law unto himself in determining modern applications of past precedents to contemporary cases.

The procedures followed by contemporary Orthodox rabbis in legal judgments are the same as those of classical rabbis, but it can be argued that in this era they show a far greater reluctance to enter into new areas of decision making than was characteristic earlier. They tend to be far stricter in their legal decisions than were their precedessors. While they have been stricter in areas where they make decisions, they have been far more willing to recognize nonrabbinic authorities in other areas affecting the life of the Jewish people than would have been the case of their rabbinic forefathers. For example, it is questionable if the rabbinic leaders of the Middle Ages would have been as willing as most contemporary Orthodox rabbis are to accept the situation in the Jewish state of Israel, where legal decisions for a Jewish polity are made by non-rabbis on non-halachic grounds. In the sense that even Israeli Orthodox rabbis, with the exception of the so-called NATURA KARTAI,* will insist that certain areas of Israeli law must be decided on halachic grounds but will not feel compelled to make this demand in other areas of Israeli law, even contemporary Orthodoxy has accepted the enlightenment distinction between the religious and the secular.[10]

Nevertheless, in theory if not always in practice, Orthodoxy is the inheritor and the preserver of classical rabbinic Judaism. Following the theology of the past, a Jew is someone whose mother is Jewish, and that person remains Jewish no matter what he or she does. For example, if a Jew becomes a Christian he is still considered to be a Jew, albeit a Jew in bad if not heretical standing. As a Jew he/she is a member of an international community called "Israel" which has a particular relationship with God. This relationship is for the Orthodox the essence of Judaism. At Sinai God directly revealed through Moses a written and an oral law. Since God is the author of this law called "Torah," and God is a perfect being, the law is unqualifiedly

---

* An extreme set of traditional rabbinic communities, located primarily in Jerusalem, that reject the legitimacy of the State of Israel as a Jewish state because the state is not ruled by traditional Jewish law and because the state was not brought into existence by the Messiah.

true when properly understood. The only body that has the right to determine this proper understanding is the rabbinate, who must follow rabbinic case precedents in making its determinations. In this sense Orthodoxy can be distinguished from liberal Judaism on the grounds that the former is "catholic" whereas the latter is "protestant." To say that Orthodoxy is catholic means that on an Orthodox view God relates primarily to the collective or catholic people Israel. Individuals in this community have relationship with God in a secondary sense, namely in virtue of their membership in the primary community. The ultimate human authority in religious matters resides in the official representatives of the religious body rather than in individual Israelites. Conversely, to say that liberal Judaism is protestant means that clearly on a Reform view and to a lesser extent on a Conservative or Reconstructionist one, God primarily relates to individuals. The collective whole, Israel, is related to God in a secondary sense in virtue of the relationship of its constituent members. Consequently, while liberal religious leaders may recommend to constituents what they should do in religious matters, these individuals are not obligated to accept their authority. They are consistent in their commitment to liberal Judaism when they make their own decisions on religious practices.

Prior to World War II, an enlightened student of contemporary Judaism might have predicted that the days of Orthodoxy in the United States were numbered. He would not have claimed that Orthodoxy would die altogether. It would have been reasonable to predict that with the birth of succeeding generations of American Jews, who were increasingly integrated into American secular life, Orthodox communities would find it increasingly difficult to maintain the loyalty and commitment of their children. The assumption, based on past experience in America, was that many children of Orthodox parents would defect to one of the more liberal branches of Judaism, while virtually no less-observant Jews would convert to Orthodoxy. However, in the 1950s and 60s Orthodoxy has successfully preserved commitment among its third and even fourth generation, while gaining many new adherents among Americans whose parents were either secular or liberal Jews. In addition, many Jews have formed new kinds of communal associations called *HAVUROT*, whose religious observance is Orthodox in almost every respect except in matters involving the separation of men and women.

At present it is too early to venture a guess as to whether or not this new trend will continue. What will be the future of either liberal or Orthodox religious Judaism in America cannot be predicted.

Undoubtedly, the religious difference between Orthodox and most liberal religious Jews, so marked in the early part of the twentieth century, is rapidly declining as religious Jews become more integrated into Western civilization. Just as rabbinic Judaism necessarily was different from biblical Judaism, so the changes in the modern world necessitate that modern, neo-rabbinic Judaism cannot be the same as classical rabbinic Judaism. The difference will not be as great as late nineteenth and early twentieth-century liberals prophesied, largely because the modern world is not as different from the past as the enlightenment messianists thought that it would be.

THE NEW THEOLOGY

In the first half of the twentieth century the United States was the center of the development of new theology as well as new institutions which enabled emancipated Jews to affirm their religious identity as Jews. During this period the concern with Jewish theology and new institutional forms of Jewish religious, communal expression were intimately tied together. The new institutions were the primary means by which the new theologies were concretized. The new theologies functioned both to explain and to justify the new communal institutions. Similarly, the important theologians and major leaders of religious institutions tended to be the same people, most of whom were rabbis. However, at the beginning of the second half of the twentieth century a change occurred. Young, Jewish, religiously-oriented intellectuals began to turn their attention to a number of Jewish theologians who tended not to be rabbis and who, for the most part, affirmed approaches to a Jewish religion that were not connected with any established Jewish religious institution. Insofar as this new, post-World War II Jewish theology has had any political influence on the established institutions of American religious Jewry, these writers encouraged their liberal Jewish readers to be far more receptive to some form of neo-Orthodoxy. Perhaps more than any other single factor the popularity of the new theology contributed to the so-called return to tradition and to Orthodoxy in the late 1950s and 1960s.

The currents of the new Jewish theology can be divided into three distinct categories. One particularly strong current in the late 1950s was "Covenantal Theology." Its most well-known spokesmen were the German theologians Martin Buber and Franz Rosenzweig.[11] These theologians advanced a form of theology rooted in biblical rather than rabbinic literature, and interpreted it in the philosophical categories of German and French Existentialism. A second current, particularly dominant in the late 1960s, is "Radical Theology." The most notable exponents of this category are a series of young American university students and teachers. Some of them aided in the formation of urban Jewish collectives called *ḤAVUROT.* These writers advanced an adaption of traditional Jewish values and practices to the 1960s' counter-culture values and practices dominant on American university campuses. Examples of individual spokesmen for this current include Zalman Schachter, Arthur Green, and Arthur Waskow. Finally, a third current, emphasizing a theme central to the popular impact of the first two categories, is "Holocaust Theology." The most notable spokesmen for this current are Eli Wiesel, Emil Fackenheim, Yitzchak Greenberg, and Eliezer Berkovits.

The following characterizations tend to be common to each category of the new non-institutional theology:

(1) The leading theological writers are individuals whose primary intellectual training is not in any traditional Jewish area. Most of these thinkers are informed Jews and many of them are rabbis, but they tend not to be involved in the leadership of synagogues. They do not function in the ministerial roles common to most American rabbis, who are spiritual leaders of congregations identified with one of the major religious institutions in American Jewry.

(2) While most of these thinkers are from liberal religious or, in some cases, even from secular backgrounds, they tend to be religious traditionalists in their teachings. Whereas the religious liberal, particularly in the nineteenth century, often felt that old practices are undesirable and new and/or innovative ones are desirable, a traditionalist tends to make the contrary judgment. That is not to say that a traditionalist will accept any religious practice simply because it is new and innovative. On the contrary, some ancient forms of Jewish expression continue to be rejected for a variety of reasons. Rather, for a traditionalist the fact that a given practice is ancient is in itself a factor in its favor, even if it is not the only factor considered.

(3) While these theologians are oriented to perpetuating and reviving past Jewish practices, they are open to introducing new ones from other cultures. Innovations are promoted because they express ancient practices in some other tradition which are judged to be capable of reinforcing a commitment to Jewish religion or they are techniques for introducing the practitioner to more important, traditionally-Jewish forms of religious behavior.

(4) Most of these thinkers are protestant rather than catholic in the sense discussed above. While the formation of a community is important to them, there is a strong emphasis on the right of a high

degree of individual independence from group behavior. Furthermore, the communities are constituted out of the private commitments of individuals. In other words, the community derives its value from the commitment of its individual members rather than the members deriving their primary religious identity from the community. The religious faith of the individual is seen to be prior to the existence of the faith community; and consequently, the community admits in principle a high degree of independent, individual variation.

(5) Most of these thinkers are at best skeptical and at worst, hostile to the great faiths that underlay the rise of modern liberal religious Jewish institutions. Their liberal predecessors believed that modern science was capable of both discovering Truth and developing instruments for improving man's life. These thinkers assert that to the extent that modern science is concerned with Truth at all, its kinds of Truth are relatively unimportant. To the extent that science can improve man's life, it does so in respects that are trivial. The major areas of intellectual and ethical human concern do not fall within the range of modern science. Their liberal predecessors believed than people freed from the so-called fetters of their superstitious past would work effectively for the betterment of all mankind. These thinkers maintain that the new man or woman is just as evil and ignorant as the old men and women were. Furthermore, their secular orientation combined with modern technology enable modern people to reach excesses of evil far beyond the capability of any past generation of human beings. In other words, the new theologians attribute some sense to a doctrine of basic human evil in opposition to the humanists' unqualified confidence in inherent human goodness. These humanists believed that increased human power would be a factor for good in all human life, while the new theologians see unrestrained human power to be a threat to mankind.

The model most often employed by the Jewish liberals to demonstrate the evil of pre-modern human society was the institution of the Spanish Inquisition. They judged it to be a product of bad social or religious thought and bad political institutions. In contrast, the new theologians fix their gaze on the Nazi concentration camps. They were the creation of what was perhaps the most modern, most secular state in all of Europe and far exceeded any evils by the Spanish Inquisition. Both periods of extreme human cruelty are judged by the new theologians to be a result of human nature rather than any particular form of political and/or intellectual society.

(6) These new theologians tend to be skeptical of the beneficent powers of human, so-called objective intellect and science. They also

generally believe that if people would work to develop their emotions they would find a key to both Truth and human moral improvement. The disciples of Spinoza and Maimonides believed that the source of good in people was their reason, and that in order to develop their rational capacities people must control or even subvert their inherently evil emotions. But Sigmund Freud taught that everything thought to be evil in the emotions resulted from their subversion and was not inherent in them as such. Freud shared the commitment of his intellectual predecessors that a life of reason was best. However, he added that unless some attention was given to emotional expression people could not be psychologically healthy, and any rational life presupposes psychological health. Using Freud's writings but rejecting his judgements, many of the new theologians asserted that the emotions, when developed, are more to be trusted than a developed intellect as forces for human, social and individual good.

(7) Finally, all of the major institutions of Western Jewish life tended to be the product of individuals who at least in theory were committed to the positive values of modern science and technology, the Western secular form of political organization, and objective rationality. In contrast, the followers of the new theology tend to be at best disinterested in and more often hostile to establishment expressions of religious life in America. Most of them prefer as little social structure as possible. Some of them even attempt to develop new forms of communal life with those who share their spirit.

Underlying the rise of this new theology were a number of political, social, and intellectual events in the mid-twentieth century. The single most important intellectual development was the new understanding of scientific experiment and truth that originated in the Vienna Circle of Logical Positivists, was promoted by the various schools of linguistic philosophy, and spread to American universities from Oxford and Cambridge in England. Briefly, these philosophers were concerned only with logic and science as sources of truth. They understand science to be limited in the following ways: The only kinds of entities that exist, be they macrocosmic or microcosmic, are particulars. General terms have meaning in contexts that refer in some essence to these particulars, but they do not name distinct kinds of entities, such as universals or Platonic Ideas. While there are ways to speak about universals and while it may be possible in some sense to say that general terms name things, the primary sense of the term "existence" applies only to particulars. If we say that A caused B to do something, what exists are A and B. There is no other kind of existent entity other than A and B called a "cause." Given that there are no such things as "essences" that have any relevance to modern, atomist science, what it means to say that A doing F is the cause of B doing G is that past experience exhibits a high coincidence of A doing F followed by B doing G. Given all we ever experience is a coincidence of two events and because neither deductions of Aristotelian-like entities such as "real causes" nor Mutakallimun acts of divine will are admissible categories in modern science, the scientist must assume that the observed conjunctions in so-called causal contexts are chance concurrences. Hence, since a scientist logically has no right to speak about causes in any literal sense, his causal statements are mere statistical generalizations about chance events which in no sense need to happen. Nothing is necessarily true in science. Although some kinds of statements are necessarily true, none giving information are ever more than conjectures whose probability is only statistical. So-called certain Truth might be possible in linguistics where statements can be made without qualification about the operational rules of man-made languages. Science, though, is concerned with information about the world, and no such statements are ever necessarily true.

Religious liberals thought that the new science could and did teach eternal, necessary, informative truths. To some extent they made their religious tradition submit to the scrutiny of what they called "Reason," dictated by the new scientific method. In contrast, Orthodox Jews insisted that certainty lay in the religious tradition rather than in any man-made methodology. The new theologians, however, tend not to deny the fallibility of a religious tradition; but they also judge science to be fallible even in its methodology. Furthermore, they tend to maintain that in a significant sense the so-called scientific method is inferior to their religious tradition. For them the kinds of ethical and cosmological judgments possible, no matter how fallible, in religion are not even admissible in the concerns of modern science and science-logic oriented philosophy. In other words religious tradition is fallible, but it deals with questions that are important; whereas, both modern science and philosophy are equally fallible and deal with relative trivia.

For the new theologians the sole importance of science lies in the fact that science-oriented engineers can develop technology that has enormous effects on human life. The negative factor is that these same engineers have no expertise which enable them to distinguish between good and perverse uses of their skill. This judgment impressed itself dramatically in their thought due to a number of events that occurred during World War II. Of particular note was the development of nuclear weapons. The atom bomb had been developed largely by European scientists for the United States, specifically to be used as a weapon against Nazi Germany. Simultaneously, German engineers worked to develop this weapon for Hitler. However, the war against Germany ended before the bomb had been perfected. To the shock of many of the scientists involved, the bomb was used by the United States on two successive occasions against the Japanese. Some of these scientists felt that on at least one, if not both, occasions there were no moral grounds for dropping the nuclear bomb on a city. Other scientists found moral justification for the act. No scientist could be *sure* that it was right to use this weapon. Even if they were certain themselves, they had little say over how their device would be employed. Scientists could develop tools with certain effects, but they had no way either to judge the moral value or to affect the use. In these most important respects science seemed to be irrelevant.

Largely on the basis of a negative judgment of Western man's ability to use his technology with any degree of moral sanity, many of the new theology's disciples reached the conclusion that there were basically perverse tendencies in Western culture itself. They reasoned only a morally weak civilization would enable people to develop such weapons without enabling them to develop comparable skill in living morally with their creations. The thought existed that at least the United States would exhibit in its internal and external relations moral behavior superior to the past behavior of European states. After World War II, the United States was in a position of world leadership; and if it was not worse in its collective behavior than its political predecessors, neither was it any better. The religious liberals of the immediate past saw in scientific dominance over religious orientation enormous power for building a better world. The new theologians saw in this same dominance enormous power for destroying humanity. Being so discouraged with the talents that Western civilization had so far exhibited, they began to examine different and older traditions which, though less technological, might be more humane. In this context considerable modern religious attention has been given to traditional Eastern religions in search of an adequate approach to spiritual life in the West. Many Jews have been part of this search, and for these very reasons many more Jews have looked at their own past. To a large extent this looking lies behind the current resurrection of Orthodoxy by American Jews from liberal backgrounds.

The factors noted above apply equally well to fundamentalist or traditionalist anti-rationalist tendencies in American Christianity. There are other considerations that apply more uniquely to American Jews. Since their emancipation, a primary goal of organized Jewish life was to gain full access to the advantages offered by citizenship in the nations of Western Europe and America. For all practical purposes, by the 1950s these goals had been achieved in the English-speaking world. Having reached their goal the second and third generation children of these immigrant Jews could evaluate the actual value of what for their parents was only a dream. They found their parental inheritance to be secure and comfortable, but they found little else. After World War II, traditional expressions of Judaism resulted from the belief of Jewish intellectuals that to achieve material gains in the Western world their parents had abandoned spiritual and moral values from their own tradition and that the virtues lost were more valuable than the profits gained.

Of far greater importance than the achieved positive comforts was the impact of the death of six million Jewish brethren at the hands of German Fascists in World War II.[12] Minimally, the new theologians saw that Jews could not abandon their Jewish identity for any form of universalist, human identity. This negative judgment is the common conceptual bond between the new religious Jews and their secular counterparts. In this connection, many Jews judged the Holocaust to have religious meaning for the Jew incomparable to any event in past Jewish history or in any other religious tradition. While there is little agreement among Holocaust theologians as to what specifically is the positive, spiritual meaning of this event, there is little question in their minds of the Holocaust's monumental importance for the Jewish people in their continuing relationship with God.

NOTES

1. See Maimonides, *Guide of the Perplexed* II, chapters 29, 32, 33, 35-47.

2. See chapter 1.

3. See chapter 11.

4. See the *Guide of the Perplexed* III, chapter 26-49.

5. See chapter 16.

6. See chapter 6.

7. In fact, at least one Conservative Jewish theologian, namely, Richard Rubenstein, has proposed such a theology.

8. See chapters 14 and 15.

9. See Solomon Freehof, *The Responsa Literature*, Philadelphia, 1955.

10. See chapter 2.

11. See chapters 14 and 15.

12. See Chapter 4.

KEY NAMES

Leo Baeck, Eliezer Berkovits, Eugene Borowitz, Conservative Judaism, The Future of the American Jew, Solomon Freehof, Yitzchak Greenberg, Abraham Heschel, Jewish Theology, Judaism as a Civilization, Kaufmann Kohler, Orthodox Judaism, Reconstructionist Judaism, Reform Judaism, Zalman Schachter, Solomon Schechter, Abba Hillel Silver, Arthur Waskow, Eli Wiesel, Stephen S. Wise.

KEY TERMS

BᶜTEY DIN, catholic, chain of tradition, civilization, covenant theology, divine inspiration, divine revelation, essence of Judaism, ethical monotheism, HALACHAH, ḤAVUROT, Holocaust theology, liberal religion, neo-orthodoxy, new theology, protestant, radical theology, rabbinic, reason, *Wissenschaft des Judentums*.

KEY QUESTIONS

1. Why are there so many divergent kinds of modern Jewish thought?

2. Why did modern Jewish theology become historical in methodology? In what sense is Jewish history an expression of theology?

3. In general terms how are the various types of religious Jewry similar and different?

4. What were the practical purposes for discussing the essence of Judaism? How did Orthodox rabbis, the classical reformers, Solomon Schechter and Mordecai Kaplan answer this question? Why were many mid-twentieth-century liberal Jews as well as Solomon Schechter not satisfied with the classical Reform answer? Why did Mordecai Kaplan not accept the answer of Solomon Schechter and Conserva-

tive Judaism? Why do the new theologians reject the question?

5. What is the basis for continuity between Jewish communities of different ages according to Orthodoxy, Reform Judaism and Conservative Judaism?

6. What is the relationship between scientific reason and religious tradition according to Orthodoxy, liberal Judaism and the new theology?

7. Describe in general terms the intellectual climate in which liberal Judaism was conceived. What explicitly and implicitly in the philosophies of Maimonides and Spinoza influenced Reform Judaism?

8. How was Judaism redefined by the reformers? In what ways was this definition ambiguous? In what sense did the reformers accept the authority of the Torah? What sorts of statements in the Torah did these theologians tend to accept and reject? How would observing Jewish rituals be judged by the classical reformers? What are three ways that their criteria are unclear? How would the modern reformers make this judgement?

9. What two major problems in the theology of classical Reform led to the development of modern Reform Judaism in the 1930s? What are the three major affirmations of modern Reform theology?

10. In what sense is it fair to characterize Conservative Judaism in terms of what Conservative Jews do rather than what they believe?

11. How did Mordecai Kaplan propose to reconstruct world Jewry? Why did he believe that a reconstruction was necessary? What did Kaplan incorporate in his proposed reconstruction from Aḥad Ha-'Am, American Pragmatism, Conservative Judaism and Reform Judaism?

12. Why was Kaplan's theology considered so valuable in the 1930s and 40s, and why was it attacked by Jewish religious thinkers in the 1950s and 60s?

13. How is modern Orthodoxy similar and different from classical rabbinic Judaism? What is the fundamental difference between Orthodoxy and liberal Judaism when it comes to determining the authority for Jewish religious practices?

14. What predictions, if any, can be made about the future of Orthodoxy and liberal Judaism? How is current American interest in

Asian religions related to the current success of Orthodoxy?

15. How did Jewish theology change in America after World War II? What are three distinct currents in this new theology? What are seven characteristics common to all three currents?

16. What social, political and intellectual events in the mid-twentieth century contributed to the development of the new theology? How did modern philosophy and the atomic bomb contribute to the anti-rationalism underlying the new Jewish theology in America? What distinctively Jewish factors contributed to American Jews having a renewed interest in Jewish tradition?

RECOMMENDED READINGS

General

Robert M. Seltzer, *Jewish People, Jewish Thought: The Jewish Experience in History*. New York: Macmillan, 1980. Chpt. 13, pp. 580-613.
Milton Steinberg, *Basic Judaism*, New York: Harcourt, Brace & World, 1947.

Orthodox

Samson Raphael Hirsch, *Judaism Eternal: Selected Essays from the Writings of S.R. Hirsch*. Translated into English by J. Grunfeld. London: Soncino, 1956.
———*Nineteen Letters*. New York: Feldheim, 1959.
———*Pentateuch*. New York: Judaica Press, 1986.

Reform

Eugene B. Borowitz, *Liberal Judaism*. New York: Union of American Hebrew Congregations, 1984.
Kaufmann Kohler, *Jewish Theology Systematically and Historically Considered*. New York: Macmillan, 1918.
Jakob J. Petuchowski, *Ever Since Sinai*. New York: Scribe, 1961.
———(ed.). *New Perspectives on Abraham Geiger: an HUC-JIR Symposium*. Cincinnati: Hebrew Union College-Jewish Institute of Religion, 1975.
———*Understanding Jewish Prayer*. New York: Ktav, 1972
Gunther W. Plaut, *The Growth of Reform Judaism: American and European Sources Until 1948*. New York: World Union for Pro-

gressive Judaism, 1965.

———*The Rise of Reform Judaism: A Sourcebook of Its European Origins.* New York: World Union for Progressive Judaism, 1965.

Noah H. Rosenbloom, *Tradition in an Age of Reform: The Religious Philosophy of Samson Raphael Hirsch.* Philadelphia: Jewish Publication Society of America, 1976.

Max Weiner (ed.), *Abraham Geiger and Liberal Judaism: The Challenge of the Nineteenth Century.* Translated into English by Ernst J. Schlochauer. Philadelphia; Jewish Publication Society of America, 1962.

Conservative

Moshe Davis, *The Emergence of Conservative Judaism: The Historical School in Nineteenth-Century America.* Philadelphia: Jewish Publication Society of America, 1965.

Robert Gordis, *Understanding Conservative Judaism.* New York: The Rabbinical Assembly, 1978

———*Aspects of Rabbinic Theology.* New York: Schocken, 1909.

———*A Book of Jewish Thoughts.* New York: Bloch, 1945.

———*Studies in Judaism.* Philadelphia: Jewish Publication Society of America, 1908.

Marshall Sklare, *Conservative Judaism: An American Religious Movement.* New York: Schocken: 1972.

6

JEWISH SECULARISM

The United States has the single largest Jewish community in the world today. Approximately two thirds of those individuals in the United States who identify themselves as Jewish do so on secular and not religious grounds.[1] Consequently, no historical treatment of contemporary Jewish thought could be complete without dealing with the kinds of thought representative of secular Jews; even more so, in light of the second largest Jewish community, the State of Israel, whose major institutions were developed along secular rather than religious lines. In this chapter attention will be given to secular Jewish thought both in North America and the State of Israel. A third major center of Jewish life continues in the Soviet Union. As of the 1980s, most Russian Jews remain positively identified in some sense as Jews, but not enough is known about them in the West to attempt any characterization of their religious or secular thought.

ETHICAL CULTURALISTS AND ETHNIC JEWRY

In North America, the primary spokesmen of secular Jewish thought have been Jews of Eastern European origin, raised in American cities like New York. Their media for expression have been either the novel, poetry, or drama. The reasons for these common characteristics already have been discussed.[2] Because of the geographic, political and religious conditions of Eastern Europe, most Jewish intellectuals from there tended to be Jewish secularists. Hence, their biological and intellectual descendants in North America also tended to be secularists. The major literary forms employed by Eastern European, primarily Russian, intellectuals were poetry and fiction. Consequently, their literary descendants in North America tended to be drawn more to the arts than to philosophy. In this regard the most representative writers to be considered will include poets such as Karl Shapiro and Allen Ginsberg, playwrights such as Arthur Miller, and novelists such as Bernard Malamud, Saul Bellow and Philip Roth. Some British writers, like the novelist William Golding and playwrights Arnold Wesker and Harold Pinter, also fit this category. Most, but not all, of them tend toward one form or another of socialism in their moral-political thinking, while remaining highly individualistic in their personal values. They are deeply influenced by Sigmund Freud's psychological categories, and they are generally products of universities in major cities like New York, where they majored in English literature. Our concern will be to discuss those aspects of their writing that speak specifically to Jewish concerns, most notably the question who or what is a Jew. While there is a great deal of similarity among them on this issue, these artists are all quite different from one another in artistic temperament, literary style, and message.

As these writers use the word "Jew," it has several distinct meanings. In one sense, a Jew is either someone whose mother is Jewish or who has undergone a religious conversion to rabbinic Judaism. In another regard, a Jew is someone raised in a working class, Eastern European home, in the predominantly Jewish (in the first sense of the word) section of some large city such as New York or Montreal. Consequently, they share a number of ethnic and cultural tastes, interests, and associations common to people with this kind of background. While the word "Jewish" is used in both of these ways, they are not the senses in which these writers tend to be interested in being Jewish. Rather, in writing as Jews, they often use the word to describe someone who, by virtue of both his circumstances and his emotional and moral temperament, is an outsider to the main currents of social and political life in the world in which he finds himself; consequently, he is one who suffers. The immediate sources of what it means to be a Jew are popular family characterizations of the Jewish people as wanderers and victims of persecution which the writers combine with literary themes learned in college from modern Russian, German, and English writers. The most important Russian influences were Leo Tolstoy, Feodor Mikhailovich Dostoevsky, and Isaac Babel. The most influential Germans were Arthur Schopenhauer and Friedrich Wilhelm Nietzsche. The single most important English author was Thomas Stearns Eliot. The more remote source was the biblical doctrine of the suffering servant.

Central to biblical thought was the view that any unnatural or immoral act produced an entity called "uncleanliness" (TAME in Hebrew) which belonged to the community in which the physically or morally wrong act was committed. When uncleanliness was attached to a community, the unclean collective, be it a family or a nation, would suffer divinely instigated catastrophes. However, the uncleanliness could be transferred to some entity that was, in all other respects, clean. By means of the slaughter of this "innocent," the uncleanliness would be removed from the guilty party. Usually the innocent was an animal. Often the animal was a goat. However, there was no inherent reason why "scapegoats" need only be goats. Hence, Second Isaiah taught that the otherwise pure prophet could undergo suffering in order to atone for—i.e., remove—the uncleanliness of his people. In time the general notion developed out of this concept that there could be individuals who in virtue of their goodness could serve as scapegoats, i.e., as the means of forgiveness for the sins of the rest of mankind. Christians interpreted their Christ to be such a suffering servant. Furthermore, they taught that Christians, in imitation of Christ, would also serve as suffering servants by which mankind would be saved from sin. This doctrine was particularly emphasized first, during the third-century C.E. persecution of Christians in the Roman Empire and later, in the modern religious writings of Dostoevsky and T.S. Eliot.

In the case of both Eliot and Dostoevsky the doctrine of the saving grace of Christian martyrdom was combined with the following teachings of nineteenth-century Christian-German theology. Schopenhauer had taught that everything that exists is either an object of mental acts or is itself a mental act. God Himself is a purely mental act, willing everything that exists in His universe. Everything other than God is, as God's creation, an object of mental acts. Furthermore, everything other than God is more or less perfect with respect to the absolutely perfect God, depending on the degree to which it is itself the subject rather than the object of mental acts. In other words, Schopenhauer projected a universe in which everything was graded in terms of moral perfection. The standard of perfection was God. Everything was more or less perfect, depending on the degree of its similarity to God; and mental acts were the respect in which things were compared to God. Any given thing was judged perfect to the extent to which it had mental acts similar to the mental acts of God. Human beings were thought to be more perfect than any other physical beings; and within this species, individual humans varied in accordance with their capacity for mental activity. The important kind of mental activity being considered here was not the abstract, mathematical reasoning of Spinoza.[3] What counted in this moral evaluation was what Schopenhauer called "will," which, as he used the word, involved empathy or identity with things other than oneself.

To the extent that one person identifies or empathizes with another person he/she feels what that other feels. Since conscious entities feel more pain than joy, the extent to which someone has perfected he/her capacity to empathize, he/she suffers pain. God is that being who most fully feels the pain of everything else. Hence, God suffers more than anything else, which is symbolized by his death in the form of a man on a cross. The more perfect a person is the more he/she is like God. This statement means that the more sensitive he/she is to the feelings of others, the greater is his/her suffering. In the writings of both Eliot (most notably "Murder in the Cathedral") and Dostoevsky (most notably *The Idiot* and *The Brothers Karamazov*), the religious saint is the person who like Christ is estranged from his/her fellowmen by his/her sensitivity and in the end suffers death.

When young American Jewish students in college read the works of Eliot and Dostoevsky, they formed very different associations with the thesis that conjoined suffering, sensitivity, and saintliness than those intended by their Christian authors. As Christian theologians had instantiated Isaiah's suffering servants with Christians, so Jewish theologians of the rabbinic period instantiated the prophet's scapegoats with the Jewish people. God chose Israel to be His people. Because of His special love for Israel, they have suffered more than other people for their wanderings from His dictated path. Israel's suffering is not only for itself; as God's holy people, Israel bears the sins of all mankind. This relationship is the reason why the children of Israel have wandered the earth and have been denied full participation in human society. In this way a number of Jewish writers identified the ideal of suffering people, found in their European-Christian literary heritage, with the biological, sociological, and historical heritage of the Jewish people.

Out of this background, the Jew was identified with any one who by virtue of his/her sensitivity was estranged from more base human society. By virtue of this estrangement, the Jew suffered the cruelty of those who were morally inferior but physically superior. This vision of the Jew by Jews was combined with a modern folk conception of Jew and gentile. The gentile was identified with natural, physical, agricultural or rural people and the Jew with the unnatural, intellectual, urban dweller. No single writer expressed this theme more explicitly than did the Soviet short story writer Isaac Babel. Babel added to this vision insights from Nietzsche's ethical application of his understanding of the Darwinian thesis of the survival and evolution of biological species.

In Babel's universe what was natural was violent, cruel, uncivilized, and immoral. Without human intellectual intervention to restructure nature, the natural is cruel. In uncontrolled nature, only the strongest—the most cruel—survive. Human beings, through the use of their intellect, are able to develop tools by which the natural order of things could be changed and made more moral. For example, a river in its natural state regularly overflows and by so doing washes away from its shore all of the benefits that it gave to those who live along side of it. People can change the natural behavior of rivers by building dams. By this unnatural means, people can make rivers yield more benefit than harm. The more unnatural people make their world, the more moral their world becomes. In the process, people grow increasingly accustomed to their "good" world, which in turn makes them less fit to survive in any "natural" environment. Similarly, people naturally are cruel to and violent with one another, but human beings have created laws which enable them to develop civilizations in which human cruelty and violence are contained. As people become more civilized and more moral, they become less capable of surviving in a natural, immoral state in competition with more natural and therefore more cruel human beings. To be moral is to be good, and to be natural is to survive; but morality and nature are inversely related, with the consequence that moral virtue and survival are inversely related.

In Babel's thought the prototype of the moral, civilized, lawgiving, unnatural creature was the Jew; while the Cossack, whom Russian romantics such as Tolstoy considered to be a "noble savage," was the prototype of the immoral, natural gentile. In Babel's writings the symbol for being Jewish was eye glasses. Glasses are a human invention which enable people to see better than they would otherwise. By improving on nature, glasses remove their wearers from natural seeing; and consequently, without glasses such people see more poorly than those who have never worn glasses.

The Bolshevik Jew, Isaac Babel was an assimilationist. He wished to abandon Judaism and become part of the proletariat. For the secular Babel to leave Judaism did not involve an act of religious conversion. It called for a change of character by which a man who was moral, bookish, and physically weak became cruel, barbaric, anti-intellectual, and physically strong. Babel often wrote about the Jewish intellectual who breaks his glasses and denies his university education. Finally, through an act of bloodletting against someone who has been kind to him, he gains acceptance among his Cossack comrades. A similar theme is found in William Golding's *Lord of the Flies*, where the only surviving ties with civilization among a group of English children lost on a South Sea island are symbolized by the glasses of a physically comic youth named Piggy. In the end the glasses are shattered; and the then primitive "pork" hunters and eaters slaughter Piggy, an act which marks the final deterioration of their civilization. What Golding's parable implies is that the Jews are the source of Christian European culture, and by persecuting the Jews the gentiles are attempting to destroy their own civilization.

Although the terms are less clear in the writings of other major English-speaking Jewish artists, the same themes appear. Some of them, such as Norman Mailer and Karl Shapiro, whose commitment to being Jewish is more peripheral, also express a desire to become more physical and more violent than their pacifistic rabbinic ancestors. Mailer presents, however unintentionally, this Jewish theme in his identity with the life style of Ernest Hemingway and in his fascination with less intellectual more brutish prizefighters such as Sonny Liston. Shapiro states it in poems such as "The Dirty Word" and "Israel." In the first, he recorded his sense of personal shame for the Jewish image of the bent-over scholar who can be victimized and mocked by any brute. In the second, his personal pride in the Jew's transformation due to the establishment of the State of Israel was revealed. Here the old negative stereotype was replaced by a new one in which the Israeli Jew is a tall, proud man who drives a tractor with one hand and shoots a rifle with the other. In part, this change of stereotype was also the appeal of Leon Uris' *Exodus* (1958) and Otto Preminger's movie (1960) based on the book. In particular, the motion picture industry regularly presented what it considered to be good Jews as assimilated, tough individuals who totally rejected any form of Jewish particularism in favor of general American values. One example among many is Dave Goodman, played by John Garfield, in the film version of Laura Z. Hobson's *Gentleman's Agreement* (1947). However, most of the American Jewish writers such as Saul Bellow, Bernard Malamud, and Philip Roth express a desire to remain Jewish—moral and sensitive—along with a willingness to accept its price in suffering and estrangement.[4]

The nineteenth-century religious reformers had based their commitment to Judaism on their affirmation of the existence of God, but they found the doctrine of Israel as God's chosen people an embarrassment which they eliminated. Later, religious liberals continued to affirm God's existence and oneness. They were more reluctant to dispose of the concept of Israel's chosenness, but it continued to be an intellectual embarrassment to them. In contrast, the secular American Jewish writers based their commitment to being Jewish on their affirmation of Israel as the chosen people, while they found the doctrine of God's existence to be at best an embarrassment. These secular Jews advocated a theology of divine chosenness without any God doing the choosing. The problem was that if to be chosen meant to suffer, such election would be understandable only if the Jewish people were chosen by God and there was nothing they could do about it. However, if there was no God to do the choosing, it would be masochistic to elect to be chosen. For this objection there was no answer except to assert that to be moral and sensitive must be better than to be immoral and insensitive, no matter what its price. This issue was to become one of the major conceptual conflicts in Zionist thought, particularly after the Arab-Israeli War in 1967.

NORMALIST AND UTOPIAN ZIONISM

Behind the great variety of different ideologies of the Zionist movement, there are two distinct, general tendencies in Zionist and Israeli thought. On one hand, there are the themes of what I choose to call here the "normalists"; and on the other hand, there are the aspirations of what I choose to label the "utopians." These general designations are used to group together tendencies in thought rather than individual Zionist theoreticians. Although some pure spokesmen wrote for both directions, such as the normalist Theodor Herzl and the utopian Aḥad Ha'am, in most instances elements of both are found in the writings of any individual Zionist theoretician. Under the category "normalist" fall all expressions of the desirability of the creation of a politically autonomous Jewish state. There Jews would live normally, i.e., live in the same way as other people. Besides Herzl

the major advocates of this Zionist orientation have been Leo
Pinsker, Max Nordau, Vladimir Jabotinsky, Haim Weizmann, and
David Ben Gurion. The "utopian" category includes all expressions
of the desirability of the creation of a culturally-autonomous Jewish
state. There Jews would develop their own art and philosophy independent of the dominant influences of a majority gentile culture.
Besides Ahad Ha'am (whose real name was Asher Zvi Ginsberg), the
leading utopian Zionists were Nahman Syrkin, Ber Borochov, Judah
Leon Magnes, and Martin Buber.

The normalists wrote defending the creation of a Jewish political
state in Palestine on the following grounds: The history of the Jews
in Christian Europe makes it clear that as long as they remain a
minority in political power within a gentile state, they will never be
able to gain all of those human rights that simply are taken for
granted by other people The present well being and equality of Jews
in countries such as the United States in not a counter-example to
this thesis. In general, all nations undergo periods of economic and
political growth that are followed by decline. While a nation is growing, it treats its Jews well; but when that nation declines, its people
turn against Jews. Generally, the better the Jews are treated during a
nation's ascendancy, the worse the Jews are treated during its decline.
No medieval state treated Jews better than did Spain, yet Spain was
the seat of the Inquisition and Spain expelled its Jews. No modern
European state treated the Jews with greater equality than did Germany, particularly during the period of the Weimar Republic; yet it
was this very Weimar Republic that gave way to the Nazis.

The cause of the persecution of the Jews lies in the fact that as
long as Jews remain a distinct people who as a minority are politically
powerless, they will constantly be used as the object upon which
declining gentile states will vent their frustrations. Some Jews have
thought that they could solve this problem by ceasing to be distinct
and by abandoning their Jewish identity. But the experience of Nazi
Germany showed the futility of this enterprise. The one positive les-
son that Hitler taught the Jewish people was that tradition is correct
in asserting "once a Jew, always a Jew." Only if the Jewish people
develop political power comparable to their gentile neighbors can
Jews be safe from this kind of historic abuse, and Jews cannot have
such power in any context other than an autonomous Jewish state.
In addition, the creation of such a state would mean security for all
Jews, whether or not they actually reside there. Frenchmen or Eng-
lishmen resident in foreign states are protected because they can
always return to France or England. Guests who have a home of their

own to which they can return always will be treated better than those who have nowhere else to go.

More than thirty years experience of the existence of an actual, politically-autonomous Jewish state has shown that in many respects this classical, normalist Zionist thesis is simplistic. A number of questions about the above argument are now apparent which were not obvious when the Jewish state was an ideal rather than a reality. It is quite correct that Jews may leave countries that persecute them and go to the State of Israel. Unquestionably, the existence of such a state in the 1930s and early 40s would have saved the lives of many European Jews. None can deny the enormous value of the existence of a Jewish state for more than one million Jews from Arab countries who since 1948 have left the hardships of their former homes and resettled in Israel. However, the mere existence of that state cannot guarantee better treatment of Jews in gentile countries. This fact has been exemplified by the treatment of Jews in the Soviet Union even after the creation of the State of Israel.

No aspect of Israeli law is more basic to the fulfillment of this normalist doctrine of Zionism than what is commonly called "The Law of Return." Still, it is not altogether clear what in practice it means for a Jewish state to grant to all Jews the right of citizenship. According to the Law of Return, all Jews, upon their first visit to the State of Israel, are entitled to become Israeli citizens; but they have no such right after their first visit. Presumably, if subsequently they should seek Israeli citizenship, they are subject to the same restrictions that any alien would face seeking citizenship in Israel. Nor is there any guarantee that this law is permanent in the Jewish state. In the early 1950s under the Law of Return, rigorously enforced by Ben Gurion, the population of the state more than doubled. Many Israelis criticized the government for this immigration policy. They argued that no state which was experiencing the kinds of economic and military difficulties that Israel had at that time could afford to admit such a high percentage of poor and sick people. Indeed, many of them were not capable of making any constructive contribution to the well-being of the state. In the 1950s the ideology of the Zionists prevailed. At that time European and Israeli Jews shared a far greater cultural and historical commonality than will be the case in future generations. Today the majority of Israeli Jews are Sephardic rather than Ashkenazic. There are signs that the common origins of American, European, and Israeli Jews in Eastern European Judaism are becoming less of a link as their generations of different cultural experiences separate Jews in different lands. In the past, the link that tied all Jews together was their common religion. Today this in no longer binding in a world where most Jews are secular, and the religious Jews are divided along sharp institutional and ideological lines.

It is no altogether clear what the term "Jewish" means in the Law of Return. According to rabbinic legislation, a Jew is someone whose mother is Jewish, but there are exceptions. In at least one case the court ruled that if a "halachicly" defined Jew (i.e. a Jew as defined by Jewish Law [halachah]) becomes a Christian, he is no longer entitled to automatic citizenship under the Law of Return, although that person may apply for citizenship through the normal channels. Because Israel is a secular Jewish state there is no reason why terms, Including the word "Jew," need function as they do in traditional, rabbinic Judaism. It is far from clear what restrictions there are on definitions of terms central to Zionist ideology, such as "Jew", once it is granted that HALACHAH need not in any sense legislate usage.

A number of problems remain concerning what is means to say that the secular, modern State of Israel is a Jewish state. Central to this question is what role the Jewish religion has to play in a secular Jewish state. As enlightened Europeans, the founders of the State of Israel intended their nation to be a democracy that distinguished between the religious and the secular. The ideal of a modern state entails a complete divorce between affairs of the state and matters of religion. Israel, however, was to be a Jewish nation. It is difficult to see how, as a Jewish state, religion can be totally divorced from some kind of political status. Even if some political role is granted to organized Judaism. it is no longer clear who its official representatives of Judaism should be. Insofar as Israeli Jews are religious at all, they are Orthodox. Does this mean that, where religion affects state law, liberal Jews must be subject to the authority of Orthodox rabbis? If yes, how can the modern principle of religious freedom be reconciled with the demands of traditional religious leaders for their proclaimed religious right to determine Jewish legislation?

Is it in fact the case that an independent Jewish state is a politically-autonomous Jewish state? In some sense, obviously, it is, but the political world is sufficiently small today that all small states are subject to the influence, if not the control, of the major world powers. To the extent that Israel is economically and/or militarily dependent on some gentile, great power, it is not politically autonomous. It is not clear that by creating a Jewish polity the Jews have overcome the problems of being a minority. Within the borders of the State of Israel, Jews are not a minority; but they remain one in the region in which they reside. Israel is part of the Middle East, and as such it remains a small, Jewish minority amidst a vast sea of predominantly Muslim Arabs.

In this context it also can be asked what constitutes normalcy? The founders of the State of Israel were Europeans for whom normalcy meant living on the model of European civilization. Now the majority of Israel's citizens are Levantine, and geographically Israel is a Levantine state. Hence, is it normal for Israeli Jews to live as Europeans or as Middle Easterners?

If religion is not to be a distinguishing factor of the Jewish state, as Catholicism distinguishes certain other states as distinctly Christian, in what respects is the State of Israel Jewish? To be a Jewish state, do the majority of its citizens have to be Jewish? Since 1967, when Israel took control of the territory west of the Jordan River, the majority of people within the authority of the Jewish state are not Jewish. How then is the secular Jewish state to remain Jewish? The immediate and obvious answer to this question would be some system of apartheid or an intentional government program to expel non-Jews. The commitment of the overwhelming majority of Israelis and Zionists to the moral values of Western civilization makes such an alternative repulsive.

Finally, many of the early Zionists realized that some Jews would not emigrate to the Jewish state but would remain identified as Jews. Still, they believed that most Jews, when given the option, would settle in Israel. Based on this belief, the normalist Zionists expressed no ideology of the relationship of a Jewish state to world Jewry other than a commitment to encourage their immigration to Israel and to protect them from attack by their host nations. However, most Jews, when given the option, have not chosen to emigrate to Israel. These Jews, while not denying the centrality of the Jewish state, have affirmed the possibility of being positively Jewish without becoming an Israeli. They implicitly insist that secular Zionist-Israel ideology must come to terms with their beliefs and the present demography of world Jewry. At least on the question of the relation between world and Israeli Jewry, the utopian Zionists have had more to say.

The utopians wrote in defense of the creation of an autonomous Jewish civilization in Palestine on the following grounds: The greatest literary, philosophic, ethical and religious achievement of the Jewish people was the various books of the Bible. While the Jewish people have produced through the ages other artistic, intellectual expressions of value, none can compare with the Bible. No Jewish work is as totally and uniquely Jewish as the Bible. The Mishnah* and the Midrash** are strongly influenced by Roman culture, the Babylonian Talmud by Sassanian culture, and Jewish medieval philosophy by Greco-Muslim culture. Generally, the more removed the Jewish people became from their autonomous roots in Palestine, the more they were influenced by the culture in which they lived, and the less inherent artistic or intellectual value could be found in their writings. In modern times Jews have produced works that are more the product of the dominant culture in which they resided than products of their own national inheritance. As such these works are inferior both to the writings of their past and to the creations of gentile contemporaries. The works of German, Russian, or French Jews are inferior to the writings of Germans, Russians, and Frenchmen because the Jews are expressing a culture that is not really their own. Only when Jews once again live in their own land will they recapture their former greatness, unequalled by any other people on earth. There they will develop an inherently valuable, natural civilization whose excellence will provide a standard for all of the world to imitate.

Political utopians such as Syrkin and Borochov envisioned Israel becoming the model socialist state whose moral, revolutionary form of government would be a paradigm for all other civilized nations.[5] Individualist moral utopians such as Buber and Magnes wrote about a state whose political structure would enable maximum individual expression and development with other persons.[6] Cultural utopians such as Aḥad Ha'am prophesied that a Jewish state would become a center for Jewish scholarship, music, art, and poetry, unequaled in either the Jewish or the gentile past. As Asher Ginsberg saw the future, a Jewish state would not be a place to which most Jews would emigrate. Rather it would be a center to which would come the most creative, artistically innovative and skilled Jews whose products would be supported and shared by Jewish communities throughout the world. Common to all of these very different visions of a Jewish homeland was that the visionaries were not merely interested in the creation of a political entity in which Jews could become like other people. They believed that Jews possessed such moral and/or intellectual and/or artistic talents that, when left alone, they would create an exemplary rather than an ordinary human society.

---

* The Mishnah is a Collection of rabbinic between 200 B.C.E. and 200 C.E., edited by Judah I who was the head ("Nasi") of the Sanhedrin in Judea from about 170 C.E. unil 217 C.E. It is the core text of rabbinic Law.
** The set of linear commentaries on the Hebrew Scriplures by the earliest rabbis who lived before the compilation of the Talmud in the sixth century C.E.

More than thirty years' experience with an existent rather than a hypothetical Jewish homeland has proved as sobering to the ideology of the utopians as it did to the thought of the normalists. It cannot be reasonably argued that the State of Israel has been less moral than any other state in the modern world. Certainly the present State of Israel has incorporated into its political practice a great deal of the idealistic teachings of the early twentieth-century socialists. Nor can it be denied that there are opportunities for Jewish education and scholarship in the State of Israel unequaled in any other nation. In an Israeli university it is possible to have the kind of specialization in all areas of Jewish scholarship that all national universities have for their own but only for their own culture. In North America and England there are chairs and even departments of Judaica in universities, but these departments consist of only a handful of people who, while they have areas of specialization, necessarily must function in their teaching as Jewish polymaths. However, in Israel, because Jewish culture is the national culture, instead of single departments of Judaica there can be and often are entire colleges of Judaica with departments for Jewish history, Jewish philosophy, Jewish religion, Jewish sociology, etc. There is no question that such a situation eventually will result in the State of Israel becoming the center for all academic studies of Judaism, just as necessarily the major centers for American studies must be in the United States and the major centers for French studies must be in France. However, it cannot be denied that the actual State of Israel has not and cannot fulfill everything that politically, ethically, and morally had been predicted by the utopians Israel is, to a large extent, a socialist state; but is is by no means an ideal political paradigm. Israelis exhibit a considerable degree of individual political self-expression, in comparison with larger and older Western states, whose populations are less homogeneous and whose political institutions are more rigid. The political and bureaucratic structure of the State of Israel has shown, to date, that it can be as unresponsive to the demands of people as any other political system. Furthermore, Israel is a state ruled predominantly by Eastern European Jews, yet the majority of its citizens are levantine. This situation has produced problems and frustrations that make it impossible to speak of the State of Israel as individualistically ideal. To say that Israel is no worse than any other state is true but irrelevant to the utopians. Their primary interest in the establishment of a Jewish state was to create a civilization superior to any other the world has known.

Furthermore. while there has been considerable artistic produc-

tivity in the young Jewish state, it is debatable in what sense this creativity is autonomously Jewish. To be sure, insofar as these artists use
the Hebrew language, their work is unique; but for theoreticians such
as Ahad Ha'am this would not have been enough. Most past Jewish
creativity, which Asher Ginsberg dismissed as gentile in influence,
was written in Hebrew. Through the first decade of the State at least
the content of many plays and novels was unique in that it dealt with
events such as the 1948 War for Independence and life on the kibbutzim. However, Israeli Jewish novelists, short story writers, playwrights, and film makers tired of the limited scope of these themes.
As they turned to new subjects and experimented with new literary
techniques, their work increasingly appeared to be the product of
American, English and/or French culture—although written in
Hebrew. If this has been so in Israeli written arts, it is even more the
case in music, painting, and sculpture. The most uniquely Jewish artists were people such as Shmuel Yosef Agnon, whose style was rabbinic and whose content came from the Eastern European Jewish
SHTETLE., i.e. the Jewish village in Eastern Europe. All of this
trend may be the result of the youth of the State of Israel; but the
causes of the cultural experience of the State of Israel may be more
drastic for utopian Zionism than that.

Technology and transportation have progressed to such an extent
that it may no longer be possible to speak in any significant sense of
a modern independent national culture in technological societies. Former cultures arose with individual differences largely because nations
were isolated. This is no longer the case. New expressions in any art
form, from music to architecture, are readily accessible to most artists.
Consequently, except for minor frills. modern culture is increasingly
international. Furthermore, to the extent that the greatest markets for
art are in the largest cities of the major world powers, new expressions
of Jewish art will continue to emanate from places such as New York,
London, and Paris more than from Tel Aviv and Jerusalem.

In fact, Ahad Ha'am's vision of the context of past Jewish literary and artistic creativity is a vast oversimplification. Even if we were
to grant that the Bible was the creation of an autonomous Jewish civilization, whereas the later classics of Jewish thought were not, it is
far from self-evident that the Bible is more uniquely Jewish and artistically or intellectually more excellent than subsequent products of
the Jewish people. More than that, the thesis of autonomy itself is
not true. The Bible was not created in a Jewish vacuum. Rather, it
was the product of Jewish life in the civilization of the ancient Near
East, a largely common culture in which biblical Jews were by no

means the majority. Nor is it clear that—all other factors being equal—Jewish art in an autonomous state is more valuable than Jewish art in states where they are a minority. Without denying the value of the Jerusalem Talmud, there is no consensus that it is superior to the Babylonian Talmud, which drew on the same sources and was written at the same time. Nor is it true that, because Jews have been influenced by the majority, gentile cultures in which they lived, their work is not uniquely Jewish.

No Jew can deny the vital importance for the Jewish people of the creation of the State of Israel. There are some who would say that Jews have committed fewer atrocities than other people only because they have not had the power and hence the opportunity to commit them. The Jewish people now have the power, for the first time in two thousand years, to determine their own fate and to disprove the above thesis.

Zionism is no longer an issue for Jews; instead, there is the question of what ought to be the role of a Jewish state as a constituent of world Jewry. Presupposed in this question is the legitimacy of both a Jewish state and a diaspora, and some acknowledgment that Jews are a people, Judaism is a religion, and Judaism and Jews cannot be dissociated from each other. The reconciliation of differing points of view is a major theme for current Jewish philosophy.

NOTES

1. See chapter 3.

2. See chapters 2 and 3.

3. See chapter 7.

4. A film story that combines both the affirmation and the negation of this type of Jewishness is Gerald Green's *The Last Angry Man* (1959). The hero, Samuel Abelman, M.D., played by Paul Muni, exhibits the kind of physical strength that characterizes the assimilationists when he arm-wrestles with a teen-age black hoodlum. Muni also portrays the moral and sensitive characteristics that mark positive Jewish identity for these secular Jews. By implication, Samuel Abelman is a synthesis of the natural gentile and the civilized Jew. Abelman is a rough (gentile), tough (gentile), highly educated (Jewish), morally dedicated (Jewish) loner (Jewish).

5. See chapter 4.

6. See chapters 5 and 10.

KEY NAMES

Shmuel Yosef Agnon, Ahad Ha'am (Asher Zvi Ginsberg), Isaac Babel, Saul Bellow, Allen Ginsberg, William Golding, Theodor Herzl, Laura Z. Hobson, Vladimir Jabotinsky, Norman Mailer, Bernard Malamud, Arthur Miller, Leo Pinsker, Harold Pinter, Otto Preminger, Philip Roth, Karl Shapiro, Naḥman Syrkin, Leon Uris, Arnold Wesker.

KEY TERMS

assimilation, chosenness, cultural utopian Zionism, diaspora, ethical culturalist, ethnic Jewry, Jew, Jewish, Law of Return, noble savage, normalist Zionist, political utopian Zionist, SHTETLE, suffering servant, uncleanliness, utopian Zionism.

KEY QUESTIONS

1. What are the three largest Jewish communities in the world? To what extent are they religious and secular?

2. What are three different meanings of the term "Jew?" What are the Jewish and non-Jewish sources of the sense in which a Jew is said to be a suffering outsider? Explain each source.

3. What does the concept of a suffering servant mean in the Hebrew Scriptures? How did the early Christian church interpret it? How did Eliot and Dostoevsky apply it? How did the Jewish community interpret the biblical concept? How did the American Jewish writers apply both the Jewish and the Christian conceptions of suffering?

4. Explain Schopenhauer's Christian ethics. How do they differ from Spinoza's ethics? How did Jewish writers absorb these ethics?

5. Explain how eye glasses function as a symbol in the writings of some contemporary Jewish authors. According to these writers, what is a Jew and what is a gentile? Are Jews and gentiles good? Is it good to be good?

6. Compare and contrast nineteenth-century liberal Jewish theology with the implicit Jewish thought of twentieth-century American,

secular literature.

7. Why was the creation of the State of Israel an event of major importance for Jewish history and thought? What new Questions arise as a result of that event?

8. Compare and contrast normalist and utopian Zionist ideology.

9. According to the normalists, why do nations treat its Jews well at some times and poorly at other times? Why is assimilation not a solution to Jewish persecution? Why would the creation of an autonomous Jewish state be a solution?

10. Evaluate what is and is not correct in the position of the normalist Zionists in the light of Jewish history since 1948. What issues are raised by (a) the Law of Return, (b) the principle of the separation of church and state, (c) the fact that Israel is a state whose population is levantine and whose geographical location is in the Middle East, and (d) the conflict between Israel's desire to be democratic and its commitment to being Jewish?

11. According to the utopians, why have Jews been unable to produce literature and philosophy equal to what they produced in biblical times? How did they propose to solve this problem? Compare and contrast the different answers of the political utopians, the individualist moral utopians, and the cultural utopians.

12. Evaluate what is and is not correct in the position of the utopian Zionists in the light of Jewish history. What issues are raised by (a) the tension between Ashkenazim and Sephardim in Israel, and (b) the quality and uniqueness of Israeli art?

RECOMMENDED READINGS

General

Robert M. Seltzer, *Jewish People, Jewish Thought: The Jewish Experience in History.* New York: Macmillan, 1980. Chpt. 15, pp. 684-766.

Secular Politics

Julius Carlebach, *Karl Marx and the Radical Critique of Judaism.* London: Routledge & Kegan Paul, 1978.
Mordecai Chertoff (ed.), *The New Left and the Jews.* New York: Pittman, 1971.

Saul L. Goodman (ed.), *The Faith of Secular Jews.* New York: Ktav, 1976.

Secular Literature

Shalom Jacob Abramovich (Mendele Mocher Seforim), *The Travels and Adventures of Benjamin the Third.* Translated into English by Moshe Spiegel. New York: Schocken, 1949.

Robert Alter, *After the Tradition: Essays on Modern Jewish Writing.* New York: E.P. Dutton, 1971.

Charles Angoff and Meyer Levin, *The Rise of American Jewish Literature.* New York: Simon and Schuster, 1970.

Abraham Chapman (ed.). *Jewish-American Literature: An Anthology.* New York: Mentor, 1974.

Bernard Cohen, *Sociocultural Changes in American Jewish Life as Reflected in Selected Jewish Literature.* East Brunswick, N.J.: Farleigh Dickinson University Press, 1972.

Milton Doroshkin, *Yiddish in America.* East Brunswick, N.J.: Fairleigh Dickinson University Press, 1969.

Allen Ginsberg, *The Fall of America: Poems of These States.* San Francisco: City Lights Books, 1972.

———*Howl and Other Poems.* San Francisco: City Lights Books, 1956.

———*Kaddish and Other Poems: 1958-1960.* San Francisco: City Lights Books, 1961.

Joseph Klausner, *A History of Modern Hebrew Literature (1785-1930).* Westport, Conn.: Greenwood Press, 1978.

Josephine Zadovsky Knopp, *The Trial of Judaism in Contemporary Jewish Writing.* Urbana: University of Illinois Press, 1975.

Joseph C. Landis (ed.), *The Great Jewish Plays.* New York: Horizon Press, 1972.

Sol Liptzin, *The Maturing of Yiddish Literature.* New York, Jonathan David, 1970.

Charles A. Madison. *Yiddish Literature: Its Scope and Major Writers.* New York: Federick Ungar, 1968.

Irving Malin and Irwin Stark (eds.). *Breakthrough: A Treasury of Contemporary American-Jewish Literature.* New York: McGraw-Hill, 1964.

Norman Podhoretz (ed.). *The Commentary Reader: Two Decades of Articles and Stories.* New York: Atheneum, 1966.

Isaiah Rabinovich, *Major Trends in Modern Hebrew Fiction.* Translated into English by M. Roston. Chicago: University of Chicago Press, 1968.

Howard Schwartz and Anthony Rudolf (eds.). *Voices within the Ark: The Modern Jewish Poets.* New York: Avon, 1980.

Karl Shapiro, *Poems of a Jew.* New York: Random House, 1958.

Ruth R. Wisse, *The Schlemiel as Modern Hero.* Chicago: University of Chicago Press, 1979.

Zionism

Shlomo Avineri, *The Making of Modern Zionism.* New York: Basic Books, 1984.

Nachman Drosdoff, *Ahad Ha'am: Highlights of His Life and Work.* Holon, Israel: Nachman Drosdoff, 1962.

Amos Elon, *Herzl.* New York: Rinehart and Winston, 1975.

Aaron David Gordon, *Selected Essays.* Edited by N. Teradyon and A. Shohat and translated into English by Frances Burnce. New York: Arno, 1981.

Ahad Ha'am, *Selected Essays.* Translated into English by Leon Simon. Philadelphia: Jewish Publication Society of America, 1912.

Arthur Hertzberg (ed.), *The Zionist Idea: A Historical Analysis and Reader.* Garden City, New York; Doubleday, 1959.

Theodor Herzl, *The Jewish State.* London: Zionist Organization, 1936.

Jacques Kornberg (ed.), At the Crossroads: Essays on Ahad Ha-Am. Albany: State University of New York Press, 1983.

Peretz Merhav. *The Israeli Left: History, Problems, Documents.* New York: A.S. Barnes, 1980.

Leon Simon, *Ahad Ha-Am, Asher Ginsberg: A Biography.* Philadelphia: Jewish Publication Society of America, 1960.

Marie Syrkin, *Nachman Syrkin, Socialist Zionist: A Biographical Memoir and Selected Essays.* New York: Herzl Press, 1961.

Melvin I. Urofsky, *American Zionism from Herzl to the Holocaust.* Garden City, New York: Anchor Press, 1975.

Part III

Modern Jewish
Philosophy

INTRODUCTION TO PART III

Let us begin by drawing a picture of the kind of world in which modern Jewish philosophy took place. Then let us note the problems that this world raised for Jewish thought. Europe does not become the center of Jewish life until after the twelfth century.[1] Because the dominant group of Jews who entered Europe then were from the Muslim world, they were considerably more advanced culturally than were their Christian neighbors. This disparity between European Jews and Christians contributed to a separation between Jews and their neighbors that had never been the case in earlier Jewish history. While Jews had been religiously and politically distinct, they were socially and culturally integrated into the general society. This integration came to an end in medieval European society. In consequence of the Maimonidean controversy, Jewish education became increasingly parochial; i.e., it was limited to traditional rabbinic texts and excluded the universal world of the arts and sciences. More should be said about this pivotal event—the Maimonidean controversy—before we continue this survey.

In the Muslim world, Jewish education incorporated what we call "secular" with "Jewish" studies. However, it is a misnomer to call the former category "secular." This term points to a separation between two bodies of information that Jews as well as Muslims would have rejected in the classic, medieval period of Jewish life. In the past, there was not only Jewish "law," as found in the Talmud and rabbinic codes. There were also Jewish science and philosophy, discovered in the writings of medieval rabbis such as Saadia, Judah Halevi, Abraham Ibn Daud, Moses Ibn Ezra, and Moses Ben Maimon (Maimonides). Just as Jews today, who have even the slightest familiarity with Jewish law, will recog-

---

* The kind of private or civil wrongs, excluding a breach of contract, for which a civil suit rather than a criminal trial is appropriate.

nize that purely legal issues such as torts* are Jewish, before the Maimonidean controversy, Jews recognized issues in the sciences and philosophy as Jewish. As contemporary Jews do not ask what religion has to do with questions about property when it is discussed by the rabbis in the traditional works of Jewish law, Jews in the past did not ask what Judaism had to do with questions about the nature of the material universe or the logical status of general terms. As there were Muslim physics, math, astronomy, and law, so there were Jewish physics, math, astronomy, and law. However, today, the curriculum of traditional Jewish schools is limited primarily to Bible, biblical commentaries, and law; and most Jews would not recognize such things, for example, as Jewish astronomy. Before the Maimonidean controversy this was not the case.

Because of this controversy, there was at least one disasterous change for the Jewish people. When the Jewish people in large numbers left the Muslim world and entered the Christian world, the Jews were thirteenth century people in the thirteenth century; whereas almost all of their Christian neighbors were barely literate. By the nineteenth century, the Christians had not only caught up to thirteenth century Muslim/Jewish science, they had significantly advanced beyond it. By the nineteenth century, Christians were culturally in the nineteenth century, whereas the Jews remained in the thirteenth century in both science and the arts.

European Jewry did make significant advancements in Jewish law and piety, but there is no comparable development in Jewish science. Thus, when the Jews were offered emancipation in Western Europe at the end of the nineteenth century, the offer—which entailed abandoning classical rabbinic Judaism as the price for entering Christian European society—was most attractive to those Jews who were brightest and most intellectually curious.[2] For the first time in Jewish history, their neighbors were more advanced in the arts and sciences than were the Jews. This discrepancy in itself made gentile Europe enormously attractive to those who were intellectually the most talented Jews. Since late medieval Judaism had systematically excluded the intellectual concerns of theoretical science and philosophy, the Jews who abandoned Judaism to pursue the life of intellect were almost universally hostile to Judaism. These individuals were dedicated to the pursuit of truth. From their personal experiences in the Jewish community, reinforced by the hostility of the gentile society, they judged religion in general and Judaism in particular to be hostile to their passion. They spoke of religion as primitive, stultifying, superstitious, etc., and their prime example was the Judaism of their childhood.

At this stage we may divide modern Jews into three categories. The great majority stayed within Jewish society and remained relatively untouched by emancipation. The second group fully entered liberal Christian society and had no interest in Judaism al all. Finally, a small group of Jewish intellectuals entered the world of the German university, but wanted, at the same time, to remain Jewish. This third group includes the Jewish philosophers whom we will study in this section.

NOTES

1. See Chapter 1.
2. See Chapter 2.

7

BARUCH SPINOZA

Baruch Spinoza had not a faithful Jewish heart though he had sucked the life of his intellect at the breasts of Jewish tradition. He laid bare his father's nakedness and said, 'They who scorn him have the higher wisdom.' Yet Baruch Spinoza confessed, he saw not why Israel should not again be a chosen nation.[1]

We begin our summary of Jewish philosophy with Spinoza's ontology. Then we turn to his ethics. In the former case, the key to understanding Spinoza's philosophy is his analysis of the term *substance*. In this instance, the key to his analysis of values, religion, and politics is the term *freedom*.

PHILOSOPHY

Substance

In Book I of *The Ethics* Spinoza presents his primitive definitions and the immediate consequences of those definitions for theology and metaphysics. He begins by defining the terms *self-caused, finite, substance, attribute, mode,* and *God.* Something is self-caused to the extent that what is true of it in the physical, extended world and in the world of thought is true solely in virtue of what that thing is. Something is finite to the extent that it is not self-caused; i.e., to the extent that it is limited; i.e., to the extent that what is true of it is determined by something other than itself. A substance is something that is self-caused; i.e., it exists in itself and it is conceived though itself; i.e., what is true of it in extension or in thought follows solely from what it is, and what it is in no way is modified by what something else is. An attribute is a way of thinking about a substance. A mode is anything that is not a substance; i.e., something that is caused by and is conceived through something other than itself. Finally, God is an absolutely infinite substance; i.e., something that exists and is conceived solely in terms of itself in every respect.

Each of these terms comes out of medieval Jewish philosophy, but each takes on a new meaning as Spinoza uses them. In fact, what Spinoza does is assume for each word a usage based on its meaning in medieval philosophy. However, Spinoza's use is more precise and rigorous than was its usage in the philosophy of his Jewish predecessors. For our purposes let us consider only one example, the term *substance*.

Spinoza's initial definition of a substance is the same as that of Aristotle and his medieval followers; viz., a substance is that which exists in itself and is conceived through itself. Spinoza's strict application of this definition was something new in the history of philosophy. Aristotle used this definition to distinguish between things like stones, buildings, trees, and properties or characteristics like soft, brown, rectangular. His distinction was based on a somewhat vague appeal to ordinary experience. For example, it is obvious that the color of a stone and a stone do not exist in the same way. The color is dependent on the stone in a way that the stone is not dependent on its color. In one sense, things like specific colors differ from things like stones. The latter can exist only in one place at one time, while the former can exist in many things in many places at the same time. In another sense, it is also true that a color can only exist in some concrete thing like a stone, whereas the existence of a stone is not dependent of any particular color in the same way. Aristotle's definition of a substance was an ambiguous attempt to express this difference. In the course of the history of philosophy, Aristotle's definition became more refined; but again, Spinoza was the first to apply it in a thoroughly rigorous, mathematical way.

The key to what is new about Spinoza's use of all of his primitive or basic terms is the adjective *mathematical*. Unlike the terms that we use in ordinary language, the terms used in mathematics tend to be completely univocal; i.e., they have one and only one precise meaning. What is useful about their rigor is that their meaning is precise. The price paid for this precision is that the terms no longer express directly what we experience. Given their Cartesian commitment to using a mathematical model to express knowledge, the continental rationalists believed that the function of precision was more important than the value of merely reflecting what is experienced. Similarly, while Aristotle's equivocal use of the term *substance* had the virtue of reflecting our every day experience, its lack of rigor limited the value of the term for stating precisely what we know.

Spinoza's mathematical rigor had the consequence that nothing that we would ordinarily recognize as a substance could count in Spinoza's use of the term as a substance. A stone is not a substance because (a) its existence is caused by something other than itself; (b) it exists in both time and space and therefore does not exist in itself; and (c) it is inconceivable that it could exist in itself or be self-caused. Given these rigorous criteria nothing in the world of experience could qualify for being a substance on Spinoza's terms. Everything of which we can think is, in Spinoza's language, a mode. Only God and the universe as such, which in the end are two different ways of talking about the same thing, qualify as substances. Hence, for Spinoza, there is one and only one substance—God. Everything else is a mode whose existence and even whose conception is dependent on God.

Spinoza (as well as his contemporary, Leibniz) made explicit with mathematical precision the implicit consequences of what he had accepted from his medieval philosophic predecessors. There is one substance, viz., God. Everything else is a mode whose existence and conception is dependent on God. Furthermore, since nothing is independent of or conceivable apart from this one substance, everything is necessarily true. There is nothing in the universe that is accidental.

Every state of affairs is logically entailed by the nature of the one substance; consequently, everything happens necessarily. Even the fact that, while I am sitting here at this particular moment, my left leg is crossed over my right leg, as opposed to any number of other options, is necessarily true. If I understood the nature of God or substance, then I would see that even this trivial state is necessarily the case; it does not merely happen to be true that my left leg is over my right leg. The only reason this fact seems to be contingent is that I am ignorant of all of its causes. If I knew them, I would see the neces-

sity. For me to know the nature of anything, I would have to understand the nature of everything, namely, of God. Once I understood
that nature, I would understand how everything that happens happens necessarily. This is ultimately what it means to say that every
event has a cause, viz., everything is necessarily the case and nothing
merely happens to happen.

If you suspect that Spinoza even uses the term *cause* in a specialized way, you are right. Recall Spinoza's initial definitions. In his system there are only two kinds of things—substances and modes. In the
former case, there is only one example in the universe—the absolutely infinite substance called "God." Everything else is a mode.
Note that *attributes* are not a third kind of thing. Rather, an attribute
is a way of thinking about a substance. Now, since God is absolutely
infinite, i.e., unlimited in every respect, there must be an infinite
number of ways to think about God, i.e., God has an infinite number
of attributes. However, human beings are capable of distinguishing
only two of them. Spinoza calls these two ways "extension" and
"thought." The attribute of thought is the entire universe of thoughts
and all of their relations. Similarly, the attribute of extension is the
entire universe (past present and future) of physical, extended, three-
dimensional objects and all of their relations. More precisely, the
attribute of thought is the thought of God which entails every other
conceivable thought; i.e., all thoughts that are not the thought of God
are logical consequences of the thought of God. Similarly, the attribute of extension is the extended universe which causes every other
extended object; i.e., all objects that are not the universe are causal
consequences of the universe.[3] In other words, the term *cause*
expresses within the extended world the counterpart of what the term
entails expresses within the thought world. For example, in Euclidean
geometry, the laws of solids are deduced from the laws of circles and
planes, which in turn follow necessarily from the definitions of a
point and a line. Similarly, the laws of physics in the world of
mechanics follows necessarily from the definitions of substance and
mode.

Freedom

In Books II and III of *The Ethics* Spinoza uses the conclusions
of Book I to spell out the general laws of physics and psychology,
which in turn lead to his claims in Books IV and V about life and
freedom. First I want to say a word about what *life* is, and then I
want to explain the sense in which Spinoza uses the term *freedom*.

The basic difference between a living thing and an inanimate object is the following: Both living and inanimate objects do things. For example, a rock rolls, shatters, goes throught the air, etc. Rocks have all kinds of activities. Everything that an inanimate thing does is caused by something other that itself. For example, a rock never initiates any behavior of its own. In contrast, a living thing has some activities of which it itself is the originator. So, to be alive it has to do something on your own rather than do something that is caused by something else.

So much for what 'life' means. 'Freedom' may be explained as follows: I will state two different notions of freedom. Spinoza believes that one of them is a viable notion, but he rejects the other. In one sense of the word, freedom means having a choice, i.e., having options: In this sense of the word, to be free means not to be determined. If you have one and only one choice, then you are not free; if you have several choices, then you are free. A second meaning of the word is self-determined. If you do something because someone or something else forces you to do it, then you are not free; but if the determination to do it comes from yourself, then you are free.

These are two radically different notions of what the term freedom means. They need not agree with each other. For example, assume that you graduate from college and you are offered six jobs. You know nothing about the jobs; you are totally ignorant. So you flip a coin, or you go by the sound of the letters of the names of the companies, or you do something else equally irrelevant to decide which job you will take. In this case, you have six choices; but the reason you have them is ignorance. Since you do not know anything about the positions, you are totally free to chose any one of the options.

In contrast, consider the following variation on this example: You study about the six jobs. As you look into them, you discover that only one of the jobs is right for you and the other five are not. At this point, you have only one choice. If you have one and only one choice, you are not free in the first sense of the term freedom. In this case you must choose the one job, because it is the only reasonable choice. Still, you are free in the second sense of the term, because you yourself determine which job you will take. The external element of luck or chance has been eliminated.

Whereas the first case involves freedom in the sense of having options, the second involves freedom in the sense that the choice is self-determined. Where you can pick six jobs through ignorance, you are simply picking by chance. This means that your choice is not self determined; the choice is due to an external factor, viz., luck or chance.

The first example is a case of freedom[1], i.e., having contingent alternatives; and the second example is a case of freedom[2], i.e., self-determination. Now let us apply these two notions of freedom to God. We always have a factor of indeterminism in our choices, because we never can work out all of the consequences. We can determine short term effects, but we cannot work them out in the long run. Therefore, given that a totally rational choice is based on knowing all of the consequences of an act, there is no way that human beings can take totally rational choices. The only entity that does not have this problem is God. God knows every consequence, and because of this knowledge God always makes a rational choice. Consequently, only God is absolutely free[2]; i.e., only God is completely self-determined, because God's choice is totally within His own control. But God has no freedom[1], at all. To make an irrational choice would be bad and God by His nature is good; therefore, He must make rational choices. Furthermore, since He is not in any sense subject to chance, because He knows every alternative, God always knows which is the best alternative. Therefore, God has no option but to make the best choice. Everything that God does is self-determined, and therefore, while God has no freedom[1], at all, God is absolutely free[2].

According to Spinoza, freedom is man's ultimate end. As explained above, we can distinguish two senses of freedom—external and internal. To say that person *a* is externally free means that to some extent what *a* does is indeterminate. On the other hand, to say that *a* is internally free means that what *a* does to some extent is determined by himself. Given Spinoza's commitment to total determinism, freedom is always internal freedom. Internal freedom[4] is discussed in an absolute and a relative sense. In keeping with this analysis, Spinoza speaks of two very different strategies for its attainment— can instantaneous strategy for achieving absolute freedom and a gradual strategy for achieving relative freedom.

We will discuss Spinoza's ethics from two perspectives. First, we will state Spinoza's philosophic ethics, which consists of definitions of the word *freedom* and the related terms *value* and *norm*. Then we will discuss the practical or applied side of Spinoza's ethics, which consists of two strategies—an instantaneous and a gradual strategy. It is with respect to this latter method, through which relative freedom may be attained, that Spinoza discusses religion and the state.

In general, *a* is free, i.e., self-determined, if and only if he is wise. To be wise is to have adequate cognition. Hence, *a* is self-determined to the extent that his existence or action is due to adequate cognition.

Conversely, a is in bondage, i.e., externally determined, if and only if he is ignorant. To be ignorant is to have inadequate cognition. Hence, a cognizes y adequately if and only if a cognizes y through its adequate cause x. x is an adequate cause of y if and only if x is a sufficient and necessary condition for y. Conversely, a cognizes y inadequately if and only if a cognizes y through an inadequate cause of x. x is an inadequate cause of y if and only if x is only a necessary but not a sufficient condition for y. Finally, a recognizes y non-adequately if and only if a cognizes y through its non-adequate cause x. x is a non-adequate cause of y if and only if x is neither a sufficient nor a necessary condition for y. With respect to means and object, a may have an adequate cognition of a singular thing y either by intuition or by reason, and he has an inadequate cognition of y by imagination. In the case of intuition, a cognizes the general essence of y through its adequate and immanent cause x, which is God, insofar as God is adequately cognized as constituted through the formal essence of His attributes. In the case of reason, a cognizes the general properties of y by subsuming y under a common notion x, provided that this notion itself can be established by intuition. Finally, in the case of imagination, a cognizes the general properties of y by subsuming y under a universal notion a, which is based merely on sense experience or heresay (i.e., on tradition) and not on reason or intuition.

As we have seen, to have a cognition of a thing is to know a thing through its cause. Hence, the degree to which cognition is adequate depends on the extent to which the cause itself is adequate. Ultimately, i.e., in an absolute sense, the only adequate cause is the whole system of nature, i.e., *natura naturans* (God's essence and existence) cognized as the cause of *natura naturata* (God's immediate and mediate infinite modes as well as His finite modes). This judgment, combined with the judgment that man as well as God may be free, determines two distinct senses of the term *freedom*.

Someone is free to the extent that he is active and has active affects. Someone is active to the extent that his existence is self-determined. Someone has active affects to the extent that his actions are self-determined. Conversely, someone is in bondage to the extent that he is passive and has passive affects. Someone is passive to the extent that his existence is due to an external cause. Someone has passive affects to the extent that his actions are due to an external cause.

There are two different respects in which activity and passivity are related to cognition. In an absolute or eternal sense, a person will be active and have active affects if and only if that person has adequate cognition. Conversely, a person will be passive and have passive affects if and only if that person has inadequate cognition. In a relative or temporal sense, a person will be active and have active affects if and only if he has inadequate cognition and he is adequately aware of this fact, so that he will not mistake his modes of imagination for real things. Conversely, a person will be passive and have passive affects if and only if he has inadequate cognition and he is ignorant of this fact, so that he will mistake his modes of imagination for real things.

Affects are the result of the interaction of a person with his environment. Spinoza distinguishes them as primary and secondary as well as positive and negative. Primary affects are the emotions of joy and sorrow and the desires that are based on them. Secondary affects are love and hate. Love is joy accompanied by an idea of its cause. Conversely, hate is sorrow accompanied by an idea of its cause. An affect is positive if and only if a's causal efficiency in relation to y either is inadequate and decreasing. Sorrow, any desire based on sorrow, and hate are always passive. All active affects are positive.

Based on this analysis of the relations among freedom, actions, cognition, and affects, Spinoza distinguishes the following senses of freedom and bondage: A person has freedom[1] when he has adequate cognition, and he has bondage[1] when he has inadequate cognition. A person who has bondage[1] has freedom[2] when he is adequately aware of this fact, and does not mistake his modes of imagination for real things; he has bondage[2] when he is ignorant of this fact, and mistakes his modes of imagination for real things.

Corresponding to these two senses of freedom and bondage are the following kinds of activity and passivity. There is an eternal and a temporal dimension to activity and passivity. In the former respect, person a acts[1] or is active[1] in relation to an object y if and only if a is the adequate cause of y through his constituted essence x and cognizes y adequately through x. Conversely, person a suffers[1] or is passive[1] in relation to an object y if and only if a is an inadequate cause of y through his constituted essense x and cognizes y inadequately through x. In the latter respect, a acts[2] or is active[2] in relation to y if and only if a is passive[1] in relation to y and has a relatively high degree of causal efficiency or control in relation to y, so that he is able to cognize y through his constituted essence x to a relatively high degree. Conversely, a suffers[2] or is passive[2] in relation to y if and only if a is passive[1] in relation to y and has a relatively low degree of causal efficiency or control in constituted essence x to a relatively low degree.

Person a has an active[1] affect in relation to y if and only if a has an affect towards y and a is active[1] in relation to y. The same is true for a having an active[2] or passive[1] or passive[2] affect towards y when a is respectively active[2], passive[1] or passive[2] in relation to y. The kind of activity corresponds to the kind of freedom, and the kind of passivity corresponds to the kind of bondage.

With respect to these definitions, Spinoza distinguishes three senses of the term *essence*. Essence[1] of a thing is the being of that singular thing insofar as it is conceived from the viewpoint of concrete duration and time. Essence[2] of a thing is the being of that singular thing insofar as it is conceived from the viewpoint of abstract duration and time. Essence[3] of a thing consists of the characteristics of that singular thing insofar as they are genetically defined in general terms and cognized by imagination as inhering in the thing. These three essences are cognized respectively by intuition, reason, and imagination.

Objects of Value (Value[1])

Spinoza speaks of values in two different senses of the term. He uses the term *value* to refer to objects of value (value[1]) and to refer to norms or standards of value (value[2]). For Spinoza objects of value are consequences of desires which in turn are consequences of emotions. Emotions are divided into feelings and attitudes. The basic feelings are the positive feeling of joy and the negative feeling of sorrow, while the primary attitudes are love and hate. Attitudes are feelings accompanied by an idea of their cause. Love arises from joy and hate from sorrow. Again, these emotions give rise to desires, which in turn are the basis for value judgments.

Values may be judged to be positive, negative, or neutral. y has a positive value for a in context c if and only if y has a positive feeling or attitude towards a: y has a negative value for a in context c if and only if y has a negative feeling or attitude towards a; and if y has neither feeling or attitude, then y is value neutral for a.

Value objects may be intuitive, in accordance with reason, or spurious for a in context c. y is an intuitive object if and only if a has an active[1] affect towards y. It is an object of value in accordance with reason if and only if a has an active[2] affect towards y. Finally, it is a spurious value if and only if a has a passive[2] affect towards y.

The principal object of value in accordance with reason is a model of human nature formed by a person's imagination. This model has no real existence, but it is nonetheless to be valued as a pragmatic device by which a person may strive to achieve freedom[2].

It has a corporeal as well as a mental dimension. With respect to the mind, again, two dimensions have to be distinguished—a cognitive and a conative side. With respect to thought, the model is the ideal of wisdom; and with respect to power or will, the model is the ideal of active love. Wisdom is defined with reference to prudence, and two different senses of wisdom can be distinguished. A person is said to have wisdom in a narrow sense to the extent that he has the power to cognize himself and other persons or things adequately by either intuition or reason. In this sense, a person has prudence to the extent that he has the power to cognize efficient means to temporal ends by intuition. A person may also be said to have wisdom in a broad sense to the extent that he has the above power of prudence that is oriented towards temporal ends that are compatible with wisdom in the narrow sense. In the narrow sense of the term, the appropriate objects of wisdom in order of causal or genetic primacy are God, oneself, and others.

Active[1] joy is called "blessedness." A person has it if and only if he directly feels that his causal efficiency in relation to the object of his feeling is adequate. Active[1] love is called "intellectual love." A person has it if and only if he has active[1] joy towards the object of his feeling, and that feeling is accompanied by an idea of its cause. The appropriate objects of love are God and the modes, i.e., everything that exists. Love of God is genetically prior. Next comes self-love, and last is love of other human beings.

Norms (Value[2])

N is a norm for a in context c if a agrees than n includes (1) an antecedent which specifies the conditions of application of the norm, (2) a consequent which specifies the theme or action idea of the norm, and (3) a modal operator which expresses the sender's particular kind of desire to influence the receiver. Linguistically, norms are equivalent expressions of declarative sentences in the form: if p, then one ought to A. Spinoza distinguishes between norms of conduct and norms of competence, the latter being stipulations of conditions for the former. The norms of conduct are normative expressions of descriptive statements derived either from natural law, reason, or divine law. The norms of competence are derived either from natural right or civil law.

The sources of norms is desire, which may be defined as power or conation determined by emotion. An alternative but equivalent definition of desire is a conscious act of will, where will is defined as power with reference to the mind. In this context, desire is to be distinguished from appetite, the latter being an unconscious act of will. In Spinoza's analysis, the most universal and basic desire of all conscious entities is to preserve their own being. Based on this desire, positive feelings are associated with what does seem to promote one's own being. Conversely, based on this desire, negative feelings are associated with what does seem to promote one's own being. Conversely, based on this desire, negative feelings are associated with what does not seem to promote one's own being. These feelings direct other, more specific desires.

There are four kinds of desires. There is an active[1] desire if and only if a's conation or power is affected by y insofar as a has an active[1] joy or love towards y. There is a passive[1] desire if and only if a's conation is affected by y insofar as a has passive[1] joy, sorrow, love or hate towards y. Similarly, there is an active[2] desire if and only if a's conation or power is affected by y insofar as a has an active[2] joy or love towards y. Also, there is a passive[2] desire if and only if a's conation is affected by y insofar as a has passive[2] joy, sorrow, love or hate towards y. All four kinds of active desires are called "fortitude." Self-regarding fortitude is called "courage," and other-regarding fortitude is called "generosity." Fortitude is the source of the norms of reason. Value preference norms are derived from courage and value distribution norms are derived from generosity. Again, these norms are value formulations of declarative statements where the expression of these statements as positive or negative is derived from desires rooted in emotions associated with the fundamental desire to preserve one's being.

The following are primary examples of value preference norms. (1) If people are going to decide between alternative courses of action, they ought to seek to obtain a reasonably well founded empirical knowledge about the alternatives and their probable consequences. (2) If people are going to decide between alternative courses of action, they ought to prefer the alternative that they feel is better and/or the more efficient alternative, i.e., the more useful means to a single end. (3) If people feel that an alternative is *prima facie* a lesser evil and they believe that by choosing it they obtain a greater good, then they ought to choose it. Conversely, if people feel that an alternative *prima facie* is a lesser good and they believe that by choosing it they obtain a greater evil, then they ought to avoid it. (4) If people feel that p will have better consequences than q in the short run but worse in the long run and that the long run consequences are better than the short, then they ought to prefer q to p. (5) People ought to prefer the alternative which they believe is more useful in strengthening or conserving their being in accordance with the requirements of adequate cognition and active joy and love. Similarly, people ought to prefer the alternative which they believe is more useful in strengthening or conserving their cognition and love of God.

The following are primary examples of distribution of value norms. (1) People ought to prefer such alternatives for themselves as can be equally obtainable for others, and they ought to help others attain them. (2) People ought to adjust their private preferences to the common good of their own civil state, as determined by the particular norms of justice of that state. More generally, people ought to adjust their private preferences to the common good of all mankind, as determined by the universal love of humanity through God and the universal norms of reason. (3) If people perceive a conflict between the common good of their own civil state and all mankind, then they ought to support reforms which are useful to integrate the former with the latter.

Spinoza also notes the following two exchange of value norms. First, people ought to repay negative value with a positive value. Second, people ought to resolve conflicts with others through love and generosity.

Strategies of Liberation

From the above analysis of freedom and value, it is clear that above all else freedom is to be sought and bondage avoided. Freedom is associated with active affects and bondage, with passive affects. The strength of an affect, and therefore the degree of one's freedom, varies as the strength of one's cognition varies. The cause of passive affects affirms the external existence of some object or state of affairs cognized inadequately. This analysis dictates the general strategy for attaining freedom: Form a clear and distinct idea of the object cognized by reflecting on it. Then cognize the idea adequately by connecting it with its adequate cause.

Again, the degree of one's freedom varies with the degree of the strength of one's cognitions. Spinoza distinguishes three modes of relative strength of cognition—temporal, ontological, and epistemological. With respect to time, if a imagines two objects or states of affairs, p and q, which both cause an affect in a, a's affect in relation to p will be stronger than a's affect in relation to q if a imagines (1) p to be present and q to be absent or past or future, or (2) p to be present in the near future or past and q to be present in the more remote future of past. a's affect will be equally slight in relation to both if a imagines p and q to be separated from the present time by a longer interval than a's imagination is able to determine. With respect to the modes of being—viz., being free or indetermined, possible and contingent or necessary, and present or absent, — if the cognition of p and q both cause an affect in a, then a's affect in relation to p will be stronger than a's affect in relation to q, if a imagines: (1) p is free and q is possible or contingent; (2) p is necessary and q is governed by some other ontological mode; (3) q is absent and contingent and p is present, or absent and possible, or belonging to a remoter future or past; and (4) p is caused by a greater number of, more constant, or more frequently present-in-a's-mind causes than is q. With respect to knowledge, if a imagines p to be more easily connected with something which a clearly and distinctly understands than is q, then a's affect in relation to p will be stronger than q's affect in relation to q.

Again, from this analysis follows Spinoza's two strategies for attaining freedom. The instantaneous strategy for absolute freedom (freedom^1) is totally independent of the gradual strategies for relative freedom (freedom^2).

The instantaneous strategy is a process of transformation by which the eternal essence of a person emerges as that person has intuitively adequate cognition of the essence, from the view point of eternity, of his/her body and then of his/her mind. This strategy involves three steps. First, form clear and distinct ideas of the affections of the body. Second, remove from these ideas any thought of external causes. Third, unite the purged ideas with all other ideas.

The gradual strategy involves social control by the individuals' environment and self-control by the individuals themselves. The central principle underlying this strategy is that an affect can only be altered by an equally strong or stronger contrary affect. Its goal is to cause the individual to alter less desirable passions with more desirable ones in order to alter in this way his/her character so that he/she can become free. First, people's society ought to create affects by which their evil passions are replaced by less evil ones. The society does this by using external norms to promote the less evil passions of repentance, humility, fear, and hope. Then people ought to create affects by which these lesser but nonetheless evil passions are replaced by good passions. Individuals do this by using internal norms to promote the good passions of love and joy, active^2 and passive^1 affects, and the desires of generosity and courage upon which, as we have seen, the norms of reason are based.

In the end the viability of the gradual strategy depends on individuals living in a good society. As individuals, they are first part of a people or social grouping, which in turn is part of a nation with a political system, which in turn is part of mankind in general. Since freedom depends on internal norms which presuppose external norms, the degree to which individuals may attain freedom, i.e., individual excellence, depends directly on the degree to which they are members of a good society; and the virtue of the society depends on the nature of its laws.

Spinoza distinguishes between descriptive and normative laws, the latter being derived from the former. There are two kinds of descriptive law—natural law and natural right. The former consists of declarative statements about the essence of things insofar as they are determined from within. The latter consists of descriptions of the conation or power of things. Natural law generates the norms of conduct, and natural right generates the norms of competence. The norms of competence are expressed in civil law; while the norms of conduct are expressed in three, ultimately equivalent forms—norms of reason, natural divine law, and universal revealed law.

The norms of reason are based on the philosophic ethics outlined above. Natural divine law is based on natural theology. Universal revealed divine law is the means by which the philosopher adapts universal truth to apply to the ignorant masses by giving conclusions without premises and by expressing descriptive truths in the form of norms. In content there is no difference between these two forms of divine law. Similarly, there is fundamentally no content difference between divine law and natural law. In fact, natural law, from a religious perspective, can be called divine guidance. There is some substantive difference between the two. They differ in both source and end. The source of natural law is human reason, whereas the source of divine law is revelation. The end of natural law is the well-being of individuals and their state, whereas the end of divine law is *summum bonum*—the true cognition and love of God.

APPLIED ETHICS

Religion and Religions

Spinoza singles out two forms of universal revealed divine law—a particularist version called "the law of Moses," and a universalist version called "the law of Christ." The law of Moses is the basis of Judaism, but it is not the same as Judaism. The law of Christ is the basis of Christianity, but it is not the same as Christianity. Ultimately, these two laws are the same. The law of Christ may be understood to be a generalization of the law of Moses. Conversely, the law of Moses may be understood to be an instantiation of the law of Christ.

Spinoza has a strong religious identity, but he has no positive commitment to any particular religion. Spinoza seems to believe that all religions are deviations from religion. Instead, Spinoza advocate a universal religion that transcends all particular religious societies. It has three dogmas: (1) God exists; God is one; and God is omnipotent. (2) There is complete divine providence or divine determinism, and to love one's neighbor is the way to the true worship of and obedience to God. (3) Those who live in accord with these dogmas will be saved; and for those who do not, there is always the possibility of repentance.

In Spinoza's understanding of the terms, true religion, like true philosophy, consists of universal, true ideas. Both have the same content and the same objective, viz., to express what is absolutely true. In fact, if we restrict our attention only to the content of each, they are identical. The end or goal of both activities is the intellectual love of God. Philosophy's laws of nature are in true religion called "divine guidance." The dogmas of true religion are also dictates of true philosophy; viz., that God exists, that God is one, that God is omnipotent, that God governs the universe absolutely, that to obey God consists in loving one's neighbor, that obedience is the path to salvation, and that it is possible to turn away from disobedience toward obedience, i.e., that there is both repentance and forgiveness.[5].

However, there is more to religion and philosophy than their content. The identity of their content means that the two are similar and absolutely coherent, but not that the two are identical. While their ends are the same, their methods are completely different. In fact, Spinoza argues that they are so distinct that they should be completely autonomous of each other. Whereas religion is intended for all people, irrespective of their intellectual abilities, philosophy is intended only for those who, through good fortune and natural disposition, have the ability to engage in abstract thought.

The truths of philosophy are discovered by philosophers, who are human beings with good intellects; whereas the truths of religion are discovered by prophets, who are human beings with good imaginations. These two excellences are inversely proportionate. Hence, in opposition to classical Jewish philosophers such as Maimonides, it is impossible to be both a philosopher and a prophet.[6]

Furthermore, the true claims of the philosopher express what is the case and are rooted in demonstrations based on mathematical modes of thought; whereas the true claims of the prophet express moral claims (what ought to be the case) and are rooted in demonstrations based on moral modes of thought that incorporate claims about human experience. Whereas contingent claims about history are not relevant to the sphere of philosophy, they are most relevant in religious demonstrations. Both in some sense express what they assert with certitude, but the kind of certitude involved is different. True philosophy has what Spinoza calls "mathematical certitude," while true religion has what he calls "moral certitude". Scripture, as an instance of true religion, is a work, addressed to the masses, which expresses certain truths; but these truths are entirely distinct from philosophy. The truths of Scripture are moral certitudes about human experience and history, which as such lie entirely outside of the sphere of philosophy. Conversely, philosophy expresses universal, timeless, mathematical truths that lie entirely outside of the sphere of religion.

Ultimately, the truths of both are coherent and consistent, since there is only one truth. At a most general level, as noted above, the truths of both can be summarized in a finite set of statements. But the mode of expression of these truths is so different that the claims of true religion and true philosophy must be treated as distinct and autonomous.

Politics

One further distinction between philosophy and true religion needs to be listed. While both state laws, obedience to which lead to salvation, they differ in their respective subjects. The agent who attains salvation through philosophy is the individual, whereas the agent who attains salvation through religion is the nation. The latter claim requires some evidence, since it is not self-evident in reading Spinoza's writings.

Spinoza states two definitions of law without at this stage distinguishing between natural and divine law.[7] According to the first definition, a law is that by which one or all members of a species act in some definite manner. He notes that the prescribed manner depends either on natural necessity or human decree. In the former case, the law expressed is a dictate of mathematical reasoning; and in the latter case, it is not.[8] But to say that the latter kinds of prescriptions, called "ordinances," are not taught by mathematical logic, i.e., by philosophy, does not mean that they are not dictates of reason. They are based on reason, but the reason involved in this case is pragmatic and/or moral and/or political. Spinoza's *Ethics* are intended to be an example of mathematical reasoning; both his *The Theologico-Political Treatise* and his *The Political Treatise* are intended as examples of pragmatic reason.

Specifically, with reference to ordinances—prescriptions dependent on human degree—Spinoza states his second definition of law. In this case, a law is a plan of life laid down by someone, either for himself or for others, with a certain object. Note that the "someone" decreeing this plan of life may be an individual, a group of individuals within a larger grouping, or the larger grouping itself. Only in the third case does the legislator legislate for himself; in the first two cases the legislators legislate for others as well. This three-fold distinction corresponds to the three forms of political states discussed in the *Treatise*, viz., monarchy (where the legislator is an individual), aristocracy (where the legislator is a subgrouping), and democracy (where the group as a whole is self-legislating). In any of these alternatives, the "object" of the legislation is "salvation." In the case of divine law, which expresses absolute truth, the object is the knowledge and love[9] of God. In the case of human law, which expresses relative truths, the object is political, viz., the life and security of the state. It is this relative, human law, whose objective is political, that constitutes, according to Spinoza, the content of the Hebrew Scriptures.

Government

As Spinoza explains in the *The Political Treatise*, ideally human beings would live by the dictates of reason as expressed in both philosophy and true religion. However, most human beings are not sufficiently developed to live in this way, and political theory must begin by assuming the human condition as it is, rather than as it ought to be. Hence, the starting point of political theory is the natural desire of all human beings to exist and to persevere in their existence. As Spinoza explains in *The Ethics*, desire is a conscious act of will which is determined by emotion. Again, political theory begins by assuming the basest emotions and desires, because these alone will be universally shared by human beings. The first desire is the desire to exist, and the first emotion is the fear of not existing. This emotion and its corresponding desire are the most fundamental cause of the existence of society. As Spinoza states in *The Political Treatise*,[10] individual fear causes association between individuals, which in turn promotes collective rights and/or power.[11] In other words, the stronger the emotion of individual fear, the stronger the power/right of the collective (i.e., the society), and the weaker the right/power of the individual. Now, as Spinoza argues in *The Ethics*, an entity is good/fulfilled/happy[12] to the extent that it is free. To be free means to be self-determined, while to be under bondage means to be determined or controlled by something other than oneself.[13]

In the lowest form of society, whose motive is solely the basest of emotions, citizens abandon all individual rights and power. In general, the nobler the citizens, the nobler the form of social organization, and the greater the power of the individual within the society. As Spinoza argues in both *The Political Treatise* and *The Theologico-Political Treatise*, democracy is preferable to aristocracy, which in turn is preferable to monarchy. This judgment of preference is made in absolute terms. In democracy—a society in which authority is vested equally in all members of the society—the individual has the maximum possible freedom. Conversely, in monarchy—a society in which authority is vested in a single individual—all other individuals have minimum possible freedom. However, this is not to say that in any concrete situation this order of preference holds.

In any particular time and place, any one of these forms of government may be best. The correct choice depends on the level of development of the citizens. Similarly, while in absolute terms, the best human being is the true philosopher; not all human beings ought to be philosophers. What a human being in a particular place at a particular time ought to be depends on the level of that individual's development. Furthermore, while all human beings desire to promote their existence, how they should promote it depends on the degree to which they are developed/free. Similarly, all political states desire to promote their existence, but what political order best promotes their well-being depends on their particular circumstances. The most important factor is the maturity/freedom of their citizens. Hence, in a world of base human beings, democracy would be the least desirable form of government and monarchy would be the best.

A good state is one which maximizes its survival. At its most fundamental level, the degree to which a state can preserve itself depends on the ability of the state to maximize internal as well as external peace. The degree to which a state can maintain internal peace depends on the degree to which the citizens of the state are willing to obey its laws. In an ideal state of highly virtuous (i.e., rational) human beings, the citizens themselves, who are governed by altruistic desires[14] and a vision of long term goods, as opposed to selfish desires and short term goods, need no external authority to move them to act in such a way as to maximize the good of the state. Hence, in such a state the best government is a democracy, which in no way legislates religion, because its citizens naturally will follow the true religion of reason. In a state whose citizens are dominated by fear, rule necessarily depends on external authority; and rule by one yields maximum law and order. In such a society the religion will be a religion of superstition, where religion appeals to the fear of its citizens to promote blind obedience to the state.[15]

Again, in absolute terms, monarchy and superstition are the basest form of government and religion. In a society of base individuals, monarchy is the best of all possible governments and religions, through which individuals will be able to advance. As they advance, they may move to appropriately higher systems of government and religion. The ultimate condition would be one in which all individuals are God, i.e., absolutely free/self-determining. In such a society, if at this level it is appropriate to speak of a society at all, there would be no law. Everyone would be self-determining; and what all individuals would determine for themselves would cohere perfectly with what everyone else determines for themselves.[16].

The steps by which human beings may develop in society from the lowest to the highest level is called "the gradual strategy of relative freedom.[17] Out of its own selfish desire to promote its own well-being, the base society will use external norms and superstitious religion to lead its base citizens to inhibit their selfish desires for self-preservation. By so acting, base individuals are conditioned to substitute for the most evil passions[18] less evil passions such as fear and hope (from the government) and repentance and humility (from religion). At this level, individual citizens are trained to internalize the formerly external norms, thereby replacing their least evil passions with good passions, such as joy and love and their corresponding desires of generosity and courage. At this level, the individual has the opportunity to achieve maximum human freedom. It is against this background that Spinoza discusses the Hebrew Scriptures and the New Testament.

The Scriptures

Both the Torah and the Gospels are expressions of universal revealed divine law. The Gospels express that law in a universal form (as the law of Jesus), whereas the Torah states it in a particularist form (as the law of Moses). The Torah establishes a system of external law in a theocracy. This form of government was best for the Hebrew people, living when and where they did. Through theocracy, this nation was able to advance to a higher form of collective existence in which external law was no longer necessary. It is the Gospels that state this higher level of human (individual and collective) existence. The Torah applies to a people who are ruled by fear, who by obedience to the Torah become a people ruled by duty. In other words, through the Torah the Jewish nation was transformed from a people of the most evil passions into a people of the least evil passions.[19]

The legislation of the Torah applies to the nation as a whole, and not to its individuals as such. The reward for national obedience is national security, and the punishment for disobedience is national destruction. Indirectly, however, obedience also rewards the citizens, since in desiring to obey—i.e., by the citizens internalizing the state's norms—the individuals become more free/self-determining. At this level of perfection, they are ready to enter into a higher grade of collective existence.

The difference in level between the prophets Moses and Jesus in itself indicates the difference between the Torah and the Gospels. Of prophets at the early national stage, Moses was the best. Prophets imagine what is real or what is imaginary by means of words or appearances. Only in Moses' case was there revelation of what is real by means of words.[20] But Jesus exceeded Moses' level, for Jesus was the only prophet to communicate directly with God, mind to mind, without the need even of words.[21]

This difference in the level of Moses and Jesus was caused by the difference in Israel's level when the Torah was revealed and later when the Gospels were revealed. So, what Moses presented as law was presented by Jesus as statements of eternal truth.[22] This claimed superiority is to be understood in two ways. First, the audience of the Gospels is more universal than the audience of the Torah, the latter being the Jewish people and the former being all mankind. Second, the propositional form of expression more clearly states what is the case than the imperative form.[23]

A proposition whose form is "If A then B" means "If you do A then necessarily B will follow"; but it says neither that necessarily you will do A, nor that necessarily B will happen. However, if the ignorant were told that to avoid A is not necessary and that B need not happen—assuming B to be a state of affairs that has negative value—then they would desire to assume that to do A is permissible and B will not happen. Hence, this propositional truth is given to the ignorant in an imperative form as "Do not do A." That Jesus abandoned the imperative mode of expression in favor of propositional claims is itself a sign that in absolute terms the Gospels address a higher level of society than does the Torah.

In summary, the Torah stipulated laws through which the Hebrew people were transformed from a base form of nation into as high a level of human existence as is possible for imperfect human beings. Then the Gospels took these excellent individuals and presented a program through which they might achieve ultimate perfection. While the Gospels, in one sense, are beyond the Torah, viz., they address a higher level of human being; in no other sense can they be said to be superior. The Torah presents the ideal system of government and religion for individuals at the level of the Hebrew nation at the particular time and place in history that God revealed His eternal truth to Moses. The Gospels, in contrast, present no system of government at all, since they address an audience that presumably is beyond the need for external authority. The Gospels address a collective whose individuals have become so fulfilled that they may move beyond the imaginative claims of prophecy. They may transcend revealed religion and enter the elite domain of the philosopher. In absolute terms, these two Scriptures are equal. Both are the best of all possible statements, for their different times and places, of that single absolute truth which is the object of true religion.

In subsequent history, Jewish intellectuals have taken radically opposite sides in judging Spinoza's attitudes towards the Jewish people. Spinoza's opponents always make specific reference to his judgements about the inferiority of Judaism and the law of Moses to Christianity and the law of Jesus. However, it may be argued in defense of Spinoza, that, based on his analysis, there exists no society in this world to which the Gospels are appropriate. Spinoza's Jesus addresses the world of the saved in the Messianic Age. While some philosophers in this world may have entered the Messianic Age, most people—both Jews and Christians—have not. Given that Jews claim that this is not yet the Messianic Age and that many Jews also claim that the Torah is no longer binding in the Messianic Age, what Spinoza says about the Gospels need not be taken to be anti-Jewish. It is always essential to remember that Spinoza's Scriptures are distinct from both Judaism and Christianity. In any case, Spinoza's statements about ethics, politics, and religion had great impact on subsequent moral and religious European and Jewish philosophy.

NOTES

1. George Eliot, *Daniel Deronda*. New York: Signet 1979. P. 489.

2. The summary presented below of Spinoza's concept of freedom is largely based on Jon Wetlesen's *The Sage and the Way: Spinoza's Ethics of Freedom*. Assen, the Netherlands: Van Corcum, 1979.

3. Many people have judged Spinoza to be a pantheist, i.e., they believe that Spinoza claims that God and the universe are the same

thing. This judgement is not correct. While it is true that according to Spinoza the term *physical universe* is a way of thinking about what God is, it is not the same as God. First of all, *extended universe* is not something real. It is an attribute, and an attribute is only a way of thinking about a substance. Second, even if we were to grant an identity between God and the universe, it still would be misleading to claim that Spinoza is a pantheist, because he does not claim that the universe is identical with everything in the universe. Consider the system of Euclidean geometry. Every proposition and theorem logically follows from the initial definitions in the system, but those definitions are not identical with the entire system. Similarly, in Spinoza's philosophy every clear and coherent thought logically follows from the definition of substance. Spinoza does not claim that, for example, the thought of God and the composite thought of the laws of physics and psychology are identical. Consequently, given Spinoza's asserted isomorphism between the attributes of extension and thought, Spinoza would not claim that the universe as an entity is identical with the totality of everything that is in the physical universe.

4. Henceforth, simply called "freedom."

5. *The Theologico-Political Treatise*, chpt. 14, pp. 186-187. This page reference and all subsequent page references to Spinoza's writings refer to *The Works of Benedict de Spinoza*, translated by R.H.M. Elwes. New York: Dover, 1955.

6. Ibid., p. 27.

7. Ibid., p. 57.

8. The latter cannot be, since the sphere of mathematical reasoning is limited to claims that are necessarily true.

9. These two words express the same thing.

10. *The Political Treatise*, p. 296.

11. The two terms *right* and *power*, have the same extension.

12. These three terms have the same extension.

13. God alone is absolutely good, i.e., absolutely free. Human beings are more or less free. Note that freedom has nothing to do with contingency. In Spinoza's universe for every state of affairs there is a necessitating cause.

14. Namely, by the love of God and their fellow human beings.

15. *The Theologico-Political Treatise*, p. 5.

16. By implication, the absolutely ideal system of government is anarchy, but in relative terms, in this imperfect world, anarchy is never a viable choice.

17. Jon Wetlesen, *The Sage and the Way*. The Netherlands: Van Gorcum, 1979. Chapter 4.

18. Namely, pure egoistic desire for self-gratification.

19. *The Theologico-Political Treatise*, p. 75.

20. To imagine what is real is better than to imagine what is imaginary, and to imagine by means of words is better than to imagine by means of appearance.

21. Ibid., p. 15.

22. Ibid., p. 65.

23. Ibid., p. 63.

KEY NAMES

Aristotle, *The Ethics*, the Gospels, Jesus, Judaism, Moses Ben Maimon (Maimonides), The Maimonidean controversy, *The Political Treatise, The Theologico-Political Treatis,* Torah.

KEY TERMS

attribute, cause, cognition, desire, emotion, essence, extension, freedom, bondage, God, infinite/finite, intellectual love, law, mathematical, mode, norm, religious, strategy (instantaneous & gradual), substance, thought, value.

KEY QUESTIONS

1. In what ways was Jewish life in Christian Europe distinct from earlier manifestations of Jewish civilization? In what way are these differences a consequence of the Maimonidean controversy?

2. According to Spinoza, why is God the only substance? What is everything else? How are thoughts and physical objects related? How are physical facts and concepts related? How is everything else

related to God?

3. Why does Spinoza assert that every event has a cause? What does this claim means?

4. What are two general senses of the term *freedom*? Which does Spinoza employ? Why? What are two further distinctions that Spinoza makes in his use of this term, and why does he make them? To what extent are human beings free? Why is God absolutely free? In what sense is He not free at all?

5. With respect to quality, when is cognition adequate and inadequate? What are two means for having adequate cognition and one means for inadequate cognition? By each of these three means, what kind of essence is cognized? What absolutely is the only adequate cause of cognition?

6. In their absolute and relative senses, when is someone active and passive? How are activity/passivity correlated with freedom/ bondage? What are Spinoza's primary and secondary affects? When are affects positive or negative? Identify and explain two kinds of emotions. What causes them? What do they produce? Of what are they the basis?

7. Identify and explain three kinds of values and three kinds of value objects. What is the principal object of value in accordance with reason? How is it formed? What are its three values? What are two senses of wisdom? What are the objects of wisdom in the narrow sense of the term? What are the objects of love?

8. What is a norm? Identify and explain two kinds of norms. What are their sources? What is the most basic desire? What are four kinds of desire? What norms do these desires direct? Give five examples of value preference norms. Give three examples of distribution of value norms. Give two examples of exchange of value norms.

9. What is the general strategy for attaining freedom? On what does its success depend? What are the three steps in the instantaneous strategy? What are the two steps in the gradual strategy? What is the goal of the gradual strategy? What principle underlies it?

10. For Spinoza, how is individual morality dependent on political morality? Identify and explain two kinds of laws. Identify and explain two kinds of descriptive law. How are laws and norms related? Compare and contrast divine and natural law.

11. What is the starting point of political theory? What is the

most fundamental cause of the existence of society? What factors determine how much power the society and its members ought to have? What are three forms of political states? What would an ideal state be like? What is a good state?

12. Compare and contrast religion and philosophy. Why ought they to be autonomous of each other? How does Spinoza judge a religion? What is the goal of true religion? What are the three dogmas of universal religion? What would an ideal religion be like? What is a good religion?

13. What are Spinoza's two examples of revealed divine law? Compare and contrast them. What goal determines their content?

14. Would you say that Spinoza was or was not anti-Jewish? Give reasons for your answer.

RECOMMENDED READINGS

General

Robert M. Seltzer, *Jewish People, Jewish Thought: The Jewish Experience in History.* New York: Macmillan, 1980. Chpt. 12, "Seventeenth-Century Science and Spinoza's Break with Judaism," pp. 547-557.

Primary Texts

Baruch Spinoza, *The Chief Works of Benedict de Spinoza.* Translated into English by R.H.M. Elwes. New York: Dover, 1955.
——*The Correspondence of Spinoza.* Translated into English by Abraham Wolf. New York: Russell and Russell, 1966.
——*Ethics.* Translated into English by W.H. White (1883) and revised by A.H. Stirling (1894, 1899). 1949.
——*The Ethics and Selected Letters.* Translated into English by Samuel Shirley. Edited and introduced by Seymour Feldman. Indianapolis: Hackett, 1982.
——*The Ethics of Spinoza and De Intellectus Emendatione.* Translated into English by Andrew Boyle (1910). New York: Dutton, 1963.
——*On the Improvement of the Understanding.* Translated into English by Joseph Katz. Indianapolis: Bobbs-Merrill, 1958.
——*Opera.* Edited by Carl Gebhardt. Heidelberg: C. Winter, 1972.

————*Principles of Cartesian Philosophy.* Translated into English by Harry E. Wedeck. New York: Philosophical Library, 1961.

————*Spinoza, Earlier Philosophical Writtings: The Cartesian Principles and Thoughts on Metaphysics.* Translated into English by F.A.Hayes. Indianapolis: Bobbs-Merrill, 1963.

————*Spinoza's Short Treatise on God, Man and His Well-Being.* Translated into English by Abraham Wolf. New York: Russell and Russell, 1963.

————*The Tractatus Theologico-Politicus.* Translated into English by A.G. Wernham. Oxford: Oxford University Press, 1965.

Secondary Texts

G. Belaief, *Spinoza's Philosophy of Law.* The Hague: Martinus Nijkoff, 1971.

J.G. van der Bend (ed). *Spinoza on Knowing, Being and Freedom.* Proceedings of the Spinoza Symposium at the International School of Philosophy in the Netherlands, Leiden, September, 1973. Assen, The Netherlands: Van Gorcum, 1974.

David Bidney, *The Psychology and Ethics of Spinoza: A Study in the History and Logic of Ideas.* New York: Russell and Russell, 1962.

John Caird, *Spinoza.* New York: Arno, 1981.

E.M. Curley, *Spinoza's Metaphysics: An Essay in Interpretation.* Cambridge, MA: Harvard University Press, 1969.

Cornelius De Deugd, *The Significance of Spinoza's First Kind of Knowledge.* Assen, Netherlands: Van Gorcum, 1966.

James H. Dunham, *Freedom and Purpose: An Interpretation of the Psychology of Spinoza.* Princeton: Psychological Review Company (Philosophical Monographs) March, 1916.

S. Dunin-Borkowski, *Spinoza.* Munster: Aschendorff, 1910.

Lewis Samuel Feuer, *Spinoza and the Rise of Liberalism.* Boston: Beacon Press, 1958.

E. Freeman and M. Mandelbaum (eds.), *Spinoza: Essays in Interpretation.* La Salle, IL: Open Court, 1973.

Marjorie Grene (ed.), *Spinoza.* New York: Doubleday, 1973.

————*Spinoza: A Collection of Critical Essays.* Garden City, Anchor, 1973.

Harold F. Hallet, *Benedict De Spinoza.* London: Athlone Press, 1957.

————*Creation, Emanation and Salvation: A Spinozistic Study.* The Hague: Martinus Nijkoff, 1962.

Stuart Hampshire, *Spinoza.* Harmondsworth, Middlesex: Penquin

Books, 1951.

S. Hessing, *Speculum Spinozanum: A Kaleidoscopic Homage 1677-1977.* London: Routledge and Kegan Paul, 1977.

———(ed.), *Spinoza: Dreihundert Jahre Ewigkeit: Spinoza-Festscrift 1632-1932.* The Hague: Martinus Nijkoff, 1962.

H.G. Hubbeling, *Spinoza's Methodology.* Anselm: Van Gaeum, 1967.

Karl Jaspers, *Spinoza.* Translated into English by Ralph Manheim. New York: Harvest Books, 1974.

Harold H. Joachim, *Spinoza's Tractatus de Intellectus Emendatione: A Commentary.* Oxford: The Clarendon Press, 1940.

———*A Study of the Ethics of Spinoza.* Oxford: Oxford University Press, 1901.

S.P. Kashap (ed.), *Studies in Spinoza: Critical and Interpretative Essays.* Berkeley: University of California Press, 1972.

R. Kennington (ed.), *The Philosophy of Baruch Spinoza.* Washington D.C.: Catholic University of America, 1980.

Barry S. Kogan (ed.), *Spinoza: A Tercentenary Perspective.* Cincinnati: Hebrew Union College–Jewish Institute of Religion, 1979.

Dan Levin, *Spinoza: The Young Thinker who Destroyed the Past.* New York: Weybright and Talley, 1970.

Barry J. Luby, *Maimonides and Spinoza: Their Sources, Cosmological Metaphysics and Impact on Modern Thought and Literature.* New York: Las Americas, 1973.

T.C. Mark, *Spinoza's Theory of Truth.* New York: Columbia University Press, 1972.

A. Naess, *Freedom Emotion and Self-Subsistence: The Structure of the Central Part of Spinoza's Ethics.* Oslo: Universitets-forlaget, 1975.

Adolph Oko, *The Spinoza Bibliography.* Boston: G.K.Hall, 1964.

G.H.P. Parkinson, *Spinoza's Theory of Knowledge.* Oxford: Clarendon University Press, 1954.

Jean Preposiet, *Bibliographie Spinoziste.* Besancon: Universite de Besancon, 1974.

L. Robinson, *Kommentar zu Spinozas Ethik.* Leipzig: F. Meiner, 1928.

Leon Roth, *Spinoza.* Boston: Little Brown, 1929.

———*Spinoza, Descartes and Maimonides.* London: Clarendon Press, 1924.

R. Shahan and J. Biro (eds.), *Spinoza: New Perspectives.* Norman: University of Oklahoma Press, 1978.

Leo Strauss, *Persecution and the Art of Writing.* Chicago, Free Press,

1952.

————*Spinoza's Critique of Religion.* Translated into English by Elsa M. Sinclair. New York: Schocken, 1965.

Jon   Wetlesen,   *A   Spinoza   Bibliography,   1940-1970.*   Oslo: Universitetsforlaget, 1971.

————*Internal Guide to the Ethics of Spinoza, Index to Spinoza's Cross References in the Ethics. Rearranged so as to Refer from Earlier to Later Statements.* Oslo: University of Oslo, 1974.

————*The Sage and the Way: Spinoza's Ethics of Freedom.* Assen, The Netherlands: Von Gorcum, 1979.

————*Spinoza's Philosophy of Man: Proceedings of the Scandinavian Spinoza Symposium, 1977.* Oslo: Universitets-forlaget, 1978.

Paul Wienpahl, *The Radical Spinoza.* New York: New York University Press, 1979.

J.B. Wilbur (ed.), *Spinoza's Metaphysics: Essays in Critical Appreciation.* Assen, Netherlands: Van Gorcum, 1976.

Harry Austryn Wolfson, *The Philosophy of Spinoza: Unfolding the Latent Processes of His Reasoning.* Cambridge, MA: Harvard University Press, 1934.

8

MENDELSSOHN AND MODERN JEWISH THOUGHT

If in no other way, Spinoza's critique of the Bible makes him the first modern Jewish thinker. In the middle ages, the following was a primary issue. Given that God is the author of the Torah, every sentence in it is true; but many of the sentences do not seem to be true. How do we reconcile this conflict? In the modern period—more specifically, in the eighteenth and nineteenth century—this question is changed as follows: Given that Scripture is at least in part a human work, and given that Jewish faith is based on the Torah, how is it possible to continue to be a Jew? Those who tried to solve this problem were the leaders of the Jewish Enlightenment, i.e., those who had a good Jewish background, knowledge of Western civilization, and a firm commitment to reconciling both in their own lives and in the lives of the Jewish people. Their most notable representative was Moses Mendelssohn (1729-1786).

MOSES MENDELSSOHN

His Life

Mendelssohn was born in Dessau, Germany, the son of a poor scribe.[1] At the age of fourteen, Moses followed his teacher, David Frankel, to Berlin where he continued his Jewish studies. From Frankel he learned Talmud and Maimonides' *Guide of the Perplexed*. There he found other teachers as well, from whom he learned German, French, Italian, English, Latin, Greek, mathematics, poetry, and philosophy. He followed his friends Friedrich Nicolai and Gotthold Ephraim Lessing[2] in politics and literature; and in philosophy he was a disciple of the teachings of Gottfried Wilhelm Leibniz (1646-1716) as they were popularized by Christian Wolff (1679-1754). In general philosophy, his most memorable accomplishment was an essay[3] that took first prize over a paper submitted by Immanuel Kant in a contest sponsored by the Berlin Academy of Sciences in 1763. However, although Mendelssohn was a well-known figure generally in eighteenth-century German intellectual circles, his fame is primarily for his Jewish writings. An event of particular importance occurred in 1769 that determined this direction in Mendelssohn's work.

A preacher from Zurich named Johann Kaspar Lavater wrote a German translation[4] of a French study in Christian apologetics by Charles Bonnet.[5] Lavater sent his translation to his acquaintance, Mendelssohn, with a letter that expressed his hope that the work would persuade Mendelssohn to convert to Christianity. Mendelssohn responded with a public letter that defended his continued commitment to Judaism.[6] The letter provided the basis for the ideas that he developed later in more detail in *Jerusalem or On Religious Power and Judaism* (*Jerusalem, oder über Religiöse Macht und Judenthum*).[7] In the letter, he distinguished between a natural religion for all mankind and the Jewish religion that is intended exclusively for the Jewish people. He argued that the two forms of religion are compatible, since Judaism only teaches specific modes of obligations for Jews that are consistent with the universal, rational teachings of natural religion. In this letter, he also explained why Judaism, unlike Christianity, is not a missionary religion. The religious truths to which all mankind ought to adhere are taught by natural religion. Since Judaism only teaches laws for the Jewish people, there is no reason to seek converts.

The Lavater affair produced a furor throughout Germany. In the end, everyone involved—Lavater, Bonnet, and Mendelssohn —regretted the entire incident. Mendelssohn himself, because of his fragile nerves, became ill. As a result of the incident, Mendelssohn became known in public as a spokesman for an enlightened form of Judaism, and a major part of his life's work was spent in this role. Among his more notable accomplishments in this respect were the work that he did to encourage the establishment of a school in 1781 that integrated Jewish and secular studies—the Judische Freischule in Berlin—and his collaboration in the 1750's with the first German periodicals in the Hebrew language—first *KOHELET MUSAR* and later *HA-ME'ASSAF.*

His Thought

Mendelssohn's major writings were *Phaedon* (1767), *Jerusalem* (1783), and *Morning Hours, or Lectures on the Existence of God* (*Morgenstunden oder Vorlesungen über das Dasein Gottes*) (1785).[8] His other writings include miscellaneous collections of sermons, a commentary on Moses Maimonides' youthful work on logic—*MILLOT HA-HIGGAYON*—in 1761, and German translations of Ecclesiastes (1770), the Pentateuch (1778-1783), Psalms (1783), and the Song of Songs (published in 1788). In addition, at the request of Solomon Dubno, Mendelssohn produced a commentary called the *BIUR*, to accompany his translation of the Pentateuch. The goal of all the translations was to wean German Jewry away from the Yiddish language, adopting instead both German and Hebrew as modern languages for both the mundane and the spiritual life of human beings who were compatibly both German and Jewish. The translations were strongly opposed by Jews who wanted to preserve the classical, traditional form of Jewish polity, as well as by defenders of Yiddish over Hebrew as the ordinary language of the Jewish people. Among Mendelssohn's most outspoken opponents were Ezekiel Landau of Prague, Raphael Kohen of Altona, and Kohen's son-in-law, Hirsch Janow.

Mendelssohn's writings on Jewish religious thought were drawn from his general knowledge of the classics of Western and Jewish philosophy, but the dominant intellectual influence on his work was Wolff's version of Leibniz's philosophy. Mendelssohn believed that natural religion teaches three doctrines—that there exists one God, that God governs the world, and that the human soul has life after its body dies. He also believed that all human beings can discover these three truths through reason without special revelation or reliance on miracles. *Morning Hours* presents Mendelssohn's demonstrations of the first dogma—the existence and unity of God. We need not look here at his argument, because it does not seem to contain anything new. It is simply a statement of Anselm's (d. 1109) ontological arguments in the form that they were stated by Leibniz. As such, they are not strong arguments; and they are significantly inferior to the version that Spinoza presented in *The Ethics*. The arguments need not concern us in a work on Jewish philosophy that is as general as is this one. The sole significance of *Morning Hours* for our purposes is that it concludes with the claim that all rational human beings, aided solely by reason, can discover that there is one God of the universe, who creates the world by an act of His will that is always aimed at the highest good. In other words, Mendelssohn believed that *Morning Hours* demonstrates solely on the basis of reason that there exists one God who is perfectly wise, righteous, merciful, and, what is most important, good.

Phaedon presents Mendelssohn's demonstration of the third dogma of natural religion—the immortality of the soul. He wrote it as a result of his correspondence with a friend, Thomas Abbt of Frankfort-am-Oder. This book is a commentary on Plato's demonstration of spiritual afterlife. In it Mendelssohn reconstructed Plato's arguments on the basis of eighteenth-century psychology and Leibniz's philosophy. In essence, Mendelssohn argued that the soul is a monad, an incorporeal, simple, self-existing substance that unites in itself all concepts and ideas. As such, it is not subject to corruption after the breakdown of a physical body. In other words, given Mendelssohn's identification of the term *soul* with Leibniz's concept of a monad, it logically follows that a soul/monad is not perishable.

However, this identification in and of itself does not entail that any individual human being preserves him/her individual identity after death. It still remains possible after this stage of the argument that a soul continues to exist, but without any memory of the form of existence that it had when it was associated with a body. If this is the case, then when a person dies, his/her soul would continue to exist; but it would not be in any intelligible sense his/her soul. For example, if your soul exists without your body and without any memories of when it was your soul, in what sense would it continue to be *your* soul? What makes it yours ultimately rests on your personality, but what constitutes your personality is inseparable from your memories of the lived experiences that formed it. Hence, if memory does not survive death, your soul may continue to exist; but it would no longer be identifiably yours.

Mendelssohn's argument for the continued individuality of the soul after death is based on the claim that God is by nature good (a claim which he attempted to demonstrate in *Morning Hours*). God's goodness, in turn, entails that this world is the best of all possible worlds. This best-of-all-possible-worlds doctrine constitutes Mendelssohn's demonstration of the second dogma of natural religion—divine providence. It provides the major premise for his argument for the preservation of individual identity after death. In the best of all possible worlds, your soul would not only continue to exist, but it would continue to exist as your soul; i.e., after death you would continue to have your self-consciousness. Furthermore, Mendelssohn argued that in the best of all possible worlds no form of punishment could be eternal. Eventually all souls, no matter how good or evil they were in life, and, most importantly, no matter whether they were or were not saved through Christ, would gain eternal bliss.

Both works—*Phaedon* and *Morning Hours*—demonstrate major claims that Mendelssohn made about natural religion in his most important work in Jewish philosophy—*Jerusalem*—which deals with the philosophy of religion. The book contains two major parts. The first is a general description of the nature of religion. Specifically, he intends to demonstrate that no concrete expression of natural religion would accept excommunication. The second part discusses the nature of Judaism as an instance of natural religion. There Mendelssohn has the specific intention of demonstrating that Judaism is more liberal than (meaning superior to) Christianity. While the book is a natural expression of the primary direction of Mendelssohn's thought throughout his adult life, there was a specific incident that motivated the book's composition.

Mendelssohn wrote a preface to the German translation by Markus Herz of *Vindiciae Judaeorum* by the Dutch Jew, Manasseh Ben Israel (1604-1657). The book defends the seventeenth-century emancipation of the Jews in Holland. Mendelssohn's preface applies its arguments to eighteenth-century Germany. In his preface, Mendelssohn argued that the general progress of mankind and the improved life of the Jewish people are directly related. He suggested that for the sake of mankind Christians must stop persecuting Jews. He also felt that for the sake of their people Jews must advocate freedom of thought and stop opposing general political freedom. The general argument entailed that all religions ought to do away with excommunication. The book and Mendelssohn's preface generated considerable public criticism, most notably from a Jewish apostate to Christianity named Josef von Sonnenfels. *Jerusalem* was written as a response to von Sonnenfels and Mendelssohn's other critics.

The themes of *Jerusalem* can be summarized as follows: True religion and the good state share the same ultimate goals. They attempt to promote human happiness in this world and bliss in the world to come. They differ only in their methods and their immediate objects of concern. The state deals with the welfare of its citizens by directing their actions. On the other hand, religion deals with the souls of its adherents by directing their beliefs and the way that they relate to God.

Every true religion is an instantiation of natural religion. Natural religion is rational religion, i.e., one that consists of true beliefs. Mendelssohn asserted that there are three kinds of truths, which he called "logically necessary," "contingent," and "temporal" truths. Logically-necessary truths are innate ideas which are self-evident to a rational mind without any necessity for demonstration. These kinds of truths are discovered through the sciences of logic and mathematics. In this case, both revelation and miracles are irrelevant. Mendelssohn's specific examples of such truths are the three claims that we have already encountered, viz., God's existence and oneness, divine providence, and the immortality of the soul. Contingent truths are ideas based on sense observation and the laws of nature of the physical sciences. Temporal truths are based on the reports of reliable witnesses about unique historical events, i.e., inferences from reliable reports of contingent events so unique that they cannot be generalized by any scientific laws of nature. In other words, temporal truths are claims based on miracles, revelation, and reliable traditions about miracles and revelation.

The content of natural religion consists of the first two kinds of truth, but natural religion itself is only a conceptual construct. Mendelssohn denied that there either is or ought to be a universal religion for all mankind. Rather, there should be multiple religions, each of which is unique because of its particular possession of truths of the third kind.

The specific consequences that Mendelssohn noted from his analysis of the nature of the state and religion are the following: (1) Since the truth of religious doctrines can be established only by means of reason, every religious institution may attempt to persuade people of its claims; but no religion may use coercion.[9] (2) Only the state has a right to use force. It properly uses this power with its right to regulate the actions of its citizens for the sake of promoting their general welfare. However, since its power is limited to actions and does not extend to beliefs, the state ought to advocate freedom of conscience, and all religious institutions should be treated with equal respect.[10] Therefore, the Jewish people are entitled to emancipation in every nation.

In the second part of *Jerusalem*, the subject matter shifts from religion in general and the state to specific religions. Three kinds of religion are mentioned—idolatry, Christianity, and Judaism. Judaism and Christianity differ from idolatry in one major respect. Where idolatry is committed to concealing truth, Judaism and Christianity are committed to teaching it. However, Mendelssohn argued that Judaism is a more perfect embodiment of natural religion than is Christianity. In at least two respects, Christianity makes claims not found in Judaism that are contrary to reason. First, it claims that there are unique Christian beliefs (dogmas) rather than behavioral obligations (laws) that distinctively define the religion. These beliefs have to do with the life and actions of Jesus. Second, it maintains that only those who accept these dogmas can know truth and gain immortal life.

In Mendelssohn's argument, of all the religions in history Judaism is the most perfect example of a natural religion. Its principles are all rational doctrines of natural religion. Judaism supplements them with positive requirements or laws that properly apply only to the Jewish people. Furthermore, it correctly maintains that these laws and only these laws are given exclusively through revelation, and no one need observe them to share eventually in eternal bliss. The laws, revealed at Sinai to Moses and transmitted to the Jewish people in every generation through the reliable witness of the rabbis, are a unique path to happiness for the Jewish people. There are many roads to this same end, and there is a distinct path proper to every people.

Mendelssohn did acknowledge that the Torah lists forms of coercion. These *prima facie* contradict his claims that no rational religion uses coercion and Judaism is a rational religion. However, he argued that these texts do not really falsify his thesis. When the Torah was given, the Jewish people belonged to their own religious political state. To the extent that the Torah speaks of coercion, it does so only for crimes against the sovereign, i.e., against the state, and not for false religious doctrines. When the Jewish people ceased to have a political state of their own, i.e., when the course of history enabled the Jewish people to achieve a separation of religion from the state, Judaism ceased to use coercion.

The specific consequences that Mendelssohn noted from his analysis of concrete forms of religion are the following. (1) Judaism is superior to Christianity. Judaism claims divine legislation and not revealed dogmas, but Christianity claims that there are beliefs that can only be known by means of revelation. Christianity attempts to coerce people's minds through dogmas, but Judaism permits freedom of thought. Finally, Christian churches emphasize tangible symbols of belief, but Judaism emphasizes deed and practice. For all of these reasons, Judaism, and not Christianity, is successful in enabling its advocates to avoid the errors of paganism. (2) The only way that Jews will differ from other citizens of a good state is that they will continue to practise their personal, divinely-ordained religious duties. A Jew may obey every duty of a state that does not infringe on these religious duties, and no state ought to pass laws that prohibit Jews from doing God's revealed word.

Immanuel Kant read *Jerusalem* and called it an "irrefutable book" that should affect "not only your nation but others as well."[11] He did not spell out how it should affect his Christian, German state. In any case, many emancipated Jews and liberal Christians studied and were influenced by Mendelssohn. At the very least, *Jerusalem* is the cornerstone upon which the Jewish enlightenment was built in the nineteenth century. Mendelssohn's life and thought had profound influence on the subsequent development of liberal Judaism, the scientific study of Judaism (*Wissenschaft des Judentums*), and nineteenth-century European Jewish philosophy.

HASKALAH (JEWISH ENLIGHTENMENT)

The single most important event in promoting the new Western, so-called scientific study of Judaism was the publication in 1832 of Leopold Zunz's study on Midrash entitled *The Sermons of the Jews* (*Die gottesdienstlichen Vortage der Juden*). It provided the model upon which so-called positive historical school of Jewish studies was established. This title refers to the approach to Jewish scholarship instituted by Zacharias Frankel (1801-1875) as the head of the Juedisch-Theologisches Seminar in Breslau. A paradigmatic product of this school is *The History of the Jews* (1853-1876) by Heinrich Grätz (1817-1891).

The major figures in the rise of German Reform Judaism were Israel Jacobson (1768-1828), Samuel Holdheim (1806-1860), Solomon Formstecher (1808-1889), Abraham Geiger (1810-1874), and Samuel Hirsch (1815-1889). With respect to Jewish philosophy, the most interesting spokesmen of this movement were Formstecher and Hirsch.

Solomon Formstecher

Formstecher's major work in Jewish religious thought is entitled

The Religion of Spirit (*Die Religion des Geistes*, 1841). Formstecher's concept of Spirit was taken from but is not identical with the notion of Spirit in the philosophy of Friedrich Wilhelm Joseph von Schelling (1775-1854). As in the case of Schelling's thought, the World Soul (Geist) is manifest in nature; but, contrary to Schelling, the World Soul is not bound by nature. Rather, Formstecher affirmed a spiritual reality that transcends nature with which he identified God. More specifically, Formstecher distinguished two major expressions of Spirit. One is the consciousness of nature that gives rise to physics. The other is the con-sciousness of consciousness itself that produces logic. The former aware-ness is the source of the ideal of aesthetic contemplation, and it leads to the development of a religion of spirit. Formstecher's paradigm of a religion of nature is paganism, where God is identified with nature and man strives to become one with God. In contrast, in religion of spirit, God transcends nature and the goal of human life is to become like (but not identical with) God through moral action. Formstecher listed Islam, Christianity, and Judaism as examples of such a religion; but he consid-ered Judaism to be the purest example of the paradigm. Formstecher observed that as paganism declined in this world, Judaism has been free to become increasingly universal. Similarly, the decline of paganism has enabled Judaism to become increasingly aware of spiritual self-consciousness. Two major stages in the history of Judaism mark this transition. First, at the end of the biblical period, Judaism overcame its identity as a nation state; i.e., it transcended political reality, and under the leadership of the classical rabbinate it became a theocracy of law. Second, with emancipation in Western Europe, Judaism can transcend itself as a theocracy and emerge as a pure spiritual religion of absolute truth.

Formstecher's Christianity is a combination of the false panthe-ism of pagan religion and the true transcendence of Judaism. The history of Christianity is the story of the internal conflict of these two opposing pure principles within the Church. Formstecher firmly believed that in the end of days, Christianity will purge itself of its pagan elements, at which time Judaism and Christianity will become identical. He believed that the instrument of this purge would be lib-eral Protestantism.

Samuel Hirsch

Hirsch presented a similar philosophy of religion in his *Religious Philosophy of the Jews* (*Die Religionsphilosophie der Juden*) (1842). He based his thought primarily on his understanding of the philoso-phy of Georg Wilhelm Friedrich Hegel (1770-1831). Hirsch discussed the philosophical cornerstones of liberal religion, viz., the relation of philosophy and religion, the nature of freedom, and the history of religion.

Concerning philosophy and religion, he claimed that their truths are identical. The sole difference is that the goal of philosophy is to transform the imaginative content of religious consciousness into the philosophic content of the mind of human spirit. Concerning freedom, he distinguished between two kinds. First, there is what he called abstract freedom. It is a contentless form that arises when the individual becomes aware of his "I" standing over and against nature. From this consciousness, the enlightened, free individual becomes aware that God transcends nature. It is this realization that led to the historical rise of Judaism. Second, there is natural freedom, which is simply the ability to do what you, the individual, desire to do. This sense of freedom leads the individual to identify nature as a divine principle. It is this identity that led to the historical rise of paganism.

For Hirsch these two senses of the term *freedom* and their consequent religious principles are the key to his characterization of this history of religion. In is analysis, only three religions are noted—paganism, Judaism, and Christianity. Paganism is, as it was for Mendelssohn, a religion that has no value; it embodies error and strives to conceal truth. In contrast, Judaism is a fully developed, true faith, whose sole remaining function is to spread its truth of ethical freedom throughout the world. It will do so through self-witness rather than through missionizing. Between these two extremes lies Christianity. Like Judaism, Christianity is committed to teaching ethical freedom to the world. However, Christianity corrupted its inherited Jewish truth when, under the influence of Paul, it incorporated the doctrines of original sin and the consequent claim that salvation is only possible through Christ. Hirsch shared Formstecher's optimism that in the end of history, Christianity will free itself of its pagan error and become identical with Judaism.

NINETEENTH-CENTURY JEWISH PHILOSOPHY

Solomon Ludwig Steinheim

Steinheim (1789-1866) was Jewish, a physician, a poet, and a philosopher; but he was neither a rabbi nor an observant Jew. Still, he published one major work on Jewish religious thought, entitled *Revelation according to the Doctrine of the Synagogue (Die*

Offenbarung nach dem Lehrbegriffe, written between 1835 and 1865). In general, he was an anti-rationalist who nonetheless reached basically the same conclusions about religion as the rationalist Reformers Formstecher and Hirsch. He claimed that the content of religion transcends what is knowable through human reason; instead, it comes directly from God through revelation. However, human reason can and does confirm the teachings of true religion, with one notable difference. Philosophy conceives all of reality in terms of necessity, but religion understands reality in terms of freedom. Steinheim went on to distinguish between natural and revealed religion. The former is exemplified by paganism, and the latter is the source of the Jewish Bible's truth. The most important difference between the two is that in paganism, God is subject to the necessity of His own nature and is limited in creation by the nature of the matter with which he must work. In revealed biblical faith, God is a creator who acts freely and creates out of nothing. The ideal example of revealed religion is Judaism. Its major truths are the concepts of revelation, freedom, the immortality of the soul, and the unity of God. Its single most important concept is freedom, which is the philosophical foundation of moral activity. Like the religions philosophy of the Reformers, Christianity also contains the true insights of Judaism, but those insights are distorted through mixture with the errors of paganism. Unlike the Reformers, Steinheim made no distinction between Protestantism and Roman Catholicism. In his judgment, both forms of Christianity were a mixture of the revealed and the natural religions.

Samson Raphael Hirsch

Hirsch (1808-1889) spent the major part of his adult life as the chief traditional rabbi of the Duchy of Oldenburg. There he wrote his major works on Jewish religious thought—*The Nineteen Letters on Judaism* (*Neunzehn Briefe über Judenthum*) (1836), and *Horeb: A Philosophy of Jewish Laws and Observances* (*Horeb, oder Versuche über Jissroel's Pflichten in der Zerstreuung*) (1838). The goal of his writings is to show Jews how to maintain a "Torah-True" commitment to their ancestral faith while integrating themselves into the life of Western civilization. Hirsch discussed ethics, Jewish law, and Jewish worship. In terms of ethics, Hirsch argued that the goal of human life is not the attainment of individual or personal happiness or perfection. Rather, individuals exist as part of a nation, and their goal is to contribute as much as possible to their nation's success. God has a plan for the universe as a whole. Within that plan each nation has its own distinct purpose. The value of the lives of individuals resides solely in their contribution to the nation in fulfilling its destiny. The Jewish people specifically have a unique purpose. The nation of Israel is to bring all other nations to recognize that God has a plan for the universe. Each individual is part of a distinct nation, and every nation must dedicate itself to fulfilling what God has intended for it.

Israel's mission is expressed in the laws of the Torah. Those laws are of five kinds. There are (1) fundamental ideas about God, the world, mankind's mission, and Israel's mission; (2) laws of social justice; (3) laws of justice for both animate and inanimate objects; (4) laws promoting love between all living things; and (5) festivals and ceremonies symbolizing Judaism's essential truths. Through its commanded acts of worship, Israel serves as a witness to the messianic ideal of human brotherhood, the fulfillment of which is part of God's ultimate plan. Emancipation also serves this end and should be accepted by the Jews. Properly understood, emancipation in no sense entails that Jews should abandon their commitment to Israel's commandments and worship.

Nahman Krochmal

Krochmal (1785-1840) is known to traditional Jews as Ranak. He was born in Brody, in the eastern part of Galicia, where his father was a wealthy merchant named Shalom Krochmalnik. Nahman lived with his father-in-law in Zolkian near Lemberg (Lvov). Eventually, he became a merchant. However, Krochmal never was successful in business. His interest was his scholarship. Primarily on his own, he studied rabbinics and the major writings of modern Western civilization. He spent the last years of his life in poverty in the home of his daughter in Tarnapol, where he continued to study and write. None of his work became public during his lifetime. In 1851, Leopold Zunz published Krochmal's *The Guide of the Perplexed for Our Time* (*MOREH NEVUKHIM HA-ZEMAN*). The book deals with philosophy of religion and history (chapters 1-7), Jewish history (chapters 8-11), Hebrew literature (chapters 12-15), and Jewish philosophy (chapters 16-17). The primary sources of Krochmal's general philosophy were Hegel, Schelling, and Johann Gottlieb Fichte (1762-1814). The primary sources of his political philosophy and history were Giovanni Battista Vico (Italy, 1668-1744) and Johann Gottfried von Herder (1744-1803).

Based on Schelling and Hegel, Krochmal became an Objective Idealist. He considered nature to be an organic unity which manifests itself progressively through Spirit (Geist). The ultimate principle of reality is Absolute Spirit or Reality-In-Itself, which he identified with God and defined as a power equal to every latent and potential form within itself. Based on this theology, he interpreted the dogma of creation out of nothing to be a transition from Absolute Reality to the generated reality of finite things. The latter is an infinite process through which God fulfills Himself. Drawing from the Kabbalah, [12] Krochmal identified the nothing of creation with God Himself. In other words, God, who was nothing, created the world for Himself in order to become God, who will become something.

Krochmal claimed that philosophy and religion differ only in form but not in content. Philosophy's goal is knowledge, and every claim of truth is at some level true. No purported knowledge is false; there are higher and lower levels of knowledge, but no error. The lowest levels of knowledge are the lessons of the imagination, which Krochmal called "ideas of mind and intellect." Every religion is a system of national worship of some true, spiritual powers. Every specific religion worships a specific spirit. Israel alone worships the general Absolute Spirit. The biblical faith of the Jewish people is unique in its purity and in the universality of its images. This analysis of the nature of philosophy and religion is the foundation of Krochmal's account of national history.

Drawing from Vico and Herder, Krochmal was a strong advocate of nationalism. Nations are collections of people who are unified through a distinct culture. Every individual nation has a unique spirituality or spiritual aptitude. It is this spirituality that constitutes the nation's 'principle' which is its reason for being or right to exist. Nations, like people, have a life of their own. Their lives vary according to how faithful they remain to their distinct cultural spirituality. Based on this principle, every nation undergoes three distinct periods. At first they grow and develop; then they reach a stage of maximum vigor and enterprise; and finally they decline and are annihilated. The one exception to this general description is the nation Israel; because Israel's spirit is the Absolute Spirit itself, Israel is an eternal nation. While it undergoes growth and development and it has distinct periods of vigor and enterprise, it does not decline and disappear. Rather, when decline sets in, Israel always undergoes renewal.

Samuel David Luzzatto

Luzzatto (1800-1875) is known to traditional Jews as Shadal. He was born in Trieste, in the north of Italy, where his father was a poor woodcutter and a student of Kabbalah. Samuel became a rabbi; and from 1829 on, he served as a member of the faculty of the rabbinical college of Padua. He wrote on the Bible, the prayer book, medieval Jewish poetry, Hebrew grammar, and theology. His major academic accomplishments were an Italian translation of the Bible and a work on Jewish philosophy entitled *The Foundations of the Torah* (*YESODEI HA-TORAH*, published in 1880). The major theme of his philosophy was the application of nineteenth-century continental Romanticism to understanding the nature of Judaism. His major intellectual sources were the apparent anti-rationalism of the medieval Jewish philosopher, Judah Halevy (1075-1141), and the radical empiricism of the modern French philosopher, Etienne Bonnot de Condillac (1715-1780).

The major themes of *The Foundations of the Torah* are epistemology, religion, and Judaism. Luzzatto rejected any claims about knowledge being based on autonomous reason. All knowledge is based on sensation, and certainty has its source in intuitive feelings rather than in intellectual demonstrations. Still, he did believe that there is certainty. Following the classical Jewish philosophers from Saadia (892-942) through Gersonides (1288-1344), he maintained that human beings cannot know God; but they can know with intuitive certainty that God exists.

Luzzatto claimed that religion is based on revelation and not on reason. The goal of religious belief is to motivate human beings to moral actions. Consequently, true religion deals with ethical conduct rather than with seemingly rational belief. Based on this judgment, Luzzatto drew a radical distinction between two kinds of religion. He called true religion "Hebraism" and false religion "Hellenism." His prime example of a false religion is that of Athens, which he called "Atticism." His paradigmatic true religion was Judaism, but he recognized that there are elements of both kinds within Judaism itself. True religion, i.e., the Judaism of rabbis such as Rashi (1040-1105) and Halevy, is directed towards human righteousness, goodness, purity, and sympathy. False religion, as can be found in the religious teachings of Moses Maimonides (1135-1204) and Baruch Spinoza (1632-1677), pursue artistic beauty as well as scientific or metaphysical understanding. True Hebraism has no dogmas. It rests on the Torah, whose primary concern is with developing emotions rather than intellect. First and foremost, the Bible seeks to develop its reader's capacity to feel compassion and pity, which are the sources of human ethics. Only secondarily does Scripture promote hope of reward, fear of punishment, and a sense in the Jewish people of *noblesse oblige* about being the chosen people. The first two feelings are useful aids to motivate human beings to behave morally. The third emotion encourages the Jewish people to strive beyond mere morality in order to accomplish moral excellence, i.e., to go beyond seeking what is good and to strive to attain what is the best.

CONCLUSION

The Jewish philosophers of the eighteenth and nineteenth centuries disagreed about whether the ultimate source of truth was reason, the emotions, or supernatural revelation. They also disagreed about the ultimate value of ritual in religion. But they shared in common the commitments that true religion deals with ethics rather than physics, that Judaism expresses religion at its best, that paganism is religion at its worst, and that Christianity is a mixture of the two. It should also be clear from the above summaries that in purely technical terms these Reformers and champions of Jewish enlightenment were not great philosophers. The first (and possibly the last) great philosopher to express their shared modern Jewish beliefs was Hermann Cohen.

NOTES

1. A few other facts of interest about his life are the following: He had a curvature of the spine from a childhhood illness. In fact, he suffered from nervous disorders for the rest of his life. He married Fromet Guggenheim (1737-1812) from Hamburg. They had three sons (Joseph, Abraham, and Nathan), and three daughters (Dorthea, Recha, and Henrietta). Moses' most famous grandchild, all of whom were Christians, was the musician Felix who was the son of Abraham.

2. Lessing was a popular German dramatist. The central character of his play, "Nathan the Wise" (1779), is modeled on Mendelssohn.

3. The title of Mendelssohn's essay was "Über die evidenz der metaphysischen Wissenschaften."

4. *Untersuchung der Beweise fur das Christenthum.*

5. *Idees sur L'Etat des etres Vivants, ou Palingenesie Philosophigue.*

6. His letter, published in 1770, was entitled, "Schreiben anden Herrn Diaconus Lavater in Zurich."

7. Henceforth to be referred to as *Jerusalem*.

8. Henceforth to be referred to *Morning Hours*.

9. In the fourteenth century, Hasdai Crescas argued that since what a man believes is caused by his background, his natural talents, his training, and his experience, people are compelled and not free to choose what they believe. Religious law can only obligate someone to choose what he is free to choose. Consequently, while a religion may stipulate obligations about actions and it may list what are true and false belief, it cannot stipulate obligations about belief. [Cf. Menachem Kellner's introduction to Isaac Abravanel's *Principles of Faith* (*Rosh Amanah*), Toronto: Associated University Presses, 1982, pp. 17-50.] Spinoza argued in the *Theologico-Philisophus Tractatus* that the state has a right to do whatever it has power to do; but, based on Crescas' argument, since the state is not able to obligate a citizen to change his beliefs, a state has no right to deny freedom of thought. Mendelssohn certainly was familiar with Spinoza's argument, and he may have known Crescas' as well.

10. Mendelssohn did place one restriction on his general political principle of religious tolerance. In his judgment a state has a right to prohibit atheism.

11. *The Jewish Encyclopedia*, vol. 8, New York: Ktav, 1901. p. 484.

12. See chapter 1.

KEY NAMES

Solomon Formstecher, *The Foundations of the Torah*, Zacharias Frankel, Heinrich Grätz, *The Guide of the Perplexed or our Time*. Samson Raphael Hirsch, Samuel Hirsch, Horeb, *Jerusalem*, Nahman Krochmal, Samuel David Luzzatto, Moses Mendelssohn, *Morgenstunden*, *The Nineteen Letters on Judaism*, *Phaedon*, The Religion of Spirit, The Religious Philosophy of the Jews, Revelation according to the Doctrine of the Synagogue, Solomon Ludwig Steinheim, Leopold Zunz.

KEY TERMS

absolute spirit, Atticism, contingent truth, Geist, HASKALAH,

Hebraism, idea of incipient thought, idea of mind and intellect, idolatry, monad, natural religion, paganism, positive historical school, principle, reality-in-itself, religion of nature, religion of spirit, revealed religion, temporal truth, world-soul.

KEY QUESTIONS

1. In what way does belief about the Bible distinguish medieval from modern Jews?

2. What are the philosophic sources of the major figures in modern Jewish philosophy?

3. In general, on what did the eighteenth and nineteenth century Jewish philosophers agree and disagree? Compare and contrast their views of the following topics:

(A) How are religions to be judged? What is natural religion? How are religion and religions related?

(B) What is Judaism? what is the function and value of Jewish law and observance? According to Samson Raphael Hirsch, what five kinds of laws are in the Torah?

(C) What is paganism? Christianity? Protestantism?

(D) What is the relationship between reason and revelation? Philosophy and religion?

(E) What will happen to all religions in the end of days?

4. Why did Mendelssohn write Hebrew translations of the classical Jewish texts?

5. How are Mendelssohn's three major works related? Why did he write each one? How does he prove God's existence? Divine Providence? Immortality?

6. Compare and contrast Mendelssohn and Samson Raphael Hirsch on emancipation. Why should gentiles grant emancipation to the Jews? Why should Jews accept it?

7. Compare and contrast the views of Mendelssohn, Samuel Hirsch and Steinheim on freedom. How did Mendelssohn limit his belief in political/religious freedom? According to Hirsch, what are two kinds of freedom, and what consequences does this distinction have for a philosophy of religion?

8. Compare and contrast Mendelssohn, Samuel Hirsch, and Samson Raphael Hirsch on the relation of religion to the state.

9. Compare and contrast Mendelssohn's, Krochmal's and Luzzatto's theories of knowledge. According to Mendelssohn, what are the three kinds of truths and how are they known? According to Luzzatto, what three emotions are the objects of the Hebrew Scriptures, and why is this the case?

10. Compare and contrast what Mendelssohn, Steinheim, and Krochmal had to say about creation. According to Krochmal, what is "creation out of nothing"?

RECOMMENDED READINGS

General

Robert M. Seltzer, *Jewish People, Jewish Thought: The Jewish Experience in History.* New York: Macmillan, 1980. Chpt. 12, pp. 557-618.

Primary

Samson Raphael Hirsch, *Horeb: A Philosophy of Jewish Laws and Observances.* Translated into English by Isidor Gruenwald. London: Soncino, 1962.

———, *The Nineteen Letters of Ben Uziel: Being A Spiritual Presentation of the Principles of Judaism.* Translated into English by Bernard Drachman. New York: Feldhiem. 1960.

Nahman Krochmal, *Moreh Nevukhim Ha-Zeman.* Edited by S. Rawidowicz. Ramat-Gan: University of Bar-Ilan, 1971.

——— *Jerusalem, or On Religious Power and Judaism.* Translated into English by Alexander Altmann. Hanover: University Press of New England, 1983.

——— *Moses Mendelssohn: Selections from His Writings.* Translated into English by Eva Jospe. New York: The Viking Press, 1975.

Secondary

Alexander Altmann (ed.), *Studies in Nineteenth Century Jewish Intellectual History.* Cambridge, MA: Harvard University Press, 1964.

Samuel Hugo Bergman, *Faith and Reason: An Introduction to Modern Jewish Thought.* Edited by Alfred Jospe. New York: Schocken, 1963.

Noah H. Rosenbloom, *Luzzatto's Ethico-Psychological Interpretation of Judaism: A Study in the Religious Philosophy of Samuel David*

Luzzatto. New York: Yeshiva University Press (Department of Special Publications) 1965.

Nathan Rotenstreich, *Jewish Philosophy in Modern Times: From Mendelssohn to Rosenzweig.* New York: Holt, Rinehart and Winston, 1968.

―――― *Jews and German Philosophy: The Polemics of Emancipation.* New York: Schocken Books, 1984.

David Rudavsky, *Modern Jewish Religious Movements: A History of Emancipation and Adjustment.* New York: Behrman, 1967.

9

HERMANN COHEN

HIS LIFE AND WORK

Cohen was born in 1842 in Coswig, where his father was the local cantor and Hebrew teacher. He acquired his Jewish education at home and his general education at the local gymnasium. At a more advanced level, he continued his Jewish studies at the Jewish Theological Seminary of Breslau; and he studied mathematics and philosophy at the University of Berlin. In 1865, he earned his Ph.D. in philosophy at the University of Halle; and in 1873, he began his academic career as a lecturer at the University of Marburg. There he wrote most of his works on mathematics and philosophy. In 1912, Cohen abandoned his purely philosophic interests and turned his attention to Jewish intellectual concerns. In 1914, he went to Wilna and Warsaw in Poland in order to help establish an independent institute of higher learning; and in 1915, he began to teach in Berlin's liberal rabbinic seminary, the Hochschule fur die Wissenschaft des Judentums. He remained at the Hochshule until his death in 1918.

The source of Cohen's philosophy is his study of the philosophy of Immanuel Kant (1724-1804) and his work in mathematics. His only book on mathematics is *The Principles of the Infinitesimal*

Method and Its History (Das Prinzip der Infinitesimalmethode und seine Geschichte), which was published in 1883. His first four books in philosophy were studies on Kant's thought—*Kant's Theory of Experience (Kants Theorie der Erfahrung)*, published in 1871; *Kant's Principles of Ethics (Kants Begruendung der Ethik)*, published in 1877; *Concerning Kant's Influence on German Culture (Von Kants Einfluss auf die deutsche Kulture)*, published in 1883; and *Kant's Principles of Aesthetics (Kants Begruendung der Aesthetik)* published in 1889. Cohen's twentieth-century books on general philosophy were all statements of his own thought—*The Logic of Pure Knowledge (Die Logik der reinen Erkenntnis)*, published in 1902; *The Ethics of Pure Will (Die Ethik des reinen Willens)*, published in 1904; and the *Aesthetic of Pure Feeling (Die Aesthetik des reinen Gefühls)*, published in 1924. In these three books, Cohen presented precisely what their titles state, viz., a study of what Cohen considered to be the three primary branches of philosophy—(1) Logic, or the systematic study of pure thinking; (2) Ethics, or the systematic study of pure willing; and (3) Aesthetics, or the systematic study of pure feeling—each of which is based respectively on Kant's three critiques. By "pure" Cohen meant what Kant meant, viz., in itself and independent of any extraneous considerations. Hence, logic deals with thought as thought, independent of the senses; ethics deals with acts of will, independent of factors such as compulsion and external consequences; and similarly, aesthetics deals with feelings, independent of their relationship to other mental and physical states of affairs.

Cohen wrote two books and more than sixty articles on Jewish philosophy. The articles were collected together into a single volume in 1924 under the title, *Jewish Writings (Judische Schriften)*. We will not deal with any of these papers in this chapter, but two of them are worthy of mention.

In 1879, a colleague of Cohen at Marburg named Treitschke published an attack on the Jews[1] in which he charged that Jews are not and cannot ever be real Germans. Cohen published a reply in 1880 called "A Confession about the Jewish Question" ("Ein Bekenntnis zur Judenfrage") in which he defended the integration of Jews into German society. In this article, Cohen argued that Jews, as the inheritors of traditional Jewish values, represent what is most worthwhile in German culture.

Cohen was called upon to provide expert witness in a law suit against an anti-Semitic public school teacher who said that the Talmud limits moral obligations for Jews to their relations with other Jews and also teaches that Jews have no moral obligations to gentiles.

Based on his testimony in 1888, Cohen published an article entitled "Brotherly Love in the Talmud" ("Die Naechstenliebe im Talmud"), in which Cohen harmonized the Jewish concepts of the chosen people and messianism by means of the Jewish concept of God. He argued that in Judaism God is understood to be the deity of the alien, which means that God presents the Jews with the ideal of making no one alien. Hence, the Jews are chosen to strive to bring about universal brotherhood, the realization of which is the fulfillment of the messianic ideal. Cohen's first book on Jewish philosophy was *The Concept of Religion in the System of Philosophy* (*Der Begriff der Religion in der System der Philosophie*), published in 1915.[2] Here Cohen argued that the purpose of religion is to fill in certain necessities of the moral life that are beyond the capacity of philosophy, viz., sin, revelation, repentance, anguish, and guilt. Philosophy cannot deal with these concepts, because it is capable only of grasping what is universal. These concepts arise only with respect to the single self, which is within the domain of religion. Hence, religion, and not philosophy, teaches the individual to face guilt and to repent without abandoning moral responsibility.

Cohen's second book on Jewish philosophy was *The Religion of Reason out of the Sources of Judaism (Die Religion der Vernunft aus den Quellen des Judentums)*, published in 1919.[3] It was edited after his death by Cohen's student, Franz Rosenzweig, and published by Cohen's wife. Here Cohen developed the argument that through their religious civilization, the Jewish people have acquired an intuitive recognition of the Kantian truths about God and ethics that reflect the best in German culture.

Cohen argued that Baruch Spinoza was a pantheist because Spinoza identified God with nature; and therefore, Spinoza's theology is both idolatrous and not Jewish. In contrast to this pagan/Spinozistic identification of God with what is, Judaism teaches ethical monotheism. According to Cohen, in Judaism man and God are correlated by means of the Holy Spirit (*RUAH HA-KODESH*). However, contrary to Christianity, this spirit is not a third entity, distinct from God and man; rather, it is the relationship between the two and nothing else. This correlation expresses itself in the religious principle of the imitation of God (*imitatio dei*), which in Cohen's interpretation, means that man strives to become like God through moral action rooted in an ideal conception of God. According to Cohen, different conceptions of God are different moral ideals; and to become like God means to strive to achieve the conceived ideal. Based on this understanding of correlation, Judaism visualizes God and man as coworkers in the creation of the world, whose end or purpose (telos) is the unification of all mankind. This goal will be approached by establishing just communities throughout the world, where the rights of the poor are defended and all classes live in peace and harmony with their society. In the end, there will be a single, just, harmonious society of all human beings. Judaism calls this state "the messianic age."

Cohen argued that this core philosophy of Judaism is the only true philosophy. It can be found in certain forms of Christianity as well. However, Judaism is philosophically superior to Christianity in two respects. First, only in Judaism does this morally-ideal conception of God, viz., ethical monotheism, function as the sole criterion by which ritual is to be judged. Second, Christianity perverts its monotheism by falsely reifying[4] the Holy Spirit.

HIS MATHEMATICAL THOUGHT

At the present time, there is a debate among students of Cohen's Jewish philosophy about the relationship between the *Concept* and the *Religion*. Some claim that the *Religion* is an extension to Jewish thought of the philosophy presented four years earlier in the *Concept*. Others claim that, in the course of just four years, Cohen radically changed his thought. They argue that in the *Concept*, Judaism is subservient to philosophy; whereas in the *Religion*, Judaism is supreme. Furthermore, they claim that in the *Concept*, the ultimate source of morality is a mere human concept, since in the *Concept* God is ideal and not real; whereas in the *Religion*, ethics are rooted in the reality and not in the mere conception of God. It is obvious that this presentation of Cohen's philosophy agrees with the former interpretation that the *Religion* is an extension of the *Concept*, but no defense of this position will be made here. Briefly, those who follow the latter interpretation are wrong because they separate the real from the ideal and they identify reality with our sense world, which Cohen, both as a Kantian and as a mathematical philosopher, would not do. What led them to their mistaken interpretation is that they think to say that the ideal is real means that mental concepts are what exists. A mathematician whose philosophic sense is as astute as was Cohen's would not agree with this judgment. In other words, Cohen's understanding of the ideal and the real was based on his understanding of mathematics. Without adequately grasping the mathematics, any interpretation of his philosophy, particularly those failing to see the unity of the *Concept* and the *Religion*, is inadequate.

It seems that Cohen's mathematics is essential to understanding not only his ontology but all of his philosophy. This dependence is unfortunate for a number of reasons. First, Cohen is the first clearly great Jewish philosopher since Spinoza.[5] However, no mere summary of Cohen's conclusions will exhibit his greatness. As long as we limit our attention to what Cohen believed, without considering why he believed it and what he really meant by what be believed, what Cohen said is hardly persuasive and does not appear to be at a qualitatively higher level than the myths of Judaism, Christianity, and Paganism that passed as history of religion in the eighteenth and nineteenth centuries.[6]

Second, the world in which scholars are competent and interested in the concerns of both scientists and humanists no longer exists, but Cohen's philosophy presupposes readers who are such modern polymaths. There are Jews who know mathematics and contemporary science; there are Jews who know religious thought and contemporary philosophy; but there are relatively few Jews who know both. In general, those who can read Cohen's mathematics are not interested in the rest of his Jewish philosophy; and those who are interested in the latter lack the background and the interest to read, let alone understand, his work on mathematics.

Third, the dependence of Cohen's philosophy on his mathematics is unfortunate. Furthermore, the assumption that the readers of this text, because they are interested in Jewish philosophy, probably do not know the relevant mathematics adds to the misfortune. Because of this dependence, in order to explain what Cohen believed as a philosopher, one must first explain something about mathematics. However, to discuss anything about mathematics, even at the simplest level, is difficult in a text such as this one that is intended to be an introduction to Jewish religious thought.

Fourth, while Cohen's general philosophy and his Jewish philosophy have had considerable influence on subsequent Western philosophy and Jewish religious thought, his mathematical writings have had no influence at all. In terms of philosophy, Cohen founded the major interpretation of Kant, called "Marburg Neo-Kantianism." This interpretation continues to be the major alternative in Continental European philosophy to the disciples of Hegel and the Romantics who rebelled against Hegel. In terms of Jewish religious thought, Cohen's philosophy provides us with the most sophisticated formulation of the religious thought available, one that underlies the kind of liberal religious Judaism that Cohen's student Leo Baeck preached.[7] Furthermore, the two most influential contemporary Jewish philosophers—Martin Buber and Franz Rosenzeweig[8]—were his students, and their thought reflects his direct influence. But no similar claims can be made about his work in mathematics.

What Cohen did was formulate an account of what is known in mathematics and physics as the infinitesimal precisely at the time when mathematicians dispensed with the necessity of employing infinitesimals to explain differential calculus and adopted Karl Weierstrass' (1815-1897) alternative account. The infinitesimal calculus is a form of mathematical thinking that rests on the conception of something called an infinitesimal. It has been used by mathematicians and physicists since the time of Archimedes (287-212 B.C.E.) to formulate theorems and solve problems in geometry and in dynamics. Most philosophers have believed that there is no way to make the notion of infinitesimals intelligible. Mathematicians were thereby forced to seek an alternative set of definitions to account for the kinds of calculations that were previously based on infinitesimals. It is generally accepted in mathematics today that Weierstrass provided such an alternative; so that by the time that Cohen published his work on infinitesimals, the scholarly world was no longer interested.

What follows below is an explanation of calculus as it is understood today using Weierstrass' definitions and approach, an explanation of how the alternative infinitesimal calculus of Cohen works, an explanation of why philosophers do not believe that infinitesimals are intelligible, and finally a defense of the Cohen alternative over that of Weierstrass. After this introduction, Cohen's understanding of the infinitesimal will be used to explain his Jewish philosophy.[9]

Weierstrass' Account of Differentials

The standard explanation of differentials used in mathematics today makes no reference to infinitesimals. Today differentials are defined as follows.

Look at the right triangles pictured in diagram 1. The increment Dx along the x-axis is the difference between the definite x of the terminal point and the definite x of the initial point. Similarly the Dy along the y-axis is the difference between the definite y of the terminal point and the definite y of the initial point. The slope (M) of a line on an x and y coordinate plane is defined as the rate of rise and fall as we move from left to right along the line, i.e., rise/run, which is equal to $(y_2-y_1)/(x_2-x_1)$, which is equal to Dy/Dx. Given a line between points P_1 and P_2 where the coordinates of P_1 are (x_1,y_1) and of P_2 are (x_2,y_2), form a right triangle by extending a line from P_1 horizontally at y_1 parallel to the x-axis and by extending a line

Diagram 1

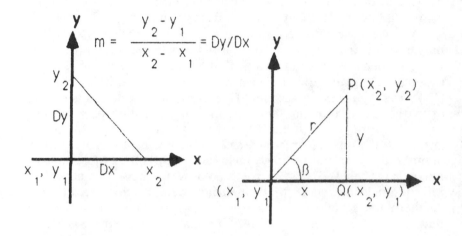

vertically from P_2 at x_2 parallel to the y-axis. Let the point of intersection of these two lines be called Q whose coordinates are (x_2, y_1). Let $x=P_1Q$, $y=P_2Q$, and $r=P_1P_3$ so that the right triangle rxy has an angle at the point of intersection of r and x. The tangent of this angle is defined as y/x.

Now also look at diagram 2. The slope (M) of a tangent line of a curve at P, whose coordinates are (x_1,y_1) is defined as follows: Where the curve is defined by a function (f) of x, take the difference between f of (x_1+Dx) and f of (x_1), divide that difference by Dx, and continuously decrease the size of Dx in this expression. The slope of the tangent is the limit of this expression as Dx in this expression approaches zero. I.e., the limit as Dx approaches zero of $[f(x_1+Dx)–f(x_1)]/(Dx)$. The name given to this slope of the tangent of a curve defined by the function f(x) at any point (x_1) on the curve is the *derivative* of the function and is represented symbolically as $f'(x)$.

Let y=f(x), in which case f'(x)=y'. We will now define the derivative of y with respect to x as dy/dx, where dy and dx are defined as follows: Let y be represented by a curve, and two points on this curve are P (at x_1, y_1) and Q (at x_1+D_x, y_1+Dy). Draw the tangent to the curve at P and extend this line in the direction of Q; then draw a vertical line through Q at (x_1+Dx) from the x-axis to the tangent and a horizontal line through P from the y-axis to the vertical line. On this triangle let dx=the length of the horizontal line, and dy=the length of the vertical line, so that the derivative of y with respect to

Diagram 2

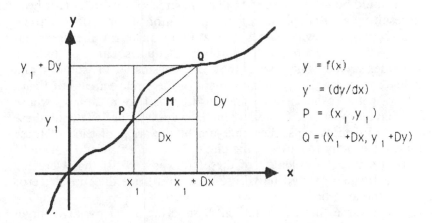

$$y = f(x)$$
$$y' = (dy/dx)$$
$$P = (x_1, y_1)$$
$$Q = (x_1 + Dx, y_1 + Dy)$$

x, y or f(x), can be said to equal dy/dx.

Now, if y=F(x) so that y'=F'(x), and y'=dy/dx, then by simple algebra dy=F' (x_0)dx, where x_0 is a specific point on the curve formed by y. dy is called the "differential of y." In other words, the differential of y, (dy), is a certain number of units of change in the y direction along the tangent of the graph of a particular finite function [F(x)]. Similarly the differential of x, (dx), is a certain number of units of change in the x direction along the tangent of the graph of the same function, and the derivative of the function is a ratio of these two differentials (dy/dx).

Infinitesimal Account of Differentials

Again, what is given above is a summary of how differentials are explained today in standard courses in calculus. The most obvious feature of this definition is that it is extraordinarily complex. There is an alternative, simpler, far more intuitive way to account for this same mathematical operation. It involves the assumption of a certain kind of mathematical entity called an "infinitesimal," which may be defined as a number or magnitude smaller than every positive rational number or magnitude but greater than zero. At an intuitive level, the infinitesimal is both simple to understand and useful. Consider the following two cases.

(1) Assume that I want to determine the area of a circle. I could divide this area into a number of equal squares, some of which

would extend beyond the circumference of the circle, the sum of which would be somewhat larger than the area of the circle. However, the resulting area is only an approximation of the area of the circle, because it is somewhat larger. If I want to make my measurement more accurate, I increase the number of equal squares by making their sides smaller. The smaller the sides, the smaller the squares, and the less inaccurate is my measurement of the circle's area; but I cannot ever get an exact measurement as long as I count squares whose sides have a positive, finite length. However, if the length of these sides are infinitesimals, then the sum of the areas of each of these squares is exactly the area of the circle. Note that it would not make sense to say that the length of these sides is zero. If that were the case, each square would have zero area, and since the sum of zeros is zero, the area of the circle would be zero.

(2) Assume that William Tell is shooting an arrow at a target which is sufficiently close that it is certain that he will hit the target; i.e., the probability that he will hit the target is 1. If I divide the target into four equal parts, the probability that he will hit any one of these parts is 1/4; if I further divide the target into n equal parts, the probability that he will hit any one of these parts is 1/n. In general, given that the probability of hitting the target is 1, then the sum of the probabilities of hitting all of the designated parts is 1. Now suppose I ask what is the probability that Tell will hit any single designated point in the target. Since the target contains an infinite number of points, the probability in this case is one over infinity. But what probability is this? It cannot be zero, for then the sum of probabilities for hitting each point would be zero; and there would be no probability that Tell could hit the target. Rather, it would seem reasonable to say that the probability of hitting any particular point, (1/i), is infinitesimal, and the sum of an infinite number of infinitesimals is 1.

The Problem of Infinitesimals

The second example points to another characteristic of infinitesimals that is their main problem. No matter how many times an infinitesimal is added to itself, the sum is always equal to or less than 1. This statement has the consequence that an infinitesimal cannot be a real number, because it violates an axiom of Archimedes (287-212 B.C.E.). This axiom states that magnitudes have a ratio to one another which are capable, when multiplied, of exceeding one another.[10] In other words, any real number or magnitude is such that if it is added to itself a sufficient number of times the sum will exceed 1. For that reason, Archimedes and all subsequent mathematicians expelled infinitesimals from the realm of real numbers and real magnitudes. This judgement led philosophers of mathematics to believe that nothing in reality can be composed of infinitesimals. Yet, infinitesimals persisted in the history of mathematics as useful entities. Archimedes himself used them to calculate the area of a parabola; Johannes Kepler (1571-1630) used them to determine the best proportions of a wine cask; and Gottfried Wilhelm von Leibniz (1646-1716) and Isaac Newton (1642-1727) used them to deal with problems of continuity. It is this very usefulness that presented the greatest perplexities about infinitesimals.

The problem can be stated as follows: On one hand, based on Archimedes' axiom, it does not seem reasonable to claim that there is in reality anything that is infinitesimal. On the other hand, infinitesimals are a key to understanding continuous motion. In the physical world, most motion seems to be continuous.[11] The question arises, how can what is not real enable us to understand what is real? For example, in the account that Newton gave in his work on dynamics, the velocity of an object in motion is to be understood as its rate of change in a given direction, i.e., a given quantity of change of place, s (measured, for the sake of this example, in feet), divided by a given amount of time, t (measured, for the sake of this example, in seconds), and instantaneous velocity, v (measured, for the sake of this example, in feet per second), is an infinitesimal change of place, ds, divided by an infinitesimal amount of time, dt, i.e., an infinitesimal change of place and an infinitesimal time.[12] Now, given a function of change of place such that $s=16t^2$, given an infinitesimal time[13], then $s_1 = 16(1)^2 = 16$, $s_2 = 16(1+dt)^2 = 16+32dt+16(dt)^2$, and $v=[16+32dt+16(dt)^2/dt - 16/dt]$. At this point Newton said that dt should be considered to be zero. Hence the determined instantaneous velocity is 32 feet per second.

George Berkeley (1685-1753) objected to this calculation as illogical. He argued that either the infinitesimal is something or it is nothing. If it is nothing, then there can be no such thing as instantaneous velocity, since $v = (ds/dt) = (0/0)$, which is meaningless. But if it is something, then the velocity determined in the case is not 32'/sec. It is at best about 32'/sec., i.e., it is some undesignated amount greater than 32'/sec., the undesignated amount being whatever 16dt is. You cannot consistently make both claims; viz., that at the beginning of the calculation, the infinitesimal is something; and at the end, the measurement is nothing.

Berkeley's reasoning seemed to be impeccable. Almost everyone agreed that infinitesimals are beyond conception and could not be real. Yet mathematicians continued to find them valuable for solving real problems in the physical world.

The dilemma seemed to be solved in the nineteenth century when Weierstrass introduced his alternative method for interpreting differentials. Instead of treating them as functions of infinitesimals, he explained them in the above way as limits on functions, and used a method based on "sandwiching" to define them.[14] Logically, the most difficult concept in Weierstrass' account of differentiation[15] is the meaning of the term *limit* in the phrase *the limit as Dx approaches zero* in the above stated standard definition of a derivative. Weierstrass defined the limit (L) of a function (e.g., L of f(x) at x_0) as follows: If, given an arbitrarily small positive number, e, another positive number, d, can be found such that for all values of x not equal to x, and differing from s_0 by less than d, the value of f(x) will differ from L by less than e. Furthermore, f(x) is a uniformly continuous function in a particular domain, and for every real number, c, of that domain and every positive e, there exists a positive d depending on e and not on c, such that the absolute value of f(x)–f(c) is less than e whenever the absolute value of x–c is less than d.

It was now possible to use differentials without the seemingly absurd interpretation of them as infinitesimals, but a major price was paid by this move. What had been intuitively a simple notion was now complex and nonintuitive. Hence, if there is a way to show infinitesimals to be mathematically intelligible, an analysis of differentials in terms of infinitesimals would be preferable to Weierstrass' limit theory account of differentials.

Cohen's Defense of Infinitesimals

Cohen raised more severe objections to the limit theory account than just an appeal to simplicity. His mathematical objection to it is that this account rests on two major undefined terms—equality and magnitude—which is not the case with the infinitesimal account. In this respect as well, the conception of differentials in terms of infinitesimals is preferable. His philosophical defense of the infinitesimal turns on its usefulness for philosophical conceptions in a way that is not possible with the limit conception. Cohen argued that infinitesimals are valuable for explaining how science deals with real objects. He showed that this way of thinking can be used as a model for understanding knowledge as historical and progressive. Furthermore, he claimed to have discovered in mathematics a new way of reasoning.

Cohen argued that in general, mathematical objects have use for reality (= nature), but they are not in themselves taken from reality. As such, mathematical objects are paradigms of a kind of thought in general, which produces but does not represent reality. That mathematical thinking is this kind of thought is apparent in the analysis of differentiation, where real areas are determined by differentials that are constructed from infinitesimals, which cannot be themselves real. In other words, the thought that constructs solutions to real area problems is created out of elements (infinitesimals) that are not themselves real, and are not anything definite (a kind of nothing), but still are not absolutely nothing. On the limit account of Weierstrass' standard analysis of differentiation, infinitesimals are nothing in an absolute sense; they can have no function in producing reality, for from such a nothing can come only nothing. In Newton's physics infinitesimals are the building blocks of the universe, for in nature everything is continuous, nothing is discrete, and continuity is constructed from fluxions of fluents.[16] For Cohen, the infinitesimal calculus as applied by Newton to physics is the model for thinking about all issues in philosophy, most notably about epistemology, ontology, ethics, theology, and aesthetics.

HIS PHILOSOPHICAL THOUGHT

Cohen spoke of an infinitesimal as a no-thing, an origin (*Ursprung*), a 0. In the world, infinitesimals are nothings that function to generate objects. Objects are defined by qualities rather than by spatial location. Qualities are definite quantities whose sums range between 0 and 1; i.e., objects are ideal products of reason constructed from infinitesimals. Every object is an infinite collection of these infinitesimal qualities, but every object is a different object. Just as two infinities differ,[17] so there are different infinitesimals; and there are different infinite collections of infinitesimals (objects).

On the basis of this model for thinking, Cohen rejected the view that Kant's noumena are unknowable metaphysical entities that underly experience. Rather, the noumena, the real, are the origins of the phenomenal objects constructed by reason for experience. Thus, Cohen's ideas (= Kant's ideals) are rational constructs that serve as models for constructing (and not for describing) reality. These ideas are the objects of both scientific theory and moral action. They are infinite goals which, in a sense, exist. The way that they exist are as asymptotes (i.e., as limits that operational curves continuously approach but never reach). This sense of existence also can be explained on a mathematical model.

Diagram 3

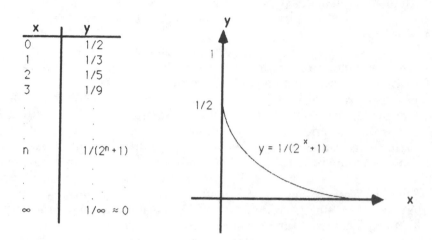

Consider the function $y=[1/(2^x+1)]$.[18] If we were to graph this function from $x=0$ to $x=$any positive number n, we would note that as the curve extends to the right along the positive x-axis the curve, which began at $y=1/2$, increasingly approximates but never reaches $y=0$. In geometric terms this is what it means to say that the limit of $f(x)$ as x approaches infinity is 0. As Cohen used this model, the function represents existent phenomenal objects whose idea is 0. This particular 0 is real and functions as the ideal limit which its generated objects continuously approach in the phenomenal world but never realize.

In Cohen's system, there are scientific objects, moral persons, and God. These three radically different kinds of entities share in common the characteristics that they are different kinds of infinitesimals whose conceptions are limits which are realized only asymptotically. In the case of ethics, the end is humanity, which the individual human being approaches; and in the case of theology, God is a rational construct which the reality of the physical world and the morality of ethics rationalizes.

The infinitesimal is a kind of nothing in that it is less than anything positive and definite, but it points to something definite, viz., the object that is its limit or ideal end. It is not itself anything real, but at the same time it is that from which all reality is generated. It is like Aristotle's "hyle," which is itself nothing at all but when informed it becomes a physical object. Cohen's concepts are also like

Aristotle's forms. Both are conceptual entities which, when unmaterialized, have no existence in the physical world. Both, in their immaterial purity, function as ideal ends, final causes that function as the goal towards which physical objects move. Cohen's ideas in their purity are ends towards which physical objects must be made to tend, which are in themselves in the transitory world[19] functions of nothings. That God created the world out of nothing means that God must be thought as of the limit of an endless summation function whose elements are all nothings, i.e., are all infinitesimals. For the "idealist" Cohen, there is a single end, God.

The idea, God, stands as the ultimate end (*telos*) of all of the processes by which the world of nature, thought, and will develop. The idea of God also functions to integrate what otherwise seems to be disparate universes. In other words, through an adequate conception of God the seemingly contradictory claims of science[20] and ethics[21] are reconciled. It is true that from the perspective of social science, the affairs of nations are determined; but it remains equally true from the perspective of political ethics, that nations are to be judged by the humanist, social-democratic standard of how justly they treat their poor. Science and ethics, as well as aesthetics, are united and coherently comprehended in the theology of that religion which understands God as the ideal limit manifest in all of the processes of creation out of what is practically nothing.

In the *Concept* Cohen identified this religion by the general term *the religion of reason*. In *Religion* he attempted to demonstrate that the only actual religion of reason is Judaism.

HIS JEWISH THOUGHT

Based on his understanding of Maimonides' so-called negative theology, statements about God are to be understood as expressions of human moral obligations. Cohen called this system of translation "the method of correlation." Cohen's method does provide a useful way to understand Maimonides' claims that (a) affirmations of God of the form 'God is F' literally mean God is not G, where G is the opposite of F; and (b) the reason that F is affirmed of God rather than G is because F expresses a human excellence whereas G expresses a human vice. Hence, the reason why it is not true to say that God is ignorant is that the predicate ignorance has no applicability to God and ignorance is a human vice. Equally, the reason why it is true to say that God is wise is that even though it is also true that wisdom, as humans understand it, does not apply to God, humans ought to become wise. In other words, "God is not ignorant" means, 'Avoid ignorance!' and "God is wise" means 'Seek wisdom!' Every divine predicate expresses a moral imperative which the believer, based on the principle of *imitatio dei*, strives to realize.[22] Cohen named this correlation of human morality with God "ethical monotheism." He identified Judaism as the one religion whose core ideal is ethical monotheism.

As understood in Jewish faith, ethical monotheism is expressed through three ideals. First is the idea of the fellowman (*Mitmensch*), which arises from human sympathy to impose on sympathizers the moral obligation to strive to create a community. The commandment that best expresses this ideal is "Love your neighbor as yourself." Second is the idea of atonement from sin, where man autonomously[23] repents and redirects his behavior towards what is good. The rite that best expresses this ideal is the Day of Atonement (Yom Kippur). Third is the idea of humanity, which posits the end to be achieved by turning through repentance toward one's fellowman. This ideal posits the unity of all human beings, which entails the commandment that believers must strive to make the *ought* of human brotherhood into an *is* of universal community. The best expression of this goal is the concept of a messianic age.

Finally, Cohen argued that all of Jewish ritual and law ultimately is about the realization of the ideal of ethical monotheism. He also noted that by striving to fulfill this ideal, its advocates would undergo suffering. Cohen believed that the people of Israel have accepted and will continue to accept their suffering as a necessary price to be God's chosen people, leading the struggle to bring about the universal human community of a just society which, according to reason, is the true (= the ideal) embodiment of God.

NOTES

1. "Ein Wort ueber unser Judentum"

2. Henceforth referred to as "*Concept.*"

3. Henceforth referred to as "*Religion.*"

4. I.e., by conceiving what is not an entity as an existent thing.

5. Here the term *great* describes a system of thought which, in terms of both technical precision and conceptual originality, belongs at the same level as the philosophy of thinkers such as Plato, Aristotle, Ibn Sina (Avicenna), Moses Ben Maimon (Maimonides),

Thomas Aquinas, David Hume, Isaac Newton, Bertrand Russell, etc. Again, it is a judgment about their technical excellence and the degree of their originality; it is not a judgment about the truth of their conclusions.

6. See chapter 8.

7. See chapter 5.

8. See chapters 10 and 11.

9. The explanation given below of Cohen's Jewish philosophy is largely dependent on a yet-unpublished manuscript about Cohen by Steven Schwarzschild. I want to acknowledge my dependence on his work as well as to thank him for his willingness to share his research with me before his own more scholarly work is ready for publication.

10. Euclid, *Elements* Df. 4, Bk. V.

11. For our purposes we can ignore the issues raised by atoms emitting discrete quantities of radiation on Niels Henrik David Bohr's (1885-1962) model in quantum mechanics.

12. Note that instantaneous velocity could neither be zero change of place in zero time nor a finite change in finite time. The latter alternative would give us an average but not an instantaneous velocity, and the former would give us no velocity at all.

13. I.e., from $t=1$ to $t=(1+dt)$.

14. It is called the "epsilon-delta" method, which is an adaption of a technique used by Archimedes called the "method of exhaustion."

15. Differentiation is the process of determining the derivatives of functions.

16. Fluxions are infinitesimally small positive changes, and fluents are infinitesimally small positive positions.

17. For example, the collection of real numbers and the collection of odd numbers are different infinities.

18. See diagram 3.

19. I.e., in the phenomenal world or world of generation and corruption.

20. E.g., that every event is necessitated by a cause.

21. E.g., that man is free to make choices.

22. In fact, no moral ideal can ever actually be realized. Like the projected limit of an asymptote, each divine ideal can be approximated but the ideal never ceases to be infinitely distant from any actual state of fulfillment.

23. I.e., without an external mediator such as Christ in Christianity.

KEY NAMES

A Confession about the Jewish Question, The Aesthetic of Pure Feeling, Archimedes, Leo Baeck, George Berkeley, Brotherly Love in the Talmud, The Conception of Religion in the System of Philosophy, Concerning Kant's Influence on German Culture, The Ethics of Pure Will, Kant's Principles of Aesthetics, Kant's Principles of Ethics, Kant's Theory of Experience, The Logic of Pure Knowledge, Marburg Neo-Kantianism, Moses Ben Maimon (Maimonides), Isaac Newton, The Principles of the Infinitesimal Method and Its History, The Religion of Reason out of the Sources of Judaism, Treitschke, Karl Weierstrass.

KEY TERMS

aesthetics, asymptote, correlation, differential, ethical monotheism, ethics, fellowman, God, Holy Spirit, humanity, idea, *Imitatio Dei*, infinitesimal, limit, logic, messianic age, object, origin, pantheist, religion of reason.

KEY QUESTIONS

1. Why is Cohen an important philosopher? A Jewish thinker? How has he influenced philosophy and Jewish thought?

2. How is Cohen's philosophy related to his mathematics? Why have his writings on mathematics not been influential?

3. Explain what is a differential equation using Weierstrass' method and Cohen's infinitesimal method. What are the advantages of each? What were Berkeley's objections to the infinitesimal calculus? What were Cohen's objections to Weierstrass' approach?

4. According to Cohen, what are the three main branches of phi-

losophy? How does Cohen relate what is actual, what is ideal, and what is real? How are mathematical objects a paradigm for thinking about reality? What is a quality? What is an object? What are the three basic kinds of objects? How are objects related to concepts? What does 'creation out of nothing' mean?

5. How are philosophy and religion related? What is the religion of reason? What is Judaism? Why did Cohen consider Spinoza's thought to be pagan and not Jewish? Why did Cohen judge Christianity to be inferior to Judaism?

6. According to Cohen, why ought Jews to be integrated into German society? What is the meaning and importance of ethical monotheism in Judaism? What are three expressions of ethical monotheism? How are they integrated in the religion of reason? What do they entail? How are they expressed in Judaism? How are Jewish rituals and laws to be judged? What is the messianic age?

7. According to Cohen, how are God and man related in Judaism? What is brotherhood? The Chosen people? God? How does the idea of God integrate chosenness and messianism?

8. How did Maimonides interpret the meaning of divine attributes? How does Cohen interpret Maimonides' explanation?

RECOMMENDED READINGS

General

Robert M. Seltzer, *Jewish People, Jewish Thought: The Jewish Experience in History.* New York: Macmillan, 1980. Chpt.16, "Herman Cohen's Neo-Kantian Philosophy of Judaism," pp. 728-736.

Eugene R. Borowitz, *Choices in Modern Jewish Thought: A Partisan Guide.* New York: Behrman House, 1983. Chpt. 2.

Primary

Archimedes, "Quadrature of the Parabola," in *The Works of Archimedes*, T.L. Heath (ed.). New York: Dover, 1953.

George Berkeley, *On Infinites* and *The Analyst* in *The Works of George Berkeley*, A.A. Luce & T.E. Jessop (eds.). London: Nelson & Sons, 1951.

Bernhard Bolzano, *Paradoxes of the Infinite.* Translated into English by D. Steele. London: Routledge & Kegan Paul, 1950.

Georg Cantor, *Contributions to the Founding of the Theory of Transfi-*

nite Numbers. Translated into English by P. Jourdain. La Salle, Il: Open Court, 1952.

Hermann Cohen, *Jüdische Schriften*. Edited by Franz Rosenzweig. Berlin: C.A. Schwetschke, 1924.

———*Kants Theorie der Erfahrung*. Olms: Hildesheiim, 1885.

———*Das Prinzip der Infinitesimal-Methode*. Frankfurt a.M.: Suhrkamp, 1968.

———*Reason and Hope*. New York: W.W. Norton, 1971.

———*Religion d. Vernunft aus den Quellen d. Judentums*. Frankfurt a.M.: 1929.

———*Religion d. Vernunft aus den Quellen d. Judentums*. Translated into English by Simon Kaplan in *Religion of Reason*. New York: Ungar, 1972.

———*Werke*. New York: Georg Olms Verlag, 1977.

Stacey Lynn Edgar, "Infinitesimals: A Defense," 1982. Ph.D. dissertation (unpublished). Syracuse University.

Gottfried Wilhelm von Leibniz, *Die Mathematischen Studien von G.W. Leibniz zur Kombination*. C.I. Gerhardt (ed.). Weisbaden: F. Steiner, 1976.

Isaac Newton, *On the Method of Fluxions and Infinite Series*, D.T. Whiteside (ed.), New York: Johnson Reprint, 1961.

———"Quadrature of Curves," in *The Mathematical Works of Isaac Newton*, D.T. Whiteside (ed.). New York: Johnson Reprint, 1964.

Abraham Robinson, *Nonstandard Analysis*, Amsterdam: North Holland, 1966.

Karl Weierstrass, *Works*, Berlin: Georg Olms, 1894-1915.

Secondary

Alexander Altmann, "Hermann Cohens Begriff der Korrelation," *In Zwei Welten: Siegfried Moses zum Fuenfundsiebzigsten Geburtstage*, H. Tramer (ed.). Tel Aviv: Verlag Bitaon, 1962, pp. 366-399.

Paul J. Cohen, *Set Theory and the Continuum Hypothesis* New York: W.A. Benjamin, 1966.

John Horton Conway, *On Numbers and Games*. London: Academic Press, 1976.

Joseph W. Dauben, *Georg Cantor: His Mathematics and the Philosophy of the Infinite*. Cambridge, MA: Harvard University Press, 1979.

M. Davis, *Applied Nonstandard Analysis*. New York: J. Wiley & Sons, 1977.

Philip J. Davis & Reuben Hersh, *The Mathematical Experience*. Boston: Houghton-Mifflin, 1982.

P. Fisher-Appelt, *Metaphysik im Horizon der Theologie Wm. Hermanns ...* Munich: Chr. Kaiser, 1965.

Kurt Gödel, "What is Cantor's Continuum Problem" in *Philosophy of Mathematics*, P. Benacerraf and H.H. Putnam (eds.). Englewood Cliffs, N.J.: Prentice-Hall, 1964.

H.L. Goldschmidt, *Hermann Cohen und Martin Buber.* Geneva: n.p., 1946.

W. Goldstein, *Hermann Cohen und die Zukunft Israels.* Jerusalem, R. Mass, 1963.

James M. Henle & Eugene M. Kleinberg, *Infinitesimal Calculus*, Cambridge, MA: M.I.T. Press, 1979.

J. Klatzkin, *Hermann Cohen.* Berlin: n.p., 1921.

William Kluback, *Hermann Cohen: The Challenge of a Religion of Reason.* Chico, CA: Scholars Press & Brown Judaic Studies, 1984.

J. Melber, *Hermann Cohen's Philosophy of Judaism.* New York: Jonathan David, 1968.

Franz Rosenzweig, "Das Neue Denken," in *Zweistrenland: Kleinere Schriften* Dordrecht: Martins Nijhoff, 1984.

Bertrand Russell, *Introduction to Mathematical Philosophy.* London: George Allen & Unwin, 1919.

———*Principles of Mathematics.* New York: W.W. Norton, 1903.

Steven Schwarzschild, "The Concept of the Infinitesimals." (a chapter from his yet unpublished study of Hermann Cohen's philosophy).

———"The Tenability of Hermann Cohen's Construction of the Self." *Journal of the History of Philosophy*, 13 (1975).

K.D. Stroyan and W.A.U. Luxembourg, *Introduction to the Theory of the Infinitesimal.* New York: Academic Press, 1976.

Uriel Tal, *Christians and Jews in Germany: Religion, Politics, and Ideology in the Second Reich, 1870-1914.* Ithaca, New York: Cornell University Press, 1975.

G.B. Thomas Jr. and R.L. Finney, *Calculus and Analytic Geometry*, Reading, MA: Addison-Wesley, 1981.

Eggert Winter, *Ethik und Rechtswissenschaft, eine Historish-Systematische Untersuchung zur Ethik-Konzeption des Marguberger Neo-Kantianismus im Werke Hermann Cohens.* Berlin: Duncker & Humbolt, 1980.

10

Martin Buber

HIS LIFE AND WORK

Buber was born in Vienna in 1878, but most of his youth was spent in Linow, Galicia, where he resided with his grandparents. His grandfather was the famous Midrash scholar, Solomon Buber. From his childhood, he gained a rich knowledge of Eastern European Polish Hasidism. He began his advanced secular studies at the University of Vienna in 1896. There he concentrated on the philosophy of Kant and Nietzsche. He was active in student Zionist activites through Die Judischen Studentenvereinigung at the University of Leipzig, married Paula Winkler in 1899, and completed his doctoral dissertation on mysticism in 1904 at the University of Berlin. There he studied with Hermann Cohen[1] and became friends with Franz Rosenzweig.[2]

In 1916, Buber became the editor of *Der Jude*, and he joined Rabbi Jeremiah A. Nobel and Franz Rosenzweig in founding Die Freier Judisches Lehrhaus in Frankfurt a.M. in 1920. In 1923, he was appointed to the University of Frankfurt as a professor of the Science of Religion and Jewish Ethics. Afterwards, he concentrated both on scholarship and on improving Jewish education. In fact, Buber became the head of the German Jewish educational establishment.

When other leading Jewish academics left Germany in the 1930s, Buber remained as long as the Nazis allowed him to work. Although he was a Zionist, he did not leave Germany because he felt that when he departed, all organized Jewish education would come to an end. Finally, in 1938, he emigrated. Buber accepted a chair in Social Philosophy at the Hebrew University in Jerusalem. Once in Palestine, Buber became politically active in attempting to reconcile the growing conflict between Jews and Arabs. In 1942, he, together with Judah Magnes, organized the Ichud Association, whose goal was to create a joint Arab-Jewish state. After the creation of the State of Israel, he turned his attention again to adult education, founding an institute for adult education in 1949. He continued to pursue educational interests in Israel until his death in 1965.

Buber's scholarly publications began with studies in Hasidism. His early books—*The Tales of Rabbi Nachman* (1906) and *The Legend of the Baal-Shem* (1908)—and his later publication of *The Tales of the Hasidim* were a major factor in reversing the negative attitudes that Western European Jewish scholars shared about the value of Eastern European Jewish literature in general and Jewish mysticism in particular. Today there is some debate among scholars about how valuable Buber's studies are compared with his contemporary and colleague, Gershom Scholem. However, the comparison is unfair. Their studies simply are not comparable. Scholem spent his academic career attempting to state clearly and accurately what were the sophisticated beliefs of the kabbalists. In other words, Scholem approached his field as an intellectual historian. In contrast, Buber was a theologian who attempted to express to his contemporaries the spirit, value, and relevance of Hasidic thought. In a sense, it was Buber's expression of this spirit that opened the minds of contemporary students of Judaica to the kind of historical study of Jewish mysticism that Scholem pioneered.

Buber's academic interests included the Bible, education, history, linguistics, philosophy, political theory, and religion. For our purposes, a complete list of all of Buber's writings would be too long. The following books are worthy of special note. In terms of biblical studies, he worked with Franz Rosenzweig in preparing a new German translation of the Bible, wrote about the messiah in *The Kingship of God* (1932), prophecy in *The Prophetic Faith* (1942), and Moses in *Moses* (1944). In terms of religion, in 1951 he published a book about Judaism and Christianity entitled *Two Types of Faith*. In terms of politics, he wrote about his commitment both to Zionism in *Israel and the World* (1944) and *On Zionism* (1944), and to a direct democratic form of socialism in *Paths to Utopia* (1949). Finally, in terms of his many works on philosophy, specific mention should be made of *I and Thou* (1923), *Between Man and Man* (a collection of essays written between 1929 and 1938), and *The Eclipse of God* (1951). Of all these books, the single most influential was *I and Thou*.

I AND THOU

Part I: Basic Words

Ich und Du (I and Thou) begins with the following words, which contain Buber's entire orientation to philosophy:

> The world is twofold for man in accordance with his twofold attitude. The attitude of man is twofold in accordance with the two basic words he can speak. The basic words are not single words but word pairs. One basic word is the word pair I-Thou. The other basic word is the word pair I-It; but this basic word is not changed when He or She takes the place of It. Thus the I of man is twofold. For the I of the basic word I-Thou is different from that of the basic word I-It.[3]

I intend now to spell out the meaning of this paragraph. What I say may seem totally unrelated at first to the above quotation, but by the end you will see what Buber is doing in this passage. Note that Buber says that the world has a two-fold "attitude" (*Haltung*). Leave aside for the moment what attitude means. First, look at what it means to say that the world is an attitude. Next, examine what it means to qualify the claim that the world is an attitude with the phrase *for man*. What does *for man* add? Is there a difference between what the world is and what the world is for man? Then, given that we understand whan at attitude is, consider what Buber means by saying that this attitude corresponds to two "basic words." What is a *basic word* (*Grundwort*)? Furthermore, what does he intend to claim when he affirms a correspondence between world, human attitude, and words?

In the above quotation Buber specifies two word pairs—*Ich-Du* (I-Thou) and *Ich-Es* (I-It). Before answering the above questions, let me say something about the word *du*. At one time, the English language distinguished between the use of the second person in intimate and in impersonal speech. *Thou* would be the second person singular used in intimate speech, whereas *you* would be restricted to impersonal speech. Grammatically, the term *du* functions in German the way the term *thou* used to function in English. The problem in this case is that English no longer makes this distinction. In fact, the use of words like *thou, thee,* and *thine* in modern English is reserved almost exclusively for *formal* worship. As we shall see, the association of the term *du* with worship is appropriate, but its association with anything formal is not. Hence, Walter Kaufmann in his English translation renders *du* as *you* rather than *thou,* but Kaufmann's translation of this term also is problematic. *You* avoids the inappropriate formal sense of the English term *thou,* but it cannot preserve the intended sense of the term *du* as something appropriate only to intimate speech. Consequently, there is no adequate way in modern English to say what Buber intends *du* to mean. In any case, it should now be clear why Buber uses this term.

Now we can ask, what is *Ich-Du*? Similarly, what is *Ich-Es*? Note that the "I" of "I-Thou" and the "I" of "I-It" and the isolated term "I" are three different things. Note also that the word "I" in isolation is not introduced until the end of Part I of *Ich und Du*. What does this mean? The answers to these questions are the key to understanding what Buber is saying and doing in this his most important work in Jewish philosophy.

The reason why Buber spoke this way has to do with his epistemology. In this paragraph, Buber states the theory of knowledge that determines much, if not most, of what he has to say about God, humanity, and the world in the rest of this book. In a word, Buber identifies himself in this paragraph as a phenomenologist.

Buber begins *I and Thou* with a statement of his contribution to an ideal language. It is the construction of this language that is the subject matter of Part I of *I and Thou*. His language has two basic or primitive words—Ich-Du and Ich-Es. Note that Ich-Du is one, simple term; it is not a compound of two words hyphenated. Similarly, Ich-Es is a single word, and Ich-Du is a different word than Ich-Es.

Buber's commitment to phenomenology is the key to understanding why in *I and Thou* he does not present formal arguments for his claims. In this respect, Buber is no different than any other phenomenologist. Formal arguments always involve premises, and the conclusions reached are no better than these starting points. Arguments can be given for the premises, but the premises become conclusions. These, in turn, require other premises; and once again our conclusions are no better than our initial assumptions. Every argument isolates new premises which, in turn, need to be transformed into the conclusions of new arguments. Either this process goes on forever and there never is a starting point, or you reach premises that require no proof. The word that describes these kinds of premises is *incorrigible*. Statements that require no proof are incorrigible statements; i.e., they cannot be proven, but they do not require proof. For example, the statement "This book *seems* to be green" is incorrigible. My honesty is all that need be assumed to establish the truth of this claim. It is for this reason that Buber begins with experience.

While statements about personal experience can be incorrigible, they are not necessarily correct. In order to describe your experience, you must use language; and in general, languages contain built-in, hidden assumptions that need not be true, i.e., that are not themselves incorrigible. For this reason, Buber attempted to construct an ideal language that avoids undesirable assumptions and, consequently, generates descriptions of experience that are incorrigible. Consequently, a critical evaluation of his claims depends solely on two factors: First, to what extent are his statements formally presuppositionless? And second, do his statements adequately describe what we, the readers, experience? The truth or falsity of what Buber says, given the presuppositions of phenomenology, are not to be determined by formal proofs. In this case, proof is irrelevant. Rather, Buber as a writer must reflect on his experience and describe it as well as he can. You as a reader must attempt to use his language to think about your own experience. Then, on reflection, conclude either "yes, that is what my experience is like" or "no, that is not what it is like."

The beginning of *I and Thou* is pre-critical. At this stage, all Buber does is spell out his language. If it is a good language, the readers will take his descriptions and agree that his experience also is theirs. In other words, Buber's claims rest on an appeal to shared experience and not on any formal argumentation. You must take his descriptions and ask yourself if you see your experience in the same way. If (and only if) you do, then you should agree with him.

The question becomes: What does it mean to say that, on reflection, you do not agree with Buber; whereas many others, upon reflection, do agree?[4] At this point, the author making the claim has two logical moves available. One possibility is that, because of your reflection, he may modify his claim or decide that he was completely wrong. For example, he may decide that he overgeneralized; he may revise his judgment to say that this claim is true for some, possibly for many, but not for all human beings. A second possibility is that he will conclude that he has done an inadequate job of expressing what he has experienced—i.e., his claim is true, but it is not universally true in the way he described it—in which case he must go back, reflect again, and either improve his language or be more careful about its use. Consequently, because of your reflective rejection, he ought to try to express himself better in the hope that you will then, on second reflection, see what he sees.

The second possibility is open to two variations. In the case described above, the assumption is that you, the reader, are honestly and openly reflecting on the author's claims. In this case, if ultimately you do not agree with him, then he is wrong; but this may not be the case. You may be rejecting what he says not because his experience does not agree with yours, but because you are insensitive or resistant to honest reflection.[5] In any case, whether or not you as a reader are honest is also something that only you can determine by your reflection. Again, the phenomenologist makes a claim based on his description of his own experience. Then you reflect first on whether his description matches your own experience; and, if it does not, whether you have honestly or sensitively (i.e., authentically) reflected. If in your judgment your honest reflection on the author's statement is that the claim does not agree with your experience, then you must conclude that he is wrong; and he, depending on his own reflection, must reevaluate his claim.[5]

Let us look again at the text of *I and Thou*. Buber begins by stating his primitive words that he will use to construct the ideal language with which he will describe reality. In the first paragraph he lists the terms, and in the next seven paragraphs he describes their meaning or function. Then, having posited the basic language of Ich-Du and Ich-Es, Buber begins to develop a fuller, richer language to describe phenomena. In this connection he talks about nature, human beings, and art. Having stipulated in his primitive language what he means by man and nature, he introduces his one relational term, *encounter* (Begegnung)

The importance of this different kind of word in Buber's language, viz., encounter, can be illustrated as follows: In arithmetic, the primitives consist of a term or entity (e.g., the number 1), and a function (e.g., +), from which all of arithmetic logically can be constructed. Similarly, Buber uses two primitive terms (Ich-Du and Ich-Es), and then introduces a function term to be used in connection with them (Begegnung).

Note that encounter is a particular kind of relation and not relation as such. The general term used by Buber for relation is *Beziehung*. Buber defines encounter in paragraphs 13 through 18;[7] and then, having defined it, he goes on to what are the two forms of encounter between human beings, positive and negative encounter. The positive encounter is called love, and the negative encounter is called hate. Buber concludes his stipulation of his basic language with a description of love and hate in human relations.[8] At this stage, he has presented his language. Book I concludes with a brief history of how his basic terms develop and how they interrelate in human events.[9]

Note that the first datum to be considered in history is language itself. The first concepts to be analysed for any contemporary philosophy are concepts of language itself, because all of your assumptions and prejudices at their most hidden (or, deepest) level are built into your understanding of language. Again, the ultimate presuppositions of thought are the underlying assumptions hidden in language.

Now that Buber has given us a new language—the language of Ich-Es, Ich-Du and Begegnung—he uses his constrruction to discuss history and the development of language itself. He presents an anthropology of language because he wants to claim that his model language is itself very close to what in human history was primitive language. The result is a history of language; viz., a language that at first is a language of I-Thou and ends up as a language of I-It, with a transition between the two extremes in a language of I-Thou/I-It. Let us now look in more detail at Buber's middle, transition stage of language.

The closest we can come to experiencing primitive language is the experience of children using language. Just as Buber uses his basic language to analyse the history of language where the best language is primitive language, so Buber turns to the language of children and presents a history of the development of their language into adult language, where the best language is child speech. Primitive language is better than sophisticated language because primitive language has less presuppositions built into it. Similarly, child speech is better than adult language because there are less presuppositions about reality built into it. In this connection, it is worth mentioning that Buber's two major concerns outside of philosophy and religion were child education and anthropology. Both interests grew out of his commitment to phenomenology.

At this point let us discuss what I-Thou and I-It are. The reality that Buber describes is the reality of phenomena and not a reality beyond phenomena.[10] Phenomena are a realm of relationship. All that we experience involves relationship. There is nothing in which we are involved that is not us in relationship. Hence, Buber begins by naming and describing two ways of experiencing relationship.

An example which will explain what Buber mens by relationship comes from a source other than Buber. The example comes from the writings of another phenomenologist named Jean Paul Sartre in his book, *Being and Nothingness.*[1]1 I am sitting and writing. While I am writing, what I am conscious of—the object of my consciousness—is what I am writing. But the object of my consciousness is not that I am writing. While I am writing, I am not thinking that I am writing. What I am thinking about is what I am writing. Then someone comes up to me and asks what I am doing. I answer that I am writing. In this second case, I have a different object of consciousness. In the first case, I was conscious of what I was writing; but in the second case, the object of consciousness is me writing. This state of affairs raises the following question: If I was not conscious that I was writing when I was writing, then how did I know afterwards that I was writing? The answer is that there was a consciousness of me writing while I was writing, but it was not an objective consciousness, I.e., I was not conscious of myself as an object.[12] In the first case, there are two different kinds of relations going on. There is the object relationship, viz., the relationship between me and the object of my act; and there is another kind of relationship that involves no object at all, viz. my consciousness that I am writing. Only in the second case, in response to the question, do I become objectively aware of myself as a writer.

This kind of object relationship is what Buber calls the I-It relationship. I-It is an objective, cognitive relationship. In contrast, the kind of non-object relationship identified above is what Buber calls the I-Thou relationship. It is a non-objective, non-cognitive relationship. It is consciousness without an object of consciousness. All relationship that involve something objective, be that object what we might call a thing, or an idea or a goal, are I-It relationships. All relationships that do not involve objectifying anything as an object of consciousness are I-Thou relationships. I believe that this description expresses the primitive sense of the difference between the two basic terms I-Thou and I-It.

Why did Buber choose these two words as his basic terms? Briefly, the answer is that Buber reconstructed Descartes' philosophy. Now let me explain what I mean by this answer. Descartes asked what claim can be the foundation for constructing certain knowledge. He asked the right question, but he was wrong in how he went about answering it. He was right when he said that scientific thinking must begin with certainty and that the only basis we ultimately have for certainty is experience. But he was wrong in assuming uncritically that experience itself is fundamental. He did not recognize that every act of experiencing the world presupposes a language through which we express that experience. He took his experience and described it. Unfortunately, he was unaware that built into his description of reality was not only his experience, but also the kind of language he used. That language itself determined the kinds of conclusions he drew from the experience. Consequently, before you can begin to describe experience, you must critically examine your language. All analysis must begin with an analysis of language. This realization is what is most distinctive about all modern philosophy, both continental and English-speaking.

Second, because of the presuppositions built into Descartes' language, he assumed that the most fundamental words were names of isolated things. The formal, grammatical structure of his language consisted of words in isolation, and from these words are constructed more complex entities such as phrases, sentences, and paragraphs. Sentences appear to be complex entities whose simples are words, and each word is taken to name some thing. As a result of this structure, Descartes assumed that ontology[13] begins by enumerating some things in isolation from each other; and he judged the first such thing to be the referent of the term *I*.

The reason an I is a starting point is that all of our experience involves an I. For example, I see a tree. The two things in this statement are tree and I. I can doubt that the tree is there, but I cannot doubt that I am there. Hence, of all possible objects with which to begin, the I is the most certain. I may be wrong about *what* I am, but I cannot be wrong *that* I am. The case is entirely different with the tree. The statement "I see a tree" is not a statement about a tree; it is a statement about me, and as such it is incorrigible. Hence, Descartes began with I, but the problem of I as a beginning is that it does not lead anywhere. Descartes failed to proceed logically from his existence to the existence of the rest of the world. No one seriously doubts that other things like trees exist. The issue is not whether those things are there. (In some sense everyone agrees that they are.) Rather, the issues are how we know that are there and the way in which they are there. Again, the questions are how do I know that the tree is there, what kind of thing is it, and in what way is it there?

From Descartes' mistakes we learn two things. One, we must be very careful about the language that we use to describe experience. Uncritical use of the vernacular will lead us astray. We need a better language than ordinary language, although ordinary language is where we begin. Our need to think clearly will force us beyond ordinary language to a more ideal one, a scientific language, a language in which we make as few uncritical assumptions as possible, a language that states with precision what we want to say. Two, the feature of ordinary language that presents phrases and sentences as compounds of isolated words does not reflect the structure of reality. Reality cannot be so constituted because from isolated entities such as an I, it is not possible to construct the world. In reality, there are no such things as isolated entities. Entities are all in relationship to other entities. Hence, the starting point must not be a language of isolated entities of which the I is one among many entities. Rather, the starting point must be relations. These relations will not be contructs from their terms; on the contrary, the terms will be deduced from the relations. Furthermore, the prime relations are the realtions into which every I enters. However, at the beginning, there is no such thing as an I, any more than there is such a thing as an object.

At the beginning, there are only relationship terms. Relations are fundamental; entities are not. The most fundamental relations are those involving an I term. The existence of an I is deduced from I relations; it is not itself a primitive. We know at this point that philosophical analysis begins by constructing a language that deals with relations, and the primary relations are ones into which every I enters. Again, there is no first I; there are only I- relational terms. Buber decided that we need assume no more than two such relations, viz., I- relations with an impersonal it and with what he calls an intimate you (Thou).

When Buber made this kind of judgment about philosophical anthropology, similar judgments were made in linguistic anthropology; viz., that the primitives of language are sentences and not single words; and that where there are single terms as primitives, these words function to express whole sentences and are not just nouns. For example, you cannot explain what "How are you?" means by explaninig the words *how, are,* and *you.* In fact, in most contexts "How are you?" is not a question, and it has nothing to do with health. The response "I'm fine" also has nothing to do with health. Words do not mean things; rather, they function in the expression of relationships. Each word has meaning only in relation to the other words that make up its context. These words themselves express complex relationships. In this respect, nouns are the most misleading terms in language; and prepositions are of most representative reality. Generally, every preposition in one language means every other preposition in another language, which is to say that you cannot learn prepositions from dictionaries or lexicons. Their meaning is totally dependent on context. Similarly, whatever things there are, what they are depends entirely on their relationship to other things in states of affairs. In other words, as sentences are linguistically prior to words, so facts (= states of affairs = relations) are ontologically prior to things.

Note that I-Thou is not a complex of two things, I and Thou. It is a single thing, viz., a form of relation. Buber's primitives are not names of things from which we construct relations. Rather, they are relations from which we deduce things. Among the things deduced are entities called I, you, and it; but these are later conclusions. They are not included in the initial I-Thou and I-It. Buber begins his ideal language with terms for relations, rather than terms for things.

One goal of any ideal language is to have as few primitives as possible. Each primitive term is an assumption; and the fewer assumptions there are, the more likely that the conclusions will be true. In Buber's language, there are linguistically two and only two assumptions—Ich-Du and Ich-Es. The primitive term *Begegnung* (encounter) functions to stipulate the rules for their usage.

This concludes the explanation of why Buber begins with relational terms and why the relational terms are I-terms. What remains to be explained is why he chooses the two right hand terms -Thou and -It and only these terms. To answer this question, recall the earlier example from Sartre's *Being and Nothingness*. Assume that in this case what I am writing is a book. Buber chooses the word I-It to express all relations involving an object (Gegenstand) in all the senses of the term, viz., physical entity, object of thought, ideal, goal, etc. Hence, my relationship to my book, both when it is just an idea in my head and after it is published, is I-It. That there is at least this kind of relationship is apparent. Why does Buber choose I-Thou as his other primitive? In part, the answer has to do with grammar, where we recognize three kinds of persons—first, second, and third. It (as well as he and she) is third person, and I is first person, leaving only one remaining person—the second. To express this kind of consciousness (this kind of I-relation) that is non-cognitive or non-objective in every sense of the term *object*, viz., to express that kind of consciousness that is not I-It (first-third persons relations) Buber coins the term *I-Thou* (first-second persons relations).

There is a second reason for choosing the term *Thou* to express non-cognitive relations. This one has to do with Kantian ethics. Kant distinguished two kinds of good. He called one of them "moral good" and he called the other "utensil good." The sentence "Running is good" is an example of using the term *good* in a utensil and not in a moral sense. Running is good because it makes you healthy, but running is not good in itself; it is only good for some purpose other than itself. Hence, it is a good that is purely a useful good. Now, says Kant, any such good is not a moral good. Something is morally good only if it is done for its own sake. Even when talking about utensil goods, these goods must be dependent on moral goods. If A is good for the sake of B and B is good for the sake of C, etc., at some point there must be some end, F, that is good for itself and not for something else. In answer to the question, what is F good for, the answer will be that it is good for nothing other than itself. Furthermore, Kant claimed that only something that is not good for anything other than itself can be morally good. Moral goods are good in themselves; they serve no practical purposes. Rather, they are ultimately what makes any practical (utensil) good both practical and good.

Kant concluded that what counts for a human being as a moral good consists in relating to another person for himself and not for any purpose, goal, end, or object other than himself. In other words, you act morally towards another person when you treat the other person as, in Kant's words, "an end in itself." For Kant, when you act morally towards a person, you in no sense use them. For Kant, love is the ultimate moral relationship; and in loving another, you do not use him. Love, like morality, is utterly useless; and as such, it is the purest expression of human morality.

It is this Kantian understanding of morality that Buber incorporates into his primitive relation of I-Thou. As in epistemology, I can become conscious of something cognitively or non-cognitively, reflectively or pre-reflectively; so in ethics, I can treat another as useful for my purposes or morally as an end in himself for no purpose whatsoever. Buber's terms I-Thou and I-It incorporate both of these kinds of distinction. I-Thou is both non-cognitive consciousness and moral relation, while I-It is both cognitive consciousness and untensil relation.[14]

In summary, the goal of Book I of *I and Thou* is to establish Buber's basic, ideal language. In that language we are given two basic words, I-Thou and I-It. These terms express relationships; they do not name entities. They are not substance terms; they are relational terms. The I of the two terms is not an entity; it is not a thing. Similarly, the Thou and the It are not things. I-Thou is one kind of relationship through which reality is experienced; I-It is another kind of relationship through which reality is experienced. All experience is relational. With these terms, Buber developed modes of relationship, viz., ways in which I-Thou and I-It function and through which we

construct the world. He described encounter, which is the basic relationship derived from I-Thou, and then he presented a history of the
I-Thou from primitive languages into complex languages, from primitive societies into complex societies, and finally from childhood into
adulthood. All of this history was presented in order to show how
I-Thou and I-It function.

History

In Book II, based on the vocabulary and the language established
in Book I, Buber presents a theory of history. His basic theme in stating the course of human flux is that in every aspect of human life we
are involved in a process of I-It taking over from I-Thou.

Note that I-It and I-Thou are both normal relationships. The
course of human history is a path on which the realm of I-It progressively takes over the realm of I-Thou. He illustrates this theme first
in the history of languages.[15] In this case, you begin with a language
of spirit and end up with the language of science. Buber sees art and
aesthetics as an attempt to overcome the conquest by I-It. This
attempt ultimately leads to a language of God.

After considering the history of language, Buber turns to social
history.[16] He starts by showing that experience is something different
than relationship, since the former is necessarily a cognitive process
and therefore a manifestation of I-It. As we move from pure relationship into experience, human institutions develop, which are an ultimate expression in the social realm of I-It. Hence, in the history of
humanity there is a tendency to increase the realm of institutions,
and each increase in institutions is an increase in the reign of I-It.

At this point, Buber notes that the I-It is not evil;[17] rather, it is
inevitable, and what is inevitable cannot be evil. This is an important
point to which we will return later.

Next, Buber uses his I-Thou to I-It progression to present a
schema for understanding the nature of the state and the nature of
economics.[18] Here Buber illustrates how the development of the state
and its economics are to be understood in terms of Buber's general
characterization of the interplay of I-Thou and I-It. Then Buber turns
to ethics,[19] and he discusses moral doctrines of freedom, determinism, and fatalism. Finally, in the last section of Book II,[20] Buber presents a history of psychology. Here Buber describes his morally-
positive types of persons, i.e., persons who maximize the I-Thou
relationship, of whom his primary examples are Socrates, Jesus, and
Goethe. Then he describes his morally-negative types of persons,
whom he calls "demonic" persons, i.e., persons who conquer and

destroy I-Thou while they themselves maximize the I-It relationship. His paradigmatic example of the latter type is Napoleon. This demon subjugates the I-Thou in himself and in others, turning himself and others into I-Its as well.

Having concluded his Book on history, Buber turns in Book III to his ultimate topic, God. In this respect it is worth noting that while Buber differs from Hegel in many important respects, his view of history is Hegelian. Like Hegel, Buber presents a schema for understanding everything in historical terms, and the ultimate topic of history is God. Buber attempts to show how all disciplines should be studied; and he exemplified this approach in the disciplines of language, politics, ethics, and psychology. In his final book of *I and Thou*, Buber applies what he has so far shown to the ultimate discipline, theology, viz., the understanding of God. However, before turning to Buber's theology, it is necessary to deal with two widespread confusions about his notion of encounter that result from the misleading way that he presents his I-Thou structure.

The first confusion has to do with what it means for an I-Thou to be personal. Normally, Buber's I-Thou and I-It are described as follows: There are, for example, two ways of being a shopkeeper and relating to a customer. In one case, no one talks except the sales person, who says, "What do you want?" There is no contact and no involvement. This is the usual way that I-It is pictured. In contrast, you go into a shop and the shopkeeper invites you to sit down, have a cup of coffee, etc. This is the usual way that I-Thou is pictured. Note that neither of these models is clearly I-Thou or I-It. The former is called I-It because neither of the participants in the relation have any concern for the other as a person. The shopkeeper is only concerned with the customer as a customer and the customer is only concerned with the shopkeeper as a shopkeeper. A customer, in this case, is a thing that is there to buy something; and a shopkeeper is a thing that is there to sell something. Their total interest in each other is as objects for profit. Both play roles, and neither is concerned with the other outside of these roles. For this reason, the relationship is impersonal. In the latter case, the impersonal functions involved seem to be irrelevant to the relationship. What counts is the opportunity for them to meet and relate. In this case, the two treat each other as persons without any concern for profit.

In reality, both relations described may have I-Thou and I-it elements. In the latter case particularly, the seemingly personal concern need not by anything more than ritual; and in the former case, the seemingly impersonal treatment may itself be merely a ritual that masks a personal contact. These descriptions in and of themselves cannot tell you whether there is or is not an encounter in either case.

The second confusion has to do with Buber's application of encounter to ethics. Normally, we associate I-Thou with being good and I-It with being bad. This too is misleading. In Book II, paragraph 4, Buber explicitly says that this is not the case. When you think about it, it could not be the case that I-It is bad while I-Thou is good. One reason for this judgment is that both are inevitable, and what is inevitable cannot be bad. A second reason is that both in their pure forms are inadequate alternatives for most lived situations. Consider the shipkeeper-customer situation again.

Shopping is a practical activity with a practical goal that in itself could not be bad. Yet, in the so-called pure I-Thou relationship between a shopkeeper and a customer, it would be practically impossible to buy anything. Now, one ought not to feel guilty about going into a store, buying something, and leaving in a relatively short amount of time. Hence, to generalize, a society in which it is not possible to do anything with anyone for any utensil goal, end, or purpose could not be a good society. At the other extreme, it should be possible to deal with someone nicely, even if being nice is in itself impractical. The salesperson knows that the shopper is there to buy something, and the shopper knows that the sales person is there to sell something. If each did not have something that the other wanted, they would not meet each other. Still, they can be pleasant to each other. Somehow between the stark I-It of complete exploitation and the naked I-Thou of no exploitation is a practical ideal for interhuman relations.

The above criticism was an immediate objection that theologians raised to Buber's *I and Thou*. However, the objection was based on a misinterpretation of what Buber was saying. The source of the misinterpretation was the misleading way that Buber himself presents his two relations. In *I and Thou* Buber presents models that are not necessarily tied to concrete human relationships. For that reason I purposely presented Buber's basic terms with reference to a non-interhuman relationship, viz., writing a book. The point emphasized with this example is that Buber proposes general structures of human reality and not merely a model of interhuman relationship. Again, Buber intended I-Thou and I-It to be true in general of all reality, and not just of one kind of relational reality. For example, Buber speaks of I-Thou relations with things like trees and rocks, examples which make very little sense when the interhuman model dominates our understanding of Buber's basic terms. Yet, Buber himself is responsible for misleading us, because of the kinds of examples he chose.

Why did Buber mislead us in this way? The answer is that Buber's primary concern in applying his basic terms was social rather than scientific philosophy. The main topic in Book II is a history of the human race in terms of language, political theory, and psychology. He did not want to deal directly with ontology, epistemology, and the like, which are all of the classical topics that interest modern philosophers of science. In contrast, Buber's contemporary, Jean Paul Sartre, presented a phenomenological structure with examples that directly suggest judgments about epistemology and ontology more than human society. Whereas Sartre in *Being and Nothingness* attempted to picture the physical universe, in *I and Thou* Buber drew a diagram of the human universe. Furthermore, in contrast to Sartre, Buber's ultimate concern was God, and he believed that the basis for talking about God-man relationship is man-man relationships. In other words, Buber was convinced that before you can talk about God, you must deal with ethics. This is the second reason for Buber's emphasis on the interhuman realm in exemplifying his basic terms. There is a third reason—the influence of his teacher, Hermann Cohen.[21]

Buber did not want to do *just* philosphy. He wanted to do *Jewish* philosophy. His answer to the question—What makes philosphy Jewish?—was Cohen's answer, viz., ethics. According to Cohen, what distinguishes Jewish philosophers from others is that for Jews ethics are primary. In Cohen's thought, the distinction of Judaism from all other religions is its emphasis on the primacy of ethics. Cohen believed that everything that we recognize as ethics has its source in Judaism; ethics are a unique and distinctive Jewish concern. Hence, the study of philosophy for the sake of ethics is what makes philosophy Jewish. Buber, sharing his teacher's belief, made the end or goal of his philosophy speculation about ethics and not speculation about the nature of the universe. Buber applied his basic terms almost exclusively to the major issues in ethics, viz., interhuman or interpersonal relationships. For non-Jews, ethics is a subtopic of philosophy, and their main topics are epistemology and ontology. For Jewish philosophers the opposite is the case. For Jews all topics in philosophy are subsumed under ethics. Even though I-Thou and I-It are applied primarily to ethics, these terms for relationship do not merely mean treating someone personally or impersonally. Clearly, the terms were intended by Buber to have a far more universal range of application.

At this point, we can spell out in general terms Buber's dialectic of I-Thou and I-It. I-It is a cognitive relationship, and I-Thou is a non-cognitive relationship. Consider a relationship between A and B where A is the subject of the relationship. That relationship is I-It if the B related to the A is in some sense an object of A's consciousness. If B is not an object of A's consciousness in the relationship, then the relationship is I-Thou. Let us take a personal and a nonpersonal example.

For months, I ran down Broad Street in Philadelphia and hardly noticed anything around me. Then someone pointed out to me that I had been running past an excellent ice cream parlor that I had never noticed, even though I ran past it every day. In a sense I had seen it, and in another sense I had not seen it. When it was pointed out to me that it was there, I noticed it. It was not as if I had never seen it before. Once I noticed it, I recognized that I had seen it before. In fact, I had seen it each time I ran down Borad Street, but now for the first time I was aware of seeing it. Here I was in a relationship with the store, but it was not a cognitive relationship.

I purposely picked an example that is neither good nor bad. Noticing or not noticing the ice cream shop is neither good not bad, although in either case I am related to it. In both cases, the relationship is morally neutral. What we learn from this example is not something about morality, but something about the two fundamental ways in which relations occur. In this case, the I-It relationship involves the shop as an object of consciousness. One way to be an object is to be an object of thought. Every act of thinking about something is an I-It relationship, because it involves an object, viz., an object of thought. Note that an object of thought does not have to be a physical object. For example, in thinking about love, love becomes an object, but love is not a physical thing. The same is true for thinking about functions or activities such as running. To think of a runner is to think of something physical, but the running itself is not. Numbers also are non-physical objects of thought. To say that something is an object need not mean that it is an entity that occupies time and space.[22]

Now let us take a more personal example. There are some things that you cannot do well unless you do them consciously, but there are other things that you may do better unconsciously than consciously. For example, some jazz musicians purposely do not study music because they believe it would negatively affect their ability to create. What they gain in flexibility by studying music they lose in spontaneity, which for jazz is critical.

Consider another, slightly more personal, example. When I was a Hillel director, there were students who wanted to have socials as opposed to lectures, concerts, and the like. Pure socials never worked out; whereas the other activities tended to have some degree of social success, viz., people met each other. Why did the social fail? If you meet someone at a concert, at least there is the possibility that both of you are there for the concert, which goal is respectable. Furthermore, you and the person you meet have something in common, viz., you like the same kind of program. It may turn out that your meeting, which was not a direct goal in attending the concert, was more important than the concert itself. Consequently, because of what happened socially, even a poor concert may turn out to be a wonderful evening.

You might want to argue that if the real purpose was to meet, then why bother to have a concert at all? The answer is that under those circumstances, the program would not succeed. The other would be there to meet someone; and since there is no other reason to be there, you would be there for the same reason. Now it will occur to the other to ask, "What is wrong with you that you go to a place to meet people?" and the same thing will occur to you about the other. If you are going to a place solely to meet people, something must be wrong with you and with them. Similarly, when singles bars were not yet knows as places to meet but were known as places to drink, people could meet at bars. When the purpose of going to the bar became to meet, bars ceased to succeed as places to meet, because no one wanted to meet the kind of person who would go to a bar to meet someone.

Ultimately, the reason why singles bars and pure socials do not work is that personal meeting cannot be a goal; such meeting takes place only when meeting is not a goal. There are certain goals that can be attained only if the goal is not present as a goal, and meeting is one of them. Meeting also may not take place where meeting is not the goal. There is no way to guarantee meeting; but once it is made the goal, not meeting is practically guaranteed. However, unless you make it a goal, there is no way to be sure that it will happen, which means that meeting is the kind of thing of which you can never be sure.

To try to control what cannot be controlled insures failure. For example, consider a husband and wife at breakfast in silence with the husband reading the paper. The wife guarantees that there will be no conversation when she says, "Why don't you talk to me?" If the goal of talking is to talk, there will be no talk. It is futile to say, "Let's talk." Rather what you do is talk, which may work if you have something to say, but it will not work if you are saying something only to talk.

In addition, you must also be open to talk to have a conversation. You have to be able to listen as well as to talk. Being open to talk does not guarantee meeting, although being closed guarantees failure in meeting. We can isolate the following three situations involving meeting: (1) You talk, but you are not yourself open to talk. (2) You are open to talk, but you cannot yourself talk. (3) You go to talk and are open to talk. Situations 1 and 2 necessarily fail; only situation 3 may succeed, but it need not succeed. Its success depends not only on you, but also on the others there as well. Should they fail to talk or to be open to talk, there is no meeting.

The problem is that if you are not open to talk, how do you become open? To make being open a goal cannot work. That is a key problem with which Buber tried to deal. His answer is that encounter occurs by chance, but it is such meeting that opens you to subsequent meeting. The more people meet, the more open they become to meeting. The more open they are, the more likely it is that they will meet someone; but meeting is never certain, since it can never be planned. Meeting ultimately is a matter of chance, but people do not like to leave things to chance. They want to have some control over what is important to them. Hence, people start doing things to control their meetings. The more they increase their controls, the less room there is for meeting; and the less they meet, the more they seek to control the meeting, until in the end there is total control and no meeting at all.

Buber considered this progression to be the central theme of human history. Things happen by chance and succeed. You try to guarantee that success, but the efforts to guarantee the success make subsequent meetings less successful. To try to guarantee meeting is natural, but inevitably that effort destroys the contin- ued meeting. For example, you see someone on a train whom you want to meet again. Either you plan to meet them again in some way, or it is most improbable that you will ever meet them again.[23] Planning is unavoidable. But planning ultimately results in people continuing to see each other only because of their memory of the meeting that took place once between them but cannot take place again.

An original I-Thou will deteriorate progressively into I-It until in the end there will be only a fossil remains of the earlier life. All spontaneity will be gone from the relationship. The relationship will have become purely objective. Everything will be predictable and knowable, but life will be gone.[24].

At this stage a revolt takes place against the I-It. A person steps outside of the relationship and regains spontaneity, and the process starts all over again. A nearly pure I-Thou moves increasingly to an I-It. When a nearly pure I-It is attained, there is a revolt in which a new, nearly pure I-Thou is attained. The new I-Thou again progressively deteriorates in an I-It direction. The movement of all history is from I-Thou to I-Thou/I-It, to I-It, and then again into a new I-Thou, which marks the recapturing of freedom at the price of security. Buber uses this progression to describe everything. In Book II, the progression is applied to the history of human beings in relationship to friends, institutions, societies, and nations. Finally, in Book III, the progression is applied to the history of God and human beings in religions.

Part III: God

Buber mentions nothing that is pure I-It.[25] Everything in the phenomenal world can be I-It and I-Thou. All of us can use and be used, while at the same time we can be open to meeting and be met by others. The same is true for all non-human objects. There is only one entity that cannot be objectified, who can only be personal, who neither uses nor is used, who is always open and to whom we can only be open. This person, who is purely person, is God. God by definition is undefinable; He is the Eternal Thou. "Eternal" means that He can only be involved in I-Thou and never in I-It.

How is this God met? Buber argued that the answer is given in the Hebrew Scriptures. For example, Jacob in the wilderness happens to encounter God while he was doing something else, viz., preparing to meet his brother.[26] While Jacob encounters God, he is not aware that it is God. They wrestle, and not until after the wrestling match is over and God is gone does Jacob say that it was God.[27] Later, after Jacob encounters God again, he builds an altar.[28] The purpose of the altar is to mark the place where he met God, so that Jacob can meet God there again. It is like meeting someone by chance on Amtrak and taking the same train to meet the person again. Building the altar is the beginning of Israel's attempt to control his meeting with God. The altar is the place where Jacob/Israel goes in the hope of meeting God again, but already the relationship has changed. With the altar, Israel has moved on from a pure I-Thou relationship to an I-Thou/I-It relationship.

As time passes, the successors of Israel increasingly structure the relationship in order to be more sure of meeting God. Their efforts result in less frequent occasions of meeting, since God is in no sense subject to control. Finally, the Israelites become so involved in ritual, they cease to be able to re-meet God. At this stage, the Israelites come to their altar in Jerusalem not to meet God, but simply to come to the altar. They do so in memory of their ancient encounters in their national youth. However, now the ritual is no longer a tool for encounter; now the ritual takes over the encounter. Before, the ritual was the form of meeting; now nothing is left but the form. At this stage, the religion is dead. Religious people only go through the mechanics of religion. God no longer is present to give life to the faith community. It is this death and absence that motivates a religious revolt by prophets, through which either the old religion is reformed or a new religion is born.

RELIGION AND POLITICS

Buber generalized the above description of the religion of Israel to apply to all religions. For Buber, religion is a human institution, subject to the same history that applies to all other expressions of human association. A religion begins when a single human I-Thou encounters the divine I-Eternal-Thou. This encounter is called "revelation."[29] Its content is entirely the meeting itself. In fact, the association of revelation with content is the first step in the process of the I-It transforming religion. Buber called this state, in which revelation has content, "faith."[30] In the end, religion becomes solely a matter of faith, while revelation is completely lost.

Similarly, religion begins with individual prayer, i.e., the encounter of God and another person. That person may be called a "prophet," although in *I and Thou* Buber does not use this term. The prophet's response to revelation is to encounter other human beings; and through his/her encounter with them, they too are brought into communion with God. As Buber expressed it, individual prayer leads to communal prayer. However, there must be some element of I-It in any form of communal worship. Communal worship requires some form of ritual.[31] It is difficult enough for an individual to encounter God. It would be all the more difficult for a multitude of individuals merely to happen to encounter God simultaneously. Since the response to relationship with God is always expressed in relationship with other human beings, the more successful a religion is in encounter with God, the larger the ranks of that religion will become. As the community of the faithful increases, the need for both dogma (from faith) and ritual (from communal worship) will increase, until, in the end, the dogma and ritual will be so dominant that there will be no room left for revelation. God Himself will become increasingly peripheral to the religion, so that the natural history of any particular religion is a continuous evolution into idolatry.

While it would seen that for Buber this process is evil, it also seems to be inevitable. Revelation necessarily produces faith, which necessarily deteriorates into idolatry. Personal prayer necessarily produces communal prayer, which necessarily transforms God into a mere lifeless cult object. What is inevitable cannot really be called evil. Buber solves this dilemma by teaching that as a religion deteriorates into an idolatrous cult, there arise new individuals—prophets—who shatter the established faith and introduce renewed revelation. As is clear from his other writings, both Jesus and the Baal Shem Tov were such prophets within the history of Judaism. Hence, in the end, nothing is lost. The revelation that results from a reaction against cult is as necessary as is the cult that develops from revelation. Similarly, I-Thou arises in reaction to I-It as inevitably as I-Thou deteriorates into I-It. The change is necessary because human beings are both I-Thou and I-It; they are neither inanimate objects nor God.

If this were all that Buber said, it would be proper to charge him with fatalism. In the end, it would seen that there is no human change at all. Inevitably, everything repeats itself; and here is no such thing as good and evil, progress and decadence. Buber is not a fatalist. At the end of *I and Thou* he states,

> But the path is not a circle. It is the way. Doom becomes more oppressive in every new eon, and the return more explosive. And the theophany comes even closer,...
> Every spiral of its path leads us into deeper corruption and at the same time into more fundamental return. But the God-side of the event whose world-side is called return is called redemption.[32]

Buber's "path" or "way" is from I-Thou, to I-Thou and I-It, to I-Thou. Buber's path/way is similar to Rosenzweig's "course" of creation, revelation, and redemption.[33] Except for those passages that deal with art, creation has no central role in *I and Thou*, but revelation and redemption do.

Buber's way is a path from revelation to redemption; and each redemption is a new, purer revelation, which inevitably leads to a new, purer redemption. Buber's man is not doomed for eternity to move back and forth between two opposing poles. Man as man cannot remain man. He stands between inanimate objects and God. The closer he comes to one pole, the more forcefully is he driven into the other. In each repetition of the cycle, man is more inanimate than he ever was before; but for the very same reason, he eventually becomes more divine than he was before. As Buber envisioned the process, it is the ultimate attainment of the God-side, in contrast to the object-side, that will mark the end of the path. This idea is Buber's vision of the messianic age as ultimate, beyond the penultimate apocalypse. In the end, God, world, and man will all be one.

It is against this background that Buber's view of the Bible is to be seen. Both the Torah and the teachings of Jesus are expressions of pure I-Thou encounter with I-Eternal-Thou. They are perpetual reminders that a human being is more than an It. As such, they can prepare an individual to reject the world as it is and to receive prophetic vision. Buber's Scriptures are political. Their political element has nothing to do with their content. For Buber, all content is in itself contrary to what is divine. Instead, they are a record of encounter which prepares the individual for encounter, which in itself is revolutionary. All revelation is inherently a rejection of all human institutions and laws. Such rejection inevitably results in new institutions and laws, which inevitably must be rejected themselves, until we arrive at the messianic age—an age when there will be no law or external forms of association, since all people will be one in communion with God.

According to Buber, in the history of Western religion, you have a pure I-Thou from the time of the patriarchs through Moses. From Moses on, Judaism is subject to increasing objectification until the time of the Pharisees. In Buber's judgment, the Judaism of the Pharisees was idolatrous; and this decadent state resulted in the spiritual revolt of the religious genius, Jesus. However, no sooner does the Jew Jesus break free than his followers, the apostles, began to create new institutions of objectification that lead to a new idolatry in the Christian Church. It is Martin Luther (1483-1546), who breaks through Christian idolatry and recaptures a living encounter with God. Similarly, the parallel idolatry of rabbinic Judaism is overcome by the genius of the Baal Shem Tov; but already in his first generation of disciples, the process of objectification has begun again.

For Buber, the great religious moments in Judaism are the period of the patriarchs, the prophets, and the first generation of the Hasidim. The rest is either itself idolatry or part of a movement towards idolatry. Although Buber nowhere explicitly says so, the implication is clear that for him rabbinic Judaism is idolatrous. In Buber's judgment, the rabbis identified God with Torah, but Torah as God as idolatry. What is critical for faith in the Hebrew Scriptures is nothing that they say. Everything that is said is an It. To give too much importance to the content of the Bible is itself idolatrous. What is important in Scripture is the encounter with God and not anything said about law or the universe as a result of that encounter. In encounter God reveals Himself, but that revelation cannot include an objective content. To see the revelation at Sinai as a revelation of laws is, according to Buber, itself idolatrous. Needless to say, traditional Jews who fully grasp what Buber said could not be very happy with his thought.

Based soled on Buber's theology, it is apparent why Buber's form of Judaism has appealed more to liberal Jews than it has to traditional Jews. Unquestionably, Buber's theology is radical and unconventional. The same is true of the political consequences of his dialectic. In political philosophy, Buber argues that the ideal society is one that is sufficiently small and structured that all members of that society can meet together and reach a consensus about all matters of state. This kind of society is called a "direct democracy." It is to be contrasted with representational democracy. In representational democracy the state already is too large for everyone to come together to reach a consensus. Consequently, the people must choose representaives who will make decisions about the state for them. In Buber's judgment, once you need a board, a senate, a parliament, or a congress, your society is too large. At this point in Buber's ideal state, the citizens will divide themselves into smaller, autonomous units. Otherwise, the citizens will have initiated a process whose end will be tyranny. No one can represent anyone else. Hence, either you continue to make decisions by meetings of the whole; or, if you are at a size where meetings of the whole are no longer functional, then you must realize that your society has become too large to be a just society.

Sometimes this form of government is called "anarchism," but anarchism does not mean a society without government. Buber's anarchist model is that of Leo Tolstoy (1828-1910). Their anarchism is government through the general consensus of those governed. Buber believed that the kibbutz was the closest approximation in modern history to this political ideal. This kibbutz ideal was an integral part of his version of Zionism.[34] While Buber opposed the creaton of the state of Israel in 1948, he did not do so because he ceased to be a Zionist. On the contrary, he believed that there should be a Jewish state; but he also believed that the price that had to be paid to create it in 1948 was too high, viz., the disenfranchisement of the Arab Palestinians. Instead of a Jewish state, he advocated a common Jewish-Arab state ruled by consensus of all who happened to be there—Arabs as well as Jews. Needless to say, the Israeli Jews are no happier with the implications of Buber's Jewish philosophy than are the traditional Jews.

NOTES

1. See chapter 9.

2. See chapter 11.

3. The translation is that of Walter Kaufmann (New York: Charles Scribner's Sons, 1970) except that I substituted "I-Thou" for his "I-You" in translating "Ich-Du."

4. For example, some Existentialists (not Buber) say that all human beings live in dread of death. Every reader must ask himself if he lives in dread of death, and he may conclude that this claim is not true. He might reflect and conclude that while he does not look forward to death dread is too strong a claim.

5. Note that at this stage, terms like "honest" and "dishonest" or "authentic" and "inauthentic" as applied to people enter the discussion of truth and error as applied to statements.

6. At this point it should be apparent to the reader that phenomenology presupposes a kind of uniformity principle that says that all authentic people upon reflection will agree, because all individual experience is uniform.

7. The paragraph numbers stated here and below are those used in Walter Kaufmann's English translation of *I and Thou* (New York: Charles Scribner's Sons, 1970).

8. Paragraphs 19-21.

9. Paragraphs 22-28.

10. For example, if we assume that the color red that we see belongs to the world of experience, but that color-appearance is caused by something in the physical world called a light wave, then Buber is talking about the world of appearance and not the physical world.

11. Jean Paul Sartre, *L'Etre et le Neant.* Translated into English by Hazel E. Barnes. *Being and Nothingness: An Essay on Phenomenological Ontology,* New York: Philoophical Library, 1956. Introduction, III, pp. iv-ivii.

12. Here "objective" means making something into an *object* of awareness.

13. I.e., the theory of the kinds of things that ex_st.

14. Note, however, that while the I-It is not moral, neither is it immoral. We will return later to this point.

15. Paragraph 2.

16. Paragraph 3.

17. Paragraph 4.

18. Paragraph 5.

19. Paragraphs 6-8.

20. Paragraphs 9-12.

21. See chapter 9.

22. Running occurs in time and space, but it does not occupy time and space.

23. The odds of meeting that person again by chance are a permutation of the number of possible places of meeting, the possible times, and the total number of people who might be at each place and time.

24. Such relationship is like a pithed butterfly. The goal is to keep the butterfly, but the living thing is lost. All that remains is its external form which can serve at best only as a memory of what was once a living thing.

25. Perhaps if he were interested in physics there might be some pure I-It, like an Aristotelian matter. Perhaps if he shared Rosenzweig's interest in creation, he might have dealt with this question; but nowhere in his writings does he show any such concerns. It is of interest to note that of all of the modern Jewish philosophers discussed in this text, only Rosenzweig is interested in creation; whereas every major classical, medieval Jewish philosopher (Abraham Ibn Daud is the one exception) gave prominent attention to creation.

26. Gen. 32:4-24.

27. Gen. 32:31.

28. Gen. 35:9-15.

29. *I and Thou.* Part III, paragraph 16.

30. Ibid., paragraph 17.

31. If nothing else, it demands a fixed time and place of meeting.

32. Martin Buber, *I and Thou*, English translation by Walter Kaufmann, New York: 1970, p. 168.

33. See chapter 11.

34. See chapter 6.

KEY NAMES

Between Man and Man, Solomon Buber, The Eclipse of God, Die Freier Judisches Lehrhaus, *I and Thou,* The Ichud Association, Israel and the World, Der Jude, The Kingship of God, The Legends of the Baal Shem Tov, Moses, Jeremiah A. Nobel, On Zionism, The Prophetic Faith, Gershom Scholem, Tales of the Hasidim, Tales of Rabbi Nachman, Two Types of Faith, Paula Winkler.

KEY TERMS

basic word, demonic person, direct democracy, encounter, Eternal Thou, faith, hate, history, I-Thou, I-It, Idolatry, it, love, object, phenomenology, prayer, prophet, religion, revelation, thou.

KEY QUESTIONS

1. Why are there no arguments in *I and Thou*? Why does Buber begin by describing experience? Why does buber create new words? How are his statements to be judged? Why does philosophy begin with a critique of language?

2. Explain how the following terms function in Buber's language: I-Thou, I-It, encounter, I-, -Thou, -It, I-Thou/I-It, I-Eternal Thou.

3. What are Buber's two primitive forms of relation? How do they differ from each other? Why did buber name them the way he named them? How and why are these terms misleading? Why might a reader think that Buber's basic relations are moral judgments? Why is this not the case? What is good and bad about each of Buber's basic relations?

4. Why does Buber discuss child speech and education? What is the basic theme of all three parts of *I and Thou*? What is Buber's primary schema or dialectic of history? Illustrate it in the following cases: language, social history, politics, religion. Is Buber a fatelist? Give reasons for your answer.

5. Why did Buber judge ethics to be prior to theology? Why did he consider himself to be a *Jewish* philosopher?

6. In general terms trace Buber's dialectic of the history of Judaism and Christianity. What is their end or goal? Why do they develop dogmas and rituals? Is this development good or bad?

7. What would it mean to label Buber's political theory as biblical anarchism? Did Buber consider the Bible to be a human work and/or the product of divine revelation? What kind of Jewish state did Buber want to create in Palestine?

8. Why would two different people who agree about what Buber said disagree about whether of not his thought is Jewish? Zionist? In other words, in what ways is Buber's thought heterodox in terms of both classical Jewish thought and classical Zionist ideology?

9. Compare and contrast Buber's philosophy with that of each of the following philosophers: Descartes, Kant, Hegel, Sartre.

RECOMMENDED READINGS

General

Robert M. Seltzer, *Jewish People, Jewish Thought: The Jewish Experience in History.* New York: Macmillan, 1980. Chpt. 16, "The Emergence of Jewish Existentialism: Franz Rosenzweig and Martin Buber," pp. 736-742.

Eugene R. Borowitz, *Choices in Modern Jewish Thought: A Partisan Guide.* New York: Behrman House, 1983. Chpt. 7.

Primary

Martin Buber, *Between Man and Man.* Boston: Beacon, 1955.

——*The Eclipse of God.* New York: Harper, 1948.

——*For the Sake of Heaven*: Translated into English by Ludwig Lewisohn. Philadelphia: Jewish Publication Society of America, 1945.

——*Good and Evil.* New York: Charles Scribner's Sons, 1953.

——*Hasidism.* New York: Harper and Row, 1949.

——*Hasidism and Modern Man.* Translated into English by Maurice Friedman. New York: Horizon Press, 1958.

——*Ich und Du.* Heidelberg: Verlag Lambert Schneider, 1977.

——*I and Thou.* Translated into English by Walter Kaufmann. New York: Charles Scribner's Sons, 1970.

——*I and Thou.* Translated into English by Ronald Gregor Smith. New York: Charles Scribner's Sons, 1958.

——*Israel and Palestine.* New York: Schocken, 1974.

——*Israel and the World.* New York: Harper and Row, 1948.

——*The Jew: Essays from Martin Buber's Journal, Der Jude, 1916-1928.* Edited by Arthur A. Cohen. University, AL: University of Alabama Press, 1980.

——*Der Jude und sein Judentum: Gesammelte Aufsatze und Reden.* Koln: Melzer Verlag, 1963.

——*The Kingship of God.* New York: Harper and Row, 1973.

——*The Knowledge of Man.* New York: Harper and Row, 1965.

——*Moses: The Revelation and the Covenant.* New York: Harper and Row, 1958.

——*On The Bible: Eighteen Studies.* New York: Schocken Books, 1984.

——*On Judaism. New York: Shocken, 1967.*

——*Paths in Utopia.* Boston: Beacon, 1958.

——*Pointing the Way.* New York: Harper and Row, 1957.

——*Prophetic Faith.* New York: Harper and Row, 1949.

——and Franz Rosenzweig, *Die Schrift.* Translation into German of the Hebrew Scriptures. Koln: Jakob Hegner Verlag, 1954-1960.

——*To Hallow This Life.* New York: Harper and Row, 1958.

——*Two Types of Faith.* London: Torch, 1951.

Secondary

Shmuel Hugo Bergmann, *HA-FILOSOFIYAH HA-DIALOGIT MIKIRGAGOR 'AD BUBER.* Jerusalem: *MUSAD BIALIK,* 1974.

Adir Cohen. *The Educational Philosophy of Martin Buber.* East Brunswick, N.J.: Fairleigh Dickinson University Press, 1983.

Malcolm Diamond, *Martin Buber: Jewish Existentialist*. New York: Oxford University Press, 1960.

Paul Edwards, *Buber and Buberism: A Critical Evaluation*. Lawrence: University of Kansas Press, 1970.

Maurice Friedman, *Martin Buber: The Life of Dialogue*. Chicago: The University of Chicago. Press, 1976.

Aubrey Hodes, *Martin Buber: An Intimate Portrait*. New York: Viking Press, 1971.

Rivka Horowitz, *Buber's Way to 'I and Thou'*. Heidelberg: Verlag Lambert Schneider, 1978.

——*Way to I and Thou: An Historical Analysis and First Publication of Martin Buber's Lectures on Religion as Presence*. New York: Seabury Press, 1984.

Donald J. Moore, *Martin Buber: Prophet of Religious Secularism*. Philadelphia: Jewish Publication Society of America, 1974.

Greta Schaeder, *The Hebrew Humanism of Martin Buber*. Detroit: Wayne State University Press, 1973.

Paul A. Schilpp, and Maurice Freidman (eds.), *The Philosophy of Martin Buber*. La Salle, Il: Open Court, 1967.

Charles May Simon, *Martin Buber: Wisdom in Our Time*. New York: Dutton, 1969.

Pamela Vermes, *Buber on God and the Perfect Man*. Brown Judaic Studies 13. Chico, Ca: Scholars Press, 1980.

11

FRANZ ROSENZWEIG

HIS LIFE

Rosenzweig was born on December 25, 1886, in Cassel, Germany. His father was a successful manufacturer and a prominent figure in his gentile community. His mother was an enthusiastic student of the arts. Both parents maintained their Jewish identity, but that identity was functionally minimal. Their son's education was primarily German, with minimal exposure to Jewish culture.[1] In his college years, his closest friends included his cousins Hans and Rudolf Ehrenberg. Their great-grandfather was Samuel Meir Ehrenberg (1773-1853), who was the superintendent of the Jewish Free School of Wolfenbuttel and a teacher of the Jewish historians Isaac Marcus Jost and Leopold Zunz.[2] Hans and Rudolph had converted to Christianity and urged Rosenzweig to do the same. To their voice was added the persuasion of another but more distant relative, Eugen Rosenstock, who also was a Christian of Jewish descent. We are told that Rosenzweig decided to convert, but that he would enter Christianity as a Jew rather than as a pagan. For that reason, he attended a Yom Kippur service in Berlin on October 11, 1913, that moved him to reverse his decision and for the first time to commit himself actively to being a Jew. In consequence of this experience, whatever it was, Rosenzweig began to study Judaism in Berlin, where he fell under the influence of Hermann Cohen and Martin Buber, the former as a teacher and the latter as a close friend.

The next major event in Rosenzweig's becoming Jewish occurred during World War I. In 1915, he volunteered for the regular army; and in 1916, he was attached to an anti-aircraft gun unit in the Balkans. Then in May and June, 1918, he was sent to an officers' training course in Rembertow near Warsaw, Poland. There he had his first contact with Jews from the Pale, whom he discovered to be adherents of Judaism who were neither primitive nor barbarian.[3]

Between July 11 and August 1, 1918, Rosenzweig was in a military hospital in Leipzig with influenza and pneumonia. He returned to the Balkan front where on August 22, 1918, he began to write *The Star of Redemption*[4] on army postcards and in letters that he mailed to his mother to have copied. He reentered a hospital in Belgrade with malaria from the end of August to the end of October, 1918, after which he returned to his unit in Freiburg, and in December, 1918, he was released from the army. He completed *The Star* on February 16, 1919.

In that same year, Rosenzweig met Rabbi Nehemiah A. Nobel in Frankfurt a.M., under whose influence he assumed the leadership of the Freies Jüdisches Lehrhaus on August 1, 1920, four months after his marriage to Edith Hahn. The Lehrhaus was representative of a number of Jewish schools in major German cities which in some way incorporated characteristics of American Jewish *Ḥavurot*[5] (i.e., small, intimate Jewish spiritual associations) and American Colleges of Jewish Studies, such as Spertus in Chicago and Gratz in Philadelphia (i.e., colleges in which university-level Jews can pursue a committed but academic study of Jewish religion and culture). The Frankfurt Lehrhaus was the most distinguished one by virtue of its students, including Erich Fromm and Shlomo Goitein, and its faculty, including Martin Buber, Nahum Glatzer, and Ernst Simon.

Approximately one year after Rosenzweig took over the Lehrhaus, viz., at the end of 1921, he noticed the first symptoms of his amyotrophic lateral sclerosis that progressively paralysed him and ultimately killed him on December 10, 1929. By August 1922, he had difficulty writing; and his speech began to deteriorate. Four months later, he could no longer write; so he began to use dictation. But in another four months he could no longer speak. In the fall of 1923, the degeneration came to a halt; but by this time the only bodily functions that worked were his life support systems. For the next six years, he lived almost literally a spiritual existence in both senses of the word, spiritual as religious and as immaterial. Barely in sensual contact with his environment, he managed to communicate with family, friends, and students and to publish works that included a German translation with Martin Buber of the Pentateuch, Joshua, Judges, Samuel, Kings, and Isaiah.[6]

Rosenzweig wrote more than forty books, monographs, essays, translations, sketches, and reviews on philosophy, religion, and Judaism. *The Star* is one of his earliest works, and he himself correctly called it his "main work."[7] In terms of his intellectual influences, Rosenzweig drew from a great diversity of disciplines in *The Star*, including a variety of branches of philosophy, linguistics, religion, history, literature, and other arts. He wrote separate works about Martin Buber, Hermann Cohen, Judah Halevi, Moses Mendelssohn, and Friedrich von Schelling, clearly suggesting that they influenced his thought. Within *The Star* considerable attention is given to Georg Wilhelm Friedrich Hegel and Johann Wolfgang von Goethe, clearly indicating that they influenced his thought. Specifically in terms of philosophy, Rosenzweig told us[8] that his study originated in the thought of Plato, Hermann Cohen, and Immanuel Kant; and in the body of the text he referred specifically to Al-Ghazzali, Aristotle, Descartes, Halevi, Hegel, Kierkegaard, Maimonides, Nietzsche, Parmenides, Schelling, Schopenhauer, and Spinoza as well. In addition, his correspondence includes references to Cassirer, Feuerbach, and Heidegger. We know that he spent extensive time studying classical rabbinic texts; and in terms of modern Jewish influences, besides Cohen and his friends associated with the Lehrhaus, he referred in his correspondence to the historian Heinrich Graetz, the poet Heinrich Heine, the novelist Franz Kafka, and the Zionist essayist Jacob Klatzkin. However, none of these influences should be seen as straight-forward connections. Rosenzweig was a highly original and creative thinker who, when he absorbed the thought of others, rejected some things; and even what he accepted was restructured in terms of his own picture of reality. It is this picturing of reality that best summarizes what *The Star* is all about.

THE STAR OF REDEMPTION

Its Purpose

The Star literally is a picture of reality. The picture is a six-pointed star, where by implication the six points suggest a second connection that contains the first star within a hexagon, from which is formed a second six-pointed star.[9] Three of the points are what Rosenzweig called "elements," which are substances out of which reality comes to be, viz., God, man, and the world. The other three points are what Rosenzweig called "courses," that are actions by the substances out of which the substances are related. God and man are linked by God's act of revelation, God and the world are linked by God's act of creation, and man and the world are linked by man's act of redemption. From these six points, the explicitly-stated star is formed.[10]

General Summary

The three parts of *The Star* exhibit considerable parallelism. To begin with, each part contains an introduction that posits possibilities presented in subsequent books, contains three books, and ends with a section that bridges a movement from one part to the next. In Part I, the three books in order are on "God," "world" and "man"; in Part II, the three books in order are about "creation," "revelation" and "redemption"; and in Part III, the three books in order are about the "fire," the "rays" and the "star." Part I ends with a "translation" that is a movement out of "death" from "mystery" to "miracle"; Part II ends with a "threshold" that is a movement from the miracle with which Part II began to "enlightenment"; and Part III ends with a "gate" that is a movement from the enlightenment with which Part III began to "life." *The Star* begins with death and concludes with life. In addition, corresponding to the ascent from "proto-cosmos" to "cosmos" to "hyper-cosmos," there is a progression in ways of picturing. Since the object of cognition in the proto-cosmos is an object, i.e., a substance, picturing can be done with "logical signs," which are no longer adequate when we move to knowledge of actions. Beyond logic and its signs in Part II is "speech" and its "grammatical symbols." Even speech is not adequate to picture the "configuration," to which is appropriate "liturgy" with "geometric terms." In addition, corresponding to the ascent through universes with progressively superior tools for picturing, Rosenzweig presented what he judged to be a progression of religious traditions that grasp reality. In Book I, we are told that the religions of ancient Greece, India, and China to some extent grasp the elements, but do so insufficiently, because their pictures do not point to a knowledge beyond elements. In Book II, we are told that Islam to some extent grasps the course, but it does so insufficiently, because its picture does not point to a knowledge beyond the course. Finally in Book III, we are told that Judaism and Christianity, each in very different ways, picture the configuration of the elements and the course, although each sees only its part of the configuration and not the whole of reality.

Explanation

The titles of the three books of *The Star* are (Part I) "The Elements or The Ever-Enduring Proto-Cosmos"; (Part II) "The Course or The Always-Renewed Cosmos"; and (Part III) "The Configuration or The Eternal Hyper-Cosmos." Again, note the parallels: elements, course, configuration; ever-enduring, always-renewed, eternal. Similarly, corresponding to the place of logical signs in Part I is the place of grammatical symbols in Part II and geometric symbols in Part III; Asian religions in Part I, Islam in Part II, and Judaism and Christianity in Part III. As the work in its totality exhibits structural parallelism, so parallels are found between subtopics at every level through all three parts.[11]

One of the things going on in the work is just aesthetic relations. Again, everything matches everything else. The topics of each book correspond to the topics of the books in the other parts, i.e., Book One of Part I parallels Book One of Part II and Book One of Part III; Book Two of Part I parallels Book Two of Part II, etc. There is a geometric order to the very structure of the work in general, independent of what each section of the book says. For example, the places in Part I where *The Star* talks about Asian religions correspond to the places in Part II where *The Star* talks about Islam, and in the same places in Part III it discusses Judaism and Christianity; the places where it talks about logical symbols in Part I correspond to the places where it talks about grammatical symbols in Part II, etc. The work as a whole exhibits an aesthetic design that in itself is important for what Rosenzweig intended. Note also that the transition that ends Part I begins the introduction to Part II; the transition that ends Part II begins the introduction to Part III; and as Part I begins with a movement from death to life, Part III ends with a movement from life back again to death, completing the circle. The circle suggests that Rosenzweig developed a system that was intended to be complete or self-contained. As you look at a painting, every part says something that is an integral part of the whole. The painting refers solely to itself and not to anything outside of itself. Each part of this work is by design connected with every other part, and all of the parts together form a picture that does not refer to anything outside of itself.

The only other book that I know of by a Jew that is as carefully plotted out as is Rosenzweig's *Star* is Spinoza's *Ethics*, but there the pattern of the parts is entirely different. Rosenzweig's structural model is art; Spinoza's is mathematics. While Rosenzweig's writing is analogous to painting or architecture, Spinoza's is analogous to geometry.

Let us now leave aside our examination of the form of *The Star* as a whole and look in general terms at the content. The goal of this work is two-fold. The first is polemical, and the second is purely philosophical. The polemical goal answers the question: Why does it make sense for an intelligent, civilized, well-educated, modern, German Jew to continue to be a Jew? It would seem that anyone who is intelligent, viz., anyone who knows and understands Hegel, would become a liberal Protestant, as all of Rosenzweig's intelligent, civilized, modern, German friends had done. Again, one goal of *The Star* is to explain why a Jew can be intelligent and civilized and still remain a Jew, even if he is modern and German.

The second goal of the book is philosophical. Rosenzweig wanted to present a picture of the universe. That picture is a *MAGEN DAVID*. Rosenzweig attempted to show that the Jewish star is the true picture of the universe. The whole work, *The Star of Redemption*, draws this picture and explains it to the reader as the true picture of the universe.

Rosenzweig pictured a world in motion. Such a picture necessarily involves some kind of things moving as well as other kinds of things that make the motion intelligible. Now, Rosenzweig's term for the things that are moved is "elements." His things are God, man, and world. The elements in isolation are static, but there are three of them. Everything in the universe is reducible to three elements—God, man, and world. These three elements stand in relationship to each other. The relationship between God and man is called "revelation;" the relationship between God and world is called "creation;" and the relationship between world and man is called "redemption." God reveals Himself to man and creates the world, and then man redeems the world. What are called "relationships" here, Rosenzweig called "courses." Thus, Rosenzweig pictured the universe as elements with courses.

What remains to be seen is the meaning of all of this motion, i.e., what is the purpose of God creating a world and revealing Himself to a man who redeems the world? Rosenzweig called that goal or end "the configuration." That is what the whole of *The Star* is about, viz., a picture of the universe, which is a *MAGEN DAVID*, in which the ultimate elements of the universe—God, man and world—are related through the courses of creation, revelation, and redemption, moving towards their configuration.

ITS DIALECTIC

Summary

Again the body of *The Star* begins with death and concludes with life. The process through which the final affirmation is achieved is dialectical. Each stage of *The Star* begins with a naught and moves either to a non-naught, which Rosenzweig called a "Yea," or to a negation of the naught, which Rosenzweig called a "nay."[12] the former movement is called "the path of affirmation" and the latter movement is called "the path of the naught."[13] Through both paths we arrive at an affirmation, the negation of which is the naught of the next stage of the process. By implication, Rosenzweig claimed that what Kant in *The Critique of Pure Reason* called a "negative judgment"[14] and an "infinite judgment"[15] are *prima facie* different but ultimately the same. In this way, each nay is a negative judgment of an initial nothing, each yea is an infinite judgment of that initial nothing, and each *and*[16] explicates the logical identity of the two forms of judgment.

From death Rosenzweig derived three objects of thought—God, man, and world. These remain distinct with progressive interrelation until the conclusion of the third part of *The Star*, when they finally are united in the affirmation of life. The initial denial of God is called "mythic God." Its nay is "concealed God"; its yea is "loving God"; and their conjunction is "the All" or the "redeemed God." The initial denial of the world is called "plastic world"; its nay is "enchanted world"; its yea is "created world"; and their conjunction is "soul." The initial denial of man is called "tragic man"; its nay is "secluded man"; its yea is "disclosed man"; and their conjunction is "created image of God." The final terms exhibit the ultimate posited unity. World becomes soul, which is what man is as the created image of God, who, redeemed, becomes the All. Part I concludes with mythic God, plastic world, and tragic man. Mythic God is God as existing life, where nature is part of God. The plastic world is the world as inspired configuration, where the whole is nothing more than its content. Tragic man is man as solitary self, where man's character or individuality as ephemerality becomes self-personality in defiance. All three are isolated elements whose isolation is their negation, for each is seen to be incomplete without some form of relation beyond itself.

Part II explores the relations of the three elements. It concludes with the enchanted world becoming created through creation (Book

I); the concealed God becoming loving through revelation (Book II); and the secluded soul of man becoming disclosed through redemption (Book III). God becomes eternal, although "He is still to become." In man, both being loved and loving combine, so that he may yet become the created image of God. In the world, merely existing and living growth combine, so that the world may yet become pure soul. In the end, God is redeemed from the labor of creation with the world and from the distress of love for the soul of man, when all three unite as the All. This ultimate unity is posited as a possibility at the end of Part II. Part III deals with Judaism and Christianity as the vehicles by which this possibility will be realized as the kingdom of God.

Explanation

There is a dialectic that runs through *The Star* that is based on Hegel's dialectic. Consider the "dialectical movements" in the diagram given in Appendix B at the end of this chapter. First, there is a general, overall structure of the movement, and then a listing of how the general structure applies to the three elements—world, man, and God. In Part I, the reader is given the elements world, man, and God. Part II begins their movement or development.

In general, the development occurs as follows. You start from nothing. Note that this is the opposite of how Hegel began. Hegel's starting point was Being. The introduction to *The Star* is a critique of Hegel's philosophy, where we are told why Being cannot be a starting point. From nothing you get an affirmation of nothing—the yea—and a negation of nothing—the nay. Then the yea and the nay come together in the and. So the movement is from nothing to yea/nay that concludes with and, where and is a positive that joins the yea and the nay in the dialectical flow.

This general movement is instantiated in each of the three cases. The World begins as plastic. The plastic world is negated as the enchanted world, and it is affirmed as the created world. Finally, the last two stages are brought together in the soul. In other words, what begins as the element world develops from being a plastic world into a soul. Man begins as tragic man. Tragic man is negated as the secluded man and is affirmed as the disclosed man. Finally, this dialectic culminates in man becoming the created image of God. Next, God begins as mythic God. Then mythic God is negated as the concealed God and affirmed as the loving God. Finally the development of God culminates in the concealed and loving God becoming synthesized, joined or fulfilled in the All, which is the redeemed God.

Note that at the very beginning of each dialectic, everything is separate. World, God, and man are all separate, distinct entities; but in the end the elements become united. World becomes soul, which is man. Man becomes the image of God. God becomes everything. When the dialectic reaches its conclusion, there no longer is any distinction between God, world, and man. When each is complete, they constitute a single thing, viz., the fulfilled universe.

Let us now look a little more closely at Rosenzweig's critique of Hegel. Hegel started with Being and only Being. Rosenzweig argues that you cannot start with only one thing, but you must start with a plurality. An analogy from mathematics may explain what both Hegel and Rosenzweig are trying to do in this case. A goal of mathematical thinking is to reduce everything to as few assumptions as is possible. With Gottlob Frege (1848-1925), the assumptions come down to a single entity (the number 1) with a single function (+). Frege argued in *The Foundations of Arithemtic* that if you assume 1 and +, you can deduce all of arithmetic. From + you deduce −, and from + and − you deduce the functions of multiplication and division.

Multiplication is only a complex form of addition, viz., a shorthand for adding additions; and division is only complex subtraction, viz., a short-hand for subtracting subtractions; and − simply is the inverse of +. Frege showed that all you need to comprehend in order to know all of arithmetic is what 1 is and how + works. Hegel tried to do in philosophy the same thing that Frege did in mathematics. He tried to demonstrate that if you know what being is (like 1), you have enough information to know everything. From the notion of Being, everything can be deduced.

Rosenzweig's critique of this claim is that with only Being, you do not have enough to know everything. In fact, Being as a starting point leads nowhere. You need multiple entities. The minimal requisite number, Rosenzweig argued, is three—God, man, and world. Furthermore, the starting point cannot be something (Being); rather, the starting point must be nothing. It is as if you built your arithmetic from the notion of zero rather than from the notion of 1. Do not push the analogy too far. In Rosenzweig's case the zero is not just 0. Rosenzweig's zero is a multiplicity. For Rosenzweig, the dialectic begins with three distinct zeros—the 0 of God, the 0 of man, and the 0 of the world.

An Example of the Dialectic:
Rosenzweig's Introduction—Nothing and Death

Note how Rosenzweig both began and ended *The Star*: "All cognition of the All originates in death, in the fear of death".[17] "Whither, then, do the wings of the gate open? Thou knowest it not? INTO LIFE."[18] Now the negation of life is death, which brings us back to the beginning of the work.

The first line quoted continues as follows:

> Philosophy takes it upon itself to throw off the fear of things earthly, to rob death of its poisonous sting, and Hades of its pestilential breath. All that is mortal lives in this fear of death; every new birth augments the fear by one new reason, for it augments what is mortal. Without ceasing, the womb of the indefatigable earth gives birth to what is new, each bound to die, each awaiting the day of its journey into darkness with fear and trembling. But philosophy denies these fears of the earth. It bears us over the grave which yawns at our feet with every step. It lets the body be a prey to the abyss, but the free soul flutters away over it. Why should philosophy be concerned if the fear of death knows nothing of such a dichotomy between body and soul, if it roars Me! Me! Me!, if it wants nothing to do with relegating fear onto a mere "body"? Let man creep like a worm into the folds of the naked earth before the fast-approaching volleys of a blind death from which there is no appeal; let him sense there, forcibly, inexorably, what he otherwise never senses: that his I would be but an It if it died; let him therefore cry his very I out with every cry that is still in his throat against Him from whom there is no appeal, from whom such unthinkable annihilation threatens—for all this dire necessity philosophy has only its vacuous smile. With index finger outstretched, it directs the creature, whose limbs are quivering with terror for its this-worldly existence, to a Beyond of which it doesn't care to know anything at all. For man does not really want to escape any kind of fetters; he wants to remain, he wants to—live. Philosophy, which commends death to him as its special protege, as the magnificent opportunity to flee the straits of life, seems to him to be only mocking. In fact, man is only too well aware that he is condemned to death, but not to suicide. Yet this philosophical recommendation can truthfully recommend only suicide, not the fated death of all. Suicide is not the natural form of death but plainly the one counter to nature. The gruesome capacity for suicide distinguishes man from all beings, both known and unknown to us. It is the veritable criterion of this disengagement from all that is natural. It is presumably necessary for man to

disengage once in his life. Like Faust, he must for once bring the precious vial down with reverence; he must for once have felt himself in his fearful poverty, loneliness, and dissociation from all the world, have stood a whole night face to face with the Nought. But the earth claims him again. He may not drain the dark potion in the night. A way out of the bottleneck of the Nought has been determined for him, another way than this precipitate fall into the yawning abyss. Man is not to throw off the fear of the earthly; he is to remain in the fear of death—but he is to remain.[19]

Rosenzweig asked, what is the whole history of thought about? What is the goal of knowing? His answer was that the motive behind knowing is fear, viz., the fear of death. What knowing seeks to do is to find eternal truths. It looks for eternal truths because what is eternal does not die. If you can know and thereby identify with what is eternal, you may think that you have overcome death. For Rosenzweig, the philosophy of Hegel is the ultimate attempt to achieve this end. In its very achievement, the enterprise loses what is most characteristic of life, for everything known becomes dead. Hence, the enterprise in its very success is doomed to failure.

In this way, Rosenzweig argued for the conclusion that the starting point of thought must be death and not life. Life must be a conclusion and not a beginning. So, the text of The Star begins with death, the opposite of life. He justified this decision in the following way: If you look at man and at what composes world, the most distinctive thing about both is that they die. Let me apply this thesis more specifically. Consider the things in the world. Everything that you see is undergoing change. Hence, to comprehend this world you must understand the change; but the new state of affairs brought about by the change is no sooner over than it too changes; i.e., no sooner is something generated than it perishes. Everything that is is only for a moment. If you try to measure it, you do not have enough time. Before you have finished thinking your thought about anything, that thing already is gone. It no longer is there. Consequently, thought can never really grasp life because life is always in the present, and the present is immeasurable. You always end up thinking about the past. For example, I want to think about my smoking; but when I try to think about it, what I am thinking about is a dead image. Consequently, knowing is an attempt to overcome death, which means that death and not life must be the starting point of thought. Everything that we think about at the moment that we think about it is dead. In essence, this is what Rosenzweig said in the first paragraph of *The Star.*

At this point it should be clear that Rosenzweig's term *death* is not the same as our ordinary term *death.* As Rosenzweig used the word, it includes everything that we call death, but it also includes much more. For Rosenzweig to say that something is dead means that it no longer exists in the present moment. Hence, as Rosenzweig used the term, everything that is not eternal, that is subject to change, is dead. In other words, to be dead means, in Aristotle's language, to be subject to generation and corruption. Now, one of the things that makes it so difficult to read Rosenzweig is that his key terms have the specialized meanings that they had in late nineteenth-century and early twentieth-century German philosophy. These words look like ordinary terms in contemporary speech, but in fact they have very different, anything-but-ordinary meanings. Death is only one of those words.

We start with negation (= death). Then we negate the negation, which gives us life. We can make the same point in another way. All growth in thinking is negative thinking. Wherever you start, you get to the next step first by negating where you were. Now in Rosenzweig's judgment, Hegel began with the conclusion and not with the real starting point. This error is the critical reason why Hegel's enterprise of knowing fails.

If you want an absolute starting point, i.e., a starting point that presupposes nothing, then the only possible starting point can be just that—nothing. The only thing that nothing presupposes is nothing. Again, if you really want to start your thinking without assumptions, then you must begin with nothing. We can show this point historically in the following way.

Descartes, the geometer, said that we accept all that we accept on the basis of tradition, but we should accept nothing on the basis of tradition. Furthermore, he claimed that the starting point of my knowledge is my act of doubting, which is an act of thought, viz., "I think, therefore I am" (The *Cogito*). Historically, we know that the *Cogito* does not lead anywhere. You cannot conclude from thinking that there is a thinker; all that you can conclude is that there is thinking. This judgment brings us to the historical stage of saying that we do not know from the *Cogito* that there is a thinker; all we know is that there is thinking. But what kind of thinking? The answer is doubting. But what is doubting? Rosenzweig's answer was that it is an act of negating. To doubt is to negate, and this negation is the proper starting point of thought. When you think about doubting, you realize that to doubt is to negate something. To assume doubt is to assume a particular kind of nothing which as such is something.

This last analytic move leads to the next step, Rosenzweig's yea. Nothing is nothing (the first nay), but as such it is something (the first yea). In this way, we pass through the first two steps of Rosenzweig's dialectic of thought. Let it suffice for our purposes to demonstrate how Rosenzweig's dialectic operated.

PART I: THE ELEMENTS

Summary

In general, Book I argues for a negation of the nothing that was the conclusion of the introduction. This negation of a negation yields a yea, a something that is mythic God, plastic world, and tragic man. The term *mythic* is used for God because that is how the Greek gods normally are understood, viz., as myths. Similarly, Rosenzweig characterized this view of man as tragic because it is the view of man that emerges through the Greek tragedies, viz., an isolated man who seeks relations with other men and with the gods.[20]

Each book contains parallels to the other books within its parts. In Part I, we are presented with a mythic God that is God's being, that is the object of the science of metaphysics; a plastic world that is the world's meaning, that is the object of the science of metalogic; and finally a tragic man who is man's self, that is the object of the science of metaethics. Each object presented is its subject as an object that does not exhaust what the subject is, because it is a picture of the subject in isolation from anything else. Each inadequate object is all that a given science can deal with as each of these sciences is meta, i.e., points to its own inadequacy and in so doing points to the possibility of a form of knowledge beyond itself. God's being is God, and in metaphysics' comprehension of God it shows that God's being is not all of God; the world's meaning is the world, and in metalogic's comprehension of the world it shows that the world's meaning is not all of the world; and man's self is man, and in metaethics' comprehension of man it shows that man's self is not all of man.

God

Moses Maimonides' negative theory of divine attributes gave Rosenzweig the initial naught of God with which his modern theology began. He claimed that the source of this theological dead end is viewing all of the divine attributes together, where each attribute is one among many and each, in view of the others, can only be interpreted as negation. Whereas classical and medieval theology began with an affirmation of God and concluded with a negation, we are to begin with a negation of what God is supposed to be,[21] and at the same time we are to affirm of God the privation of every individual naught. In medieval terms, what is affirmed is God's infinite essence. The affirmation posits that from God there are infinite possibilities of reality. At the same time what is denied is that what we affirm as God's essence is God. This denial is in itself an affirmation of divine freedom.

The logical symbol introduced to express this cognition of God is $A=A$.[22] The general logical form $y=x$ asserts that a grammatical subject y is in some form of intransitive relation with a predicate. To affirm y entails affirming x, where y is a nay and x is a yea, such that x constitutes an essence, so that $y=$ is freedom over and beyond the posited essence. In $A=A$, the A on the left of the equation is divine freedom, and the A on the right is divine essence, both of which are God. Again, note that the relationship asserted is intransitive, so that while divine freedom becomes divine essence, divine essence does not become divine freedom. Classical theology had nowhere to go, because it began with God's essence. Freedom entails the power to act, so that divine essence is seen not as an entity, but as unlimited power for—. Note that the sentence is incomplete. God's essence is unlimited power for something, and that something cannot be expressed as long as attention is focused on God in isolation to anything else.

Rosenzweig claimed that primitive atheism and the religions of Greece, India, and China embody the error of thought about God that begins by affirming God's essence in isolation. His Greek religion includes both the religion of classical mythology and the religion of the classical philosophers, most notably Plato and Aristotle. His Indian religion is Buddhism, his Chinese religion is Taoism, and his prime example of primitive atheism is Sophism.

God or the gods of Greece are alive or vital in the sense that they are immortal, but they are not alive in the sense that they are involved with the world. Rather, as the gods are interpreted by the philosophers, it is more the case that the world is made part of them than that they are part of the world. The association of the gods with nature makes nature divine, but it excludes the gods as gods from nature. In contrast, the gods of Asia are outside of nature, but they are not alive; they are a naught that is a mere abstraction. Whereas Rosenzweig also would have theology begin with a negation, his naught is both from and to an aught; but in the religions of Asia, no aught appears in the thought movement. Asia's religious thought posits a negated naught, a nay-nay, as the essence of deity. As such, it is a retrogression from the elemental and not a progression beyond it. Whereas Rosenzweig would posit a movement from an initial naught to a yea, Asian religion moves backward from the initial negation to a not-naught. In Indian Buddhism, this negation is the appeal beyond God to Nirvana, where presumably nothing exists; an in Chinese religion, the ideal of Tao is a simple negation, viz., an atheism where at every moment anything and everything is denied. Greek theology fails because it is unable to move beyond the physical world, and Asian religion fails because it is unable to move beyond the initial naught.

Rosenzweig noted attempts by both peoples to move beyond this limit. He cited the mystery cults, the philosophies of Greece, and the Friends of God of India. He credited them as monotheisms but condemned them as inadequate because they did not reverse the initial method of their theology. Their one God becomes so remote in nature from man and the world that its isolation cannot be transcended.

We began by doubting God. Then we negated the negation, which gave us the affirmation of mythic God. Now we negate this second affirmation. At first, we denied that there is nothing, and we said that there is something. The something that we got were the gods of Greek and Asian religions, but these deities are not related to empirical reality. They are either nothing at all or mere objects among other objects in the perceived universe. Hence, we derive the nay of our initial yea. There is a God (yea), but He has not yet been revealed to us (nay).

World

Classical and medieval philosophy made knowledge of God the starting point of all knowledge. To the extent that there is doubt about the existence of God, there also is doubt about the existence of the world. According to Rosenzweig, Descartes' *Cogito* points to the inadequacy of pre-Hegelian cosmology in the same way that Maimonides' theory of divine attributes illustrates the inadequacy of previous theology. While Descartes seemed to begin with negation, i.e., doubt; in fact, his doubt is only hypothetical. For Descartes there is no real question about the existence and nature of God, the world, or man. His doubt was only intended to exhibit that given knowledge, but his effort failed. As in the case of theology, the failure is not due to doubt but to beginning with an affirmation and attempting to deal with everything in the world as an "all" (*omnibus*), where each thing is viewed as one among many things, all of which are knowable together. This initial naught, i.e., doubt about knowledge of the world, gives rise to an affirmation (which Rosenzweig called an "aught") of logos, or world-order.

Everything in the world is subject to an order that can be known by reason, but this reason cannot show the unity of all. We can move beyond our original doubt to affirm a yea of the universal, which Rosenzweig identified with world-spirit. World-spirit is not the world, it is a plastic world. The word *plastic* means visible or tangible. It is something that is (a) known through the senses in the sense world; (b) is subject to sight, taste, hearing, smelling and touch; and (c) sensually present. This world is a plenitude of individual, continuously-created objects reported by the external senses. In medieval terms, the sensible world is affirmed and it is knowable insofar as each object in it is universal and hence spiritual, i.e., incorporeal; but as God is not His essence, so the world is not its logos.

Insofar as the world is living, i.e., vital, it is logos, i.e., reasoning. Reason lacks the plenitude, i.e., the totality of sense objects. As such the world is not rational. Yet, if anything is alive in the world, it is the sensate object. Rosenzweig's thought leads to the paradox that life (the plenitude) is lifeless (without logos). The paradox is overcome only when we cease to focus on the world as a whole and turn our attention to particulars in the world. Insofar as the individual is universal, it is passive and unmoved. Its life resides in its particularity, but life is activity and motion. Insofar as the particular is alive, it is active. Its motion is towards an end, viz., to penetrate into its species, i.e., as particular to become universal. In medieval terms, the particular is its species, which is all of the individual that can be known; but no particular is identical with its species. Rather, every particular strives to become its species, i.e., to become a particular universality.

The logical symbol introduced to express this cognition of the world is B=A. The connective = expresses penetration, which is an intransitive relation. B strives to penetrate A, but A does not strive to penetrate B. A is world-spirit or logos, and B is the individual, particular instance within the plenitude. B=A expresses the life of the isolated sensory individual, whose life is the project of penetrating its rationality or universality, viz., world-spirit or logos. In medieval terms, the particularity of the individual is its matter, and its universality is its form. B=A also expresses that the content of the world is that which is becoming the form of the world, that the particular is becoming universal, and ultimately what is active seeks to become passive. Also, =A is the divine essence. Hence, B=A states that the world as a plenitude of sensate individuals is alive with an end to penetrate the essence of God.

In the religion and philosophy of Greece, the cosmos and the world are plastic, i.e., they are posited single entities that contain all individuals solely as parts without any individuality of their own. In the Idealist vision of the plastic world stated above by Rosenzweig, the plenitude of distinct individuals is striving to become unified, but for the Greeks this unity already is itself posited. Whereas Idealism's world is all-filling, the Greek's world is all-filled. Their plastic world is structured, but not created. The world is finite, whereas God is infinite. Given the posited completeness of the world, viz., that the sensate objects of the world plenitude are in fact united in a whole, there is no way to relate the finite world to the infinite God. However, it is precisely this relation that is the unity of the world. Plato and Aristotle could not resolve this contradiction. In their world-view, individuals come into existence solely as part of a community; but in doing so, they lose their individuality. The community itself is only one particular among other particulars. Community is not a real unity. This failure led Sophism to rebel against the notion of community by affirming the individual in isolation, independent of any collective. In the end, Sophism failed as well because it cannot make intelligible how individuals are related to each other. Its failure provokes a second rejection, which gives rise to the development of the great polis of Rome, where community again vanquishes its individual parts.

In contrast to the Greek view of the world, which affirms the plenitude over spirit and community over the individual, Indian religion affirms spirit over and against the plenitude and the individual over and against community. In so doing, Indian religion posits the nay of the world while rejecting its yea. Although it failed, the Greeks attempted to conjoin the nay of universality that is spirit with the yea of particularity that is in the plenitude. Instead, Indian religion posits the universal concept that is spirit while it rejects all individuality as a mere illusion.

Chinese religion also falls short of Greek religion's effort to unite form and matter, but it moves in an opposite direction from that of Buddhism. In China, spirits become corporeal; and corporeal individuals become the spirits of ancestors. Whereas India closes its eyes to the world, China totally submerges itself into the world, losing the realization that the world in isolation, viz., the plastic world, is essentially and vitally incomplete.

We began by doubting the world. Then we negated the negation, which gave us the affirmation of the plastic world. Now we negate this second affirmation. At first, we denied that there is nothing, and we said that there is something. The something that we got was the sensual world, but the world that we have come up with is not real. The reality of this world is not what we know about this world, because what we know is always something dead. Hence, we derive the nay of our initial yea. There is a world (yea), but the world is dead (nay).

Man

Kant claimed that the self lies beyond what is given in the world of experience, so that the existence of a self is not self-evident. Rosenzweig argued that this claim gives the initial naught of man with which modern psychology begins. In theology, this naught led to the yea of God's immortal, unconditioned, essential existence beyond knowledge. In cosmology, this naught led to the yea of the world's essential and necessary existence in knowledge (logos). In the case of man, essence is finitude,[23] which, in comparison with the other elements of God and world, is man's distinctiveness. Ephemerality constitutes man's essence because it is universally true of all men, but it does not constitute any man's individuality.

The understanding of the self that has now been reached is the concept of tragic man. Tragic man is simply man in isolation as an object among objects. The logical symbol used to express this understanding is B=B. The B in the left hand place of the grammatical subject expresses man's permanent essence as ephemerality. It is a yea that functions as a counterpart of the A on the left hand in the equation A=A, which is divine freedom. The grammatical subject B is human free will, which is an expression of man's universal and permanent character. This B of man differs from the A of God in that human freedom is finite, i.e., ephemeral; whereas divine freedom is infinite power. Since it is infinite, divine freedom acts because it is power (A=A), whereas human freedom only wills (B=B). The B of the predicate place in the equation is a nay. It expresses a direction but not a content, and as such it is defiant will. Thus, B=B expresses the claim that man's finite will becomes a defiant will. This defiance transforms man's character into self-consciousness; and in being self-conscious, man becomes a peculiar person, viz., a self. The first man (Adam) who resided in the Garden of Eden only had character and did not attain a personality until he became defiant. B alone is merely character. When it strives to penetrate world-spirit as expressed in the equation B=A, it is world content in relation to the world form, whose symbol also is the essence of God.[24] Furthermore, when B strives in defiance to become itself, as expressed in the equation B=B, it is man with personality and not merely an object in the world. A=A expresses God's unadulterated infinity; B=B expresses man's unadulterated finiteness; and as of yet there is no connection between them other than the possibility of connection through the world (B=A).

In defiance, man passes beyond what he is in isolation; just as in freedom God transcends His essence. Beyond man's character and individuality is his personality as himself. In terms of Greek thought, where the content of ethics is character, man is projected beyond ethics, as God is beyond physics[25] and the world is beyond logic. Just as in their thought about the world and God, where the Greeks could point beyond physics and logic to metaphysics and metalogic, here too they could envisage a metaethics. Unfortunately, their metaethics is no more successful than their other sciences of the elements because the elements remain only elements, isolated from the configuration that they need for completion. In this case too, Asian religions avoid the paradoxes of Greek religion only by reversing the thought process and not by advancing beyond the level that the Greeks achieved. The Asians posit character but reject defiance. In so doing, they deny the self. In Indian Buddhism, character loses all distinctiveness. As God and world return to their initial negation, so the self returns at death to its initial naught. In Buddhism, this retrogression results from too strong an emphasis on character. In Chinese religion, the same effect results from too little emphasis on character, where the ideal of Confucius is an ideal of an ordinary man, viz., a man without excellence, i.e., without character.

We began by doubting man. Then we negated the negation, which gave us the affirmation of tragic man. Now we negate this second affirmation. At first we denied that there is nothing, and we said that there is something. The something that we got was tragic man, i.e., an isolated thing among things; but the man that we have presented is not real. In his radical freedom, he has no relationship to the world; as such, he is without content, and therefore he is nothing at all. Hence, we derive the nay of our initial yea. There is man (yea), but man is nothing (nay).

Explanation

Part I deals with the elements, Part II with the course, and Part

III with the goal, purpose, or configuration. These elements are proto-cosmos, where proto means before, and cosmos means the universe. The isolated elements are prior to the universe.

Suppose that I explain what it means for a man to run by showing a series of pictures of the different states of the man's muscles. I display the pictures in order to enable us to understand the man's motion. The pictures necessarily are false, because the reality consists of motion while the pictures are static. In other words, the very device used to understand the motion is itself a distortion of the reality it is trying to explain. Similarly, modern physics tries to reduce every physical thing to its most basic components or elements, and then from these elements to construct a picture of the physical universe. Everything in the universe is a compound of those elements, and what exists will be seen to be compound. However, the elements never exist as elements, i.e., in isolation. In this sense, the elements do not exist; they are a mental construct by which we explain the compounds which do exist. In our universe—the one we experience—there are no elements, i.e., there are no basic things in isolation outside of their configuration with each other.

Part I began with three things—God, man, and world—that are separate. Our initial God is a thing among things. At first, there is no consciousness of the world as such. The only sense in which there is a world is as the collection of all the things in it. All we mean initially by the world is the collection of all of these things. The things in the world are divided into objects and subdivided into living and non-living objects. The living objects, called "persons," divide into the categories of men and supermen. These supermen are the initial gods. And so we come to the stage of Greek religion.

Initially, we become aware only of things that are sensually present. All of them are separate and isolated. We think of the world as a list or bundle of distinct objects. Among those objects are humans and gods. All of these things together make up this world, although they remain separate and distinct. This is man's vision at the stage of Greek religion.

The next stage of realization negated the world laid out for us in Part I. As we initially think about these separate, isolated things, we soon become aware that they are not really like this at all. For example, you want to think about a butterfly; so you catch one, stick a pin through it, and mount it on a board. However, you no longer have a butterfly. What you have instead is the cadaver of a butterfly.

The first stage of learning is classification. That is why you stick pins in the butterflies. The beginning of knowledge involves classifying separate, distinct things. You classify gods into families of gods. You classify human beings into different kinds as well. Finally, you think about the various kinds of objects, and you put them into classes as well. This process is the beginning of science.

All science initially is a classification of objects. Aristotle's writings on the natural sciences are an example of such a beginning. However, having done this for a while, you become aware that you are not thinking about anything real. All of those pithed butterflies are not butterflies. All of John James Audubon's birds are not birds. They are only pictures of birds. Cadavers of people are not people.

How do you go from the cadaver, which is all that the scientist can give you, to the living, real thing? The problem with grasping the reality is that it is continually in motion; and as soon as you try to capture it, it is dead. But even if you were merely to watch it, you still only see the thing; you do not see its motion. For example, Galileo tried to capture motion in a series of sketches. They were his attempt to transcend our knowledge of an object in order to grasp the object in motion. However, he also failed. What he produced was a series of still pictures imposed upon each other, which also is not real.

This situation is why scientific thinking necessarily is limited; it inescapably distorts what it tries to represent. To know reality is to picture it, but everything that we picture scientifically is dead. This state of affairs is another reason why the starting point of true philosophy is death.

The next step in formulating an adequate picture of reality requires that we negate this initially-affirmed world. Reality must be other than this God, world, and man. In this connection, it is valuable to mention two Pre-Socratic philosophers, Heraclitus and Parmenides.

Recognizing that what we know through the sciences could not be reality, Heraclitus and Parmenides tried to go beyond this level of sensible cognition to characterize reality. They went in opposite directions. Parmenides said that reality is what is permanent, while Heraclitus claimed that change itself is reality.

In order to understand their views, consider the following metaphor. To know a river is to know its course. A river is neither a bundle of drops of water, nor is it the banks. The drops of water are always changing. To see a river is not to see the drops of water. To think of a river as the sum total of its drops of water is to think only of a collection of drops of water and not to think of a river. Rather, the river is those drops in a course, and the course is the reality of the river. The drops are only the elements of the river. If by the river you mean its elements, then the river is always changing. The river, however, is something else that is relatively unchanging. What in the river is unchanging is its course, but the course is nothing. The thing that is most critical in knowing the river itself is not a thing; it is nothing, no-thing (*LO DAVAR*).

Heraclitus claimed that the river itself is reality. In contrast, Parmenides said that what is always in the process of becoming, of changing, cannot be reality. What changes is immediately past; when it is past, it is gone; and therefore, it no longer is real. Nor can what is real be future, since the future, by definition, is that which is not yet. If the world of becoming is what is real, its reality cannot be past or future. Its reality must be what is in the present; but nothing changing is in the present, since in an instant it goes from being future (what is not yet) to being past (what is no longer). if we picture time as a line, the present is merely the point that divides past from future, and a point is nothing. Anything that has any duration is past or future. If we think that this world of change is reality, then nothing is real. Therefore, Parmenides said that reality is what does not change. He claimed that there are two worlds—the world of becoming or change that is always changing and always becoming, and the real world which is a world of permanence. The real world is a world of being rather than a world of becoming. What resides in this world are thoughts. Whereas thoughts are real, other things are not.

Parmenides' claim that the real is what is permanent and does not change entails the assumption that this apparent world is not real. Similarly, Heraclitus' claim that the real is the change itself entails the same conclusion. In spite of their differences, both philosophers arrived at the same conclusion, that there is something beyond this world. If this world is what is, then this world is not real. Reality is something else. In Rosenzweig's terms, they reached the stage where thinking man steps outside of and beyond the world of plastic things, mythic gods, and tragic men. For the first time, man is able to negate this universe. By so doing, he calls the negation—what is not this plastic universe—"reality."

What this reality is is nothing. Now we are at the stage of Asian religions. Historically, we know that these Greek philosophers' insights came from the influence of Indian thought in Buddhism and Hinduism. From these two religions, we first derive the insight that reality is something, and something is an illusion.

According to Rosenzweig, the insight of Asian religions is that as long as we depend on scientific thinking, we will have things without motion, viz., things merely in isolation. If we truly think about these things, we will know that this cannot be the way they really are.

We come to posit the negation of the things that are, viz., the negation of the elements. The negation of the world as element gives us what Rosenzweig called the "enchanted" world, i.e., the world of mystery. We come to the awareness that beyond the sensible world there is manifest a non-sensible world of which we know nothing. We know that it is, but we do not know what it is. Similarly, the negation of man as an element gives us what Rosenzweig called the "secluded" man, i.e., man in isolation, knowing that what he is is not isolated. Likewise, the negation of God as an element gives us what Rosenzweig called the "concealed" god, i.e., a god who is nothing until He reveals Himself.

By the end of Book I, those following Rosenzweig's thought have reached the conclusion that the conception of isolated elements is only the beginning of knowledge. The elements of the universe are not yet the universe. The world is composed of compounds in motion. Rosenzweig's discussion of his elements—God, man, and world—is not a description of the universe, the cosmos; rather, it is a discussion of what is prior to the universe—a proto-cosmos. Only when the elements are seen in motion, i.e., in interaction with or in relationship to each other, can we be said to be discussing the cosmos, i.e., the existent, empirical world.

As we begin to think about this negation which concludes the first part of the *Star*, we are ready to negate the negation, which leads us to the next step. Book II is the next step. Here reality again becomes something positive, but the affirmed universe is a universe of movements rather than of things, one of relations rather than of elements. We now move beyond the elements world, man, and God, turning to creation, revelation, and redemption. Creation is the act of God on the world; revelation is the act of God to man; redemption is the act of man on the world. In this way, we move from the terms (elements) of relations to the relations themselves.

PART II: THE COURSE

Rosenzweig said that this proto-cosmos is ever-enduring, meaning that it stands outside of time. The configuration is said to be eternal which again is a non-temporal reference. Of the three—the ever-enduring proto-cosmos, the always-renewed cosmos, and the eternal hyper-cosmos—only the second, the always-renewed cosmos, i.e., our universe (with its past present and future), is subject to time. This and this cosmos alone is the realm of history.

Remember that Part I deals with the elements, Part II with the course, and Part III with the configuration. As *The Star* moves through each part, a progression in method takes place. The symbols used in Part I were logical symbols. Now, in Part II, the symbols are grammatical; and then, in Part III, the symbols will be liturgical or geometric. Similarly, as *The Star* develops, the focus on religion changes. In Part I Rosenzweig discussed Asian and Greek religion; Part II deals with Islam, and Part III discusses Judaism and Christianity.

Each part is to be viewed as an advancement towards a total picture of reality. Presupposed in this progression is the judgment that logic, the language of science, has limited validity. Beyond logic is grammar. Grammar is the language of art.[26] For Rosenzweig, art has the ability to grasp truth beyond the ability of science.

Similarly, beyond art is religion. The first religions to have insight into reality were the Asian and Greek religions, and Islam improves on them; but Judaism and Christianity have the best grasp of reality. After presenting a general overview of Rosenzweig's work, we will return to look at his judgments about religion, particularly Judaism and Christianity, in more detail.

Summary

In Part II, the three books are divided by basic divisions of time. The cosmos is the present universe, which is the domain of time. Both the proto-cosmos and the hyper-cosmos are beyond time. In time, there is creation at the beginning, which occurred in the past; there is revelation now, in the present; and there is the expectation of redemption, in the future. Creation is the ever-enduring base of things. Revelation is the ever-renewed birth of the soul, and redemption is the eternal future of the kingdom. The three acts are not eternal, for eternal is not subject to time as Rosenzweig used this term. Rather, they are endless. As long as there is time, but only as long as there is time, there is past creation, present revelation, and future expectation of redemption.[27] From the present revelation, we glimpse reality's beginning in creation and reality's end in the Kingdom of God that constitutes the redemption of the present.

In addition, Rosenzweig explicated all three courses in terms of the Hebrew Scriptures. He presented his treatment of creation as an interpretation of the first three chapters of Genesis, revelation as an interpretation of the Song of Songs, and redemption as an interpretation of Psalms 111-118.[28]

Creation and Creature

The inadequacy of an enchanted world, i.e., a world that is divine but is not related to God, is overcome by the doctrine of creation. Creation, though, is empty without revelation. Here creation is a past event. God remains as remote from man and the world as he is in the enchanted world, without revelation in each present moment. Rosenzweig judged this to be the inadequacy of Islam's doctrine of creation, which, inadequacy, he claimed, occurs because the Quran, unlike the Talmud and the New Testament, is independent of the Old Testament. He asserted that the source of this error is Islam's misunderstanding of miracles.

In classical Jewish and Christian theology, miracles are not events that express divine freedom over and against natural law. In this sense, either there are no miracles or every event is miraculous. If a miracle means an act contrary to natural law, then no event is a miracle, for natural law simply expresses divine will. If a miracle means an act of divine will, then all act are miraculous. What distinguishes miracles from other events is that they are signs that, as interpreted by prophets, motivate belief or faith. It is in this sense that creation itself is miraculous It is not the sense in which the eternal Quran or creation itself is viewed as miraculous in Islam. Both are inexplicable givens of divine will. As such, they are capricious, as the acts of pagan deities have no purpose.

The Star's Islam is the Islam of the atomist philosophers of Kalam. In Kalam, every act is miraculous because at each moment the spiritual atom, who is God, is continuously rewilling a world. Thus, the world is an unconnected bundle of indistinguishable atoms that exist only for an atomic moment, where one moment is identical with every moment before and after it. This world has no essence; and therefore, it also lacks purpose. In this Islam, God's acts are totally free, and hence capricious; whereas in Judaism God acts through wisdom from His attributes of love and/or righteousness. Thus, there is some inner necessity to God's act, in consequence of which the world has purpose. Because in Islam God's acts are capricious, its world cannot endure beyond the moment. Islam's creation negates the world. In contrast, Judaism's creation from divine essence, expressed as love or righteousness, is world-affirming, yielding a world that persists. In Judaism the created world exists, but it is not complete. It is the process of becoming, moving towards an end, that is the created world's being. In Rosenzweig's Islam of the Kalam, nothing created exists beyond the moment; so what is created is continuously complete and never renewed. Here Islam fails to distinguish between existence and being. What exists is what is and is nothing more than what it is. While Islam's God continuously creates and at each moment a new world is created, there is no real relation between the two.

The result is a view of reality that Rosenzweig described as "pagan monotheism." There is one God of the world, but God and world are isolated from each other. Islam reaches beyond the plastic world and the mythic God of the pagans to an enchanted world with a concealed God; but its creation is not really creation, because its God does not really love. Hence, its movement beyond paganism is only appearance and not reality.

Revelation and Soul

Creation by itself, in isolation from any other act, is merely a past event. In contrast, love by itself is entirely a present event. Through revelation, the two are joined together as a present that rests on a past. The concealed God, who is the negation beyond the mythic God, becomes a manifest God through revelation. His first act is creation. Creation expresses God's essence as power; but it is only a past manifestation, and hence a past power. Revelation expresses God's essence as love in the present. In the present, God is an active lover who daily loves his loved one more time. This love is an act rather than an attribute, because it does not persist through time. Love is always present and must be renewed at each new present until the end of time. Furthermore, because love is not an attribute, it is not universal. At each moment, God loves individuals, be they humans, nations, epochs, or things; and at each new moment God loves more individuals: but in the cosmos of time, God does not love every individual.

As Islam affirms creation but does not understand it, so it posits but fails to comprehend revelation. For Islam, revelation is a universal, and therefore an essential, attribute of God that is given to every individual. Consequently, revelation is a past (and not a living, present) event that is always the same and never develops. Whereas in Islam God gives a book (the Quran), in Judaism God gives His presence in love. For Judaism the Torah is not a book;[29] it is a living, growing oral law, as is Christianity's living revelation in the sayings of Christ.

As Islam's misunderstanding of God's act of creation distorts the created world, so its misunderstanding of God's act of revelation in love distorts the loved one who receives the revelation, viz., the soul. Through humility, the defiant, tragic man recognizes his seclusion, and in this recognition he becomes open to receive revelation; but humility is not an act. Man plays no active role in a love where revelation is entirely a gift from God. The faithful man can do no more than be open to the gift and accept it. In contrast, the believer of Islam is an active agent. Since Islam's revelation never changes, it is always available from the past. To believe requires no special divine act in the present. Those who do not have faith need nothing more than what already has been given. Their lack of faith is entirely their own responsibility. Islam's believers become active seekers and not passive receivers of God's word. Thus, in Islam there can be divine mercy, but no love, since man receives faith through his own works.

Redemption and Kingdom

God's first revelation in the past, i.e., at the beginning of man and the world, is creation. Its grammatical expressions are in the root sentence:[30] "It is very good."[31] The objects of the world are expressed through indefinite, temporal nouns that are passive, for God and only God is active. The adjective *good* expresses the attribute or quality of God that gives the world its essence, not as what it is, but as what it is becoming through prophecy. The term *very* points beyond creation to subsequent revelation.

The second revelation is the giving of the Torah at Sinai, whose grammatical expression is the root-word I that begins the revelation.[32] The I is really an "I, however" or "I, not otherwise," where the not otherwise means not otherwise than everything. Hence, God's call of I points to a soul beyond God, expressed by the root-word Thou. At creation this root-word is expressed to Adam in the root-sentence: "Where art thou?"[33] which is the offer of the gift of love in the present. The proper response is "Here I am," which expresses man's readiness in humility to receive the gift. It means "What am I commanded?" (i.e., what is the revelation) to which God responds, "And you shall love the Lord" (i.e., Love me).[34] The proper human response to this command is "I am thine," which posits shame because to acknowledge love is to admit weakness. It is equivalent to saying, "I have sinned" (i.e., I accept your love as a gift, for I cannot love on my own). It is an altogether different response than Islam's "God is God," which admits no sin and no gift, but instead affirms that man can do God's will. Islam's response acknowledges only the concealed God.

In contrast, God becomes manifest only when man in humility opens himself to God's gift and God responds, "Thou art mine." Most important about this root-sentence is that the "Thou" and not the "I" of God is the subject. This answer posits man's relation to God as a relationship to the world, where the commandment to love the Lord becomes the commandment to love the loved one's neighbor.[35] Thus, the secluded self, through divine love, is commanded to love his neighbor; and in so doing, he turns from his isolation towards the world.

Rosenzweig argues that Judaism's way of God as love of neighbor is distinct form Islam's love of Allah. The difference is not the content, but the form. The way of Allah is expressed by a set of positive laws, whereas the way of God is expressed by negative laws. Positive commandments prescribe specific actions, leaving no room for an unpredictable response to God's love in the moment of being loved. In contrast, negative commandments set limits on possible responses, but they do not dictate the responses. Islamic positive law leads Muslims to a historical approach to law in which the past rules the present, while Judaism's and Christianity's negative law leads Jews and Christians to a deductive approach where the present rules the past.

Islam's doctrine of redemption looks the same as that of Judaism and Christianity, but in reality it is quite different. The love of neighbor in Judaism and Christianity is directed through the individual neighbor, who is the object of love only because he happens to be there. Ultimately, the focus of love of the other is the entire world. Each redeemed individual turns from being loved to loving his neighbor who, when loved, turns to his neighbor. As more and more objects in the world become not objects but loved souls, ultimately all of the will be transformed into soul. To the extent that the objects of the plastic world become soul, the world becomes redeemed as living.

The Star's term for this redeemed, living world is *kingdom*. The kingdom in Judaism and Christianity is markedly different from Islam's kingdom. The most significant difference is that the kingdom of Allah cannot exhibit growth. Instead, Islam posits an imam, i.e., a spiritual leader, who directs each age in the consensus of the living community (*IJMA*). Judaism's oral law is always new, because it is a logical deduction from Sinai; Islam's *IJMA* is the voice of the past guarding against innovation in the present.

Behind the difference between oral law and *IJMA* is a different conception of time. In Islam every moment is the same. There is no eternity. There is only an endless succession of identical moments ruled by the past. In contrast, for Judaism and Christianity the future is an unpredictable expectation of redemption, where any moment can be the last moment, viz., the eternity that initiates the fully-redeemed world of the kingdom of God.

Explanation

Note the parallelism between the terms creation, revelation, and redemption; ever-enduring (a time word), ever-renewed (also a time word), and eternal future. Ever-enduring and ever-renewed are both time words, but eternal-future is not. Future is, but eternal is not. Rosenzweig's use of these terms indicates that his ultimate future is not in time, but at the end of time.

Creation corresponds to things or world; revelation corresponds to the soul or the human being; and the kingdom points to God. We have the world, man, and God. Only here, in Part II (i.e., in the present), the world is the totality of things, man is a soul, and God is a kingdom. God is identified with a kingdom that is the state of the universe at the end of days. God, through creation, is understood to be engaged in a process of self-actualization.

Prima facie creation is in the past, redemption is in the future, and revelation is in the present. Since the language of knowledge at the stage of the course is grammar or art, Rosenzweig picked three works of literature on which to base his descriptions—the Genesis Story, the Song of Songs, and the Psalms. The latter two are works of poetry. Psalms deals with redemption and the future; Song of Songs is about revelation and the present; and Genesis is about creation and the past.

This, in general, is the over-all structure of Book II. Now let us look in slightly more detail at what Book II is about and how it fits into the overall structure and purpose of *The Star*.

The Inadequacy of Isolated Elements

At the end of Book I, we had the elements of the universe, but they stood in isolation. However, as we thought about the elements in Book I, we saw that this isolation did not make sense. Neither man, God, nor the world are intelligible in isolation.

MAN: Man is a social animal. This human characteristic is not accidental. It is essential. Man in isolation cannot live. He remains dependent on human society, and society presupposes community. This is our tragic man, our isolated man, closed within his own world, á la Descartes. He cannot get outside of himself, so he is not real. Only in relationship is man real.[36] We see man going from tragic man, being enclosed, to becoming disclosed, i.e., living in society, in relationship. Man is no longer defined as the individual, but as part of a society or community. Therefore, Rosenzweig's basic entity is not the individual, it is the community; and the individual exists only as part of the community. This realization begins Book II.

WORLD: At the beginning the world was simply a collection of things. It was a bundle of trees, rocks, etc. In itself, over and beyond the individual things collected within it, the world was nothing. However, the world itself does not function in this way., Everything in the world is interrelated. The laws that define what a thing is define it in terms of its interaction with everything else. You cannot know what a physical thing in the universe is in isolation. A physical thing can only be known by laws that describe not the thing itself, but the object as it is related to and involved with everything else. In this way, we begin to sense that there is something more to the world than what is in the world. The things in the world are not all of the world. There is something beyond the world that makes sense out of the world.

At this level of realization we have arrived at the enchanted world. We recognize that there must be some relationship between the things in the world and the forces that are beyond these physical things. These unknown, non-physical or spiritual things are what make the world enchanted or magical. It is magic in the sense that primitive religion is called magic. There is a recognition that there are forces to the universe other than the visual, oral, tactile, sensory things in the universe. This insight leads to the notion of the world as a created entity.

If the world is something created, something other than the world creates it. The universe stands in relationship of creator and creature. All of these physical objects are creatures; and if there are creatures, there must also be a creator.

GOD: The initial gods are not entities beyond the universe, but part of the universe. The differences between Zeus and Socrates, for example, are quantitative and not qualitative. Socrates lives in Athens and Zeus on Mt. Olympus. Mt. Olympus, a part of the world, is a physical entity, just as Athens is a physical entity. The other differences are quantitative. For example, Socrates is very smart; if he were smarter, he would be divinely smart. Odysseus is very cunning; if he were even more cunning, he would be divinely cunning. Some human beings are capable of making all kinds of disguises or transformations. If someone is extremely talented, e.g., he can turn himself into a bull and from a bull he can turn himself into something else, he would be divinely talented. Gods are human creatures who have talents that are the same as human talents, only more so. To have divine wisdom, divine cunning, or divine strength (like Atlas) is to have a human virtue to an extent beyond a human being. In other words, gods are supermen. Consequently, all of the problems of man in isolation also apply to the gods. Just as there must be something beyond men and objects, so there must be something beyond these gods. There must be gods who are not just more than men. Gods must exist who are qualitatively different from men.

Islam

Rosenzweig argued that the Asian religions grasped the inadequacy of man, the world, and the gods in isolation. Still, they only grasped this insight at the level of recognizing that the things that appear to be real are really nothing at all. For them, the ultimate is nothing. Now, the value of talking about nothing is that it points to something beyond what is, but still the end of this level of reflection is only a nothing. At this level we progress from the mythic god to the concealed god, viz., to the awareness that there is something more than this world, which is totally different. It is an absence, a lack, nothing. However, this nothing, this no-thing, is God. God is nothing material or sensual. Still, this deity creates the world and brings human beings into relationship. Through his act of creation, this God establishes things in relationship through love. In this way *The Star* moves us from the concealed God to the loving God. The religion that rises beyond the Asian religions to this level of insight is Islam.

Rosenzweig's Islam[37] posits man as part of society in which he alone is nothing. This great religion of the Middle Ages has man existing as part of a divine society, the society of the *Muslim*.

The word *Muslim* comes from *SALAM*, which is the same as the Hebrew word *SHALEM*. *SHALEM* means whole, complete, or perfect. In Rosenzweig's Islam, wholeness, completeness and perfection come from being part of this divine community, i.e., this human community that stands in relationship to deity. However, *SALAM* also means submissive. In Islam, the word *SALAM*, unlike the Hebrew word *SHALOM*, has a primary meaning of submission. A Muslim is he who submits to God.

Properly speaking, a Muslim is not a member of a particular religion. Judaism is the name of one religion among many; Christianity is the name of another religion among many. The word *Islam* does not name a religion. Similarly, the word *Muslim* simply means a religious person. In this way the word Islam simply means religion, i.e., *true* religion that worships the *true* God. Here in Rosenzweig's Islam, we first encounter the worship of God as He truly is, which means through a society of people related to God. Islam is the community that is related to God. The community is the primary entity, and the individual gets fulfillment through his participation in this community.

This community of Islam also stands in relationship to the world. The world and the community of human beings are all created entities, and all of them ultimately stand in relationship to a God who is their creator.

The Lack of Freedom

In this Muslim structure, man has no freedom because he is only part of a community. As such, man has neither rights nor freedom, just like the parts of your body. Your parts exist to serve your body and only your body; they have no other function or purpose. They are not entitled to independence. A part that becomes independent is a bad part. If your lung starts doing its thing rather than your thing, you must do something about it. Your lung is not entitled to worry about itself. It is only entitled to serve you well. When it does not serve you well, it is to be corrected. If you cannot correct it, you get rid of it. It has no inherent right to anything, including existence.

Similarly, human beings who exist as parts of communities have no rights, no freedom, and no independence. Their identity is defined solely in terms of the community of which they are part. Just as individuals have no freedom, because they are defined solely within the society, so the society is part of the planet earth, the earth is part of the solar system, the solar system is part of its constellation. Everything is a part of something else. In the end, there is one entity, which is the universe itself, i.e., the universe ruled by God on which everything within that universe has only one choice—to submit or not to submit, to obey or not to obey. However, in either case there is no freedom. This is the bind to which Rosenzweig's dialectic has led us at the end of Book II.

It is the desire for freedom that is the motive that breaks thought out of Part II into the continuation of Rosenzweig's dialectic in Part III. Man has found relationship as disclosed man, but he has lost self-identity. World has found order and existence as a created universe, but it lacks vitality. God is a loving God, but there is no one for God to love, because all of the creatures must do what they do. Thus, God is unfulfilled. He merely exists. The world also exists, but it is not free. Man exists, but he has no self-determination. As we arrive at the end of Part II, we have man without freedom, world without life, and an unredeemed God.

PART III: THE CONFIGURATION

Summary

In Part III, we have the fire within the star that is the eternal life of Judaism, the rays from the star that are the eternal way of Christianity, and what lies beyond both, the star in its totality that is the eternal truth. Eternal truth is the goal of Rosenzweig's *Star*. It is the total picture of reality. It is God, man, and the world unified within their elements[38] as single entities that, through their course, are unified into a single reality that transcends both elements and courses.

Judaism and Christianity

Rosenzweig's Islam grasps reality to as great an extent as it can be grasped by a community that is not redeemed. It is not pagan like the religions of Greece and Asia, whose belief is basically flawed. Both pagan peoples achieve a conception of plastic world, tragic man, and mythic God; but they have no conceptual tools to bring these isolated elements into configuration. Asian religion cannot transcend the isolation, so it retreats into the initial nothing out of which the elements were projected. The Greeks do not retreat, but they have no means to resolve their new negations of an enchanted but isolated world, a secluded man, and a concealed God. In content, Islam succeeds in relating the elements with creation, revelation, and redemption. But it misunderstands all three; and for that reason, its conceptions are inadequate. The creation of Islam's created world has an inadequate form that renders the world only verbally different from the enchanted world; the revelation of Islam's loving God is misinterpreted, so that He is only verbally different from the concealed God; and the redemption of Islam's disclosed man is misunderstood, so that he is only verbally different from the secluded man. Islam's content is correct, but its form is wrong. It cannot transcend its logic and its grammar to the level of prayer that holds the key to entreating the kingdom of God. There the redeemed God loves man as His created image who transforms the created world into soul.[39]

The symbol through which Rosenzweig expressed ultimate reality is the six-pointed star in which God, man, and world are united in a redemption that is brought about through prayer. In this picture

Judaism and Christianity are seen as mirror images of each other. Their characteristics are isomorphically but inversely related to each other. Judaism lies at the core of the star. Judaism is a fire that lives off itself, perpetually turned inward, without need of the unredeemed world of time and space; Christianity stands at the periphery of the star, rays from the fire, perpetually turned outward, drawing the unredeemed world of time and space into itself. Jews are an eternal people, but Christians are not a people; Christians are individuals[40] on an eternal way. Jews are joined by blood community; Christians are joined by a shared mission. Jews stand outside of time; Christians master time by transforming the present into an epoch that marks a transition from its eternal beginning in Christ to its eternal end in the kingdom. In that both the Jewish people and the Christian way are eternal, each encompasses within itself all possibilities that are expressed as contradictions.

(1) In Judaism, God is both king and father, an omnipotent, just creator on one hand and a loving, merciful creator on the other hand. In Christianity, He is father and son. The father preserves God's remoteness, while the son paganizes God. God becomes man so that pagans can enter the kingdom.

(2) In Judaism, man is both patriarch and messiah, a soul loved by God on one hand and a lover who loves his neighbor on the other hand. In Christianity, man follows the divergent paths of priest and saint. The priest is a vessel of revelation in the image of God who conceals within himself Dostoyevsky's Grand Inquisitor; the saint is a vehicle of redemption, guided by God who conceals within himself heretical caprice.

(3) In Judaism, the world is both this-world and the world-to-come. It has the existence of a creature longing backward for creation on one hand and a life that grows forward towards the kingdom on the other hand. In Christianity, the world is on one hand a state and on the other hand a church.

(4) Judaism has the liturgical year of a holy people; Christianity has the liturgical year of a sanctified soul, i.e., a redeemed world, effected by individuals who only superficially are in community. Both the Jewish Sabbath and the Christian Sunday are occasions for listening in community. The Sabbath at the end of the week commemorates the redemption of an already redeemed (i.e., united) community. Sunday at the beginning of the week commemorates creation, since Christians are individuals not yet in community and hence not yet redeemed. Jews have festivals commemorating revelation, whose expression is the communal meal of a truly united people. Christians

have festivals commemorating revelation. whose expression is the communal meal of individuals not yet united as a people. Pesach and Christmas note the beginning of the beginning of revelation. Shavuot and Easter mark its beginning: Sukkot and Pentacost recall its completion, while pointing to the kingdom.

This isomorphism breaks down at the Days of Awe, which express the Jewish people's redemption through communal prayer. Christianity has no counterpart because it is not yet redeemed. Through baptism Christianity has the power to redeem individuals, but these individuals remain individuals; only at the end of the way will they form a real community. Since Christians are not yet a community, the sense of unity, expressed through prayer as we and ye, must be prepared for and generated through the use of art. On Sunday, church architecture serves this purpose; and on the religious festivals, this is the role of music. Christianity only approaches redemption in its secular festivals of the yet-to-be-redeemed world for which poetry prepares the way and dance parallels Judaism's communal prayer.

Explanation

Each part of *The Star* has a religion that captures the insight of the dialectic of that level. We moved from Greek to Asian religion in Book I, advanced to Islam in Book II, and now in Book III we move to Judaism and Christianity. Note that the conclusion lies beyond any particular religion. Judaism and Christianity are religions in so far as religious insight has developed. The conclusion of Book III is beyond any particular religion. This claim is not meant to put down Judaism, for the conclusion is the messianic age, which is the fulfillment of history. This end is a quite traditional Jewish belief. Even if we judge Judaism to be the best of religions, Judaism ends with the coming of the messiah. the messianic age ends this world; everything that is true of this world ends at the messianic age.

The Messianic Age

Jewish law (*HALACHAH*) relates the following about the messianic age: The temple will be rebuilt; the Davidic Monarchy will be reestablished; the dead will be resurrected; and you should not talk about any of it. At least the last claim has been ignored for 2,000 years. Jews engaged in considerable speculation about the messianic age inspite of the rabbis' clear prohibition. They believed that when it comes, it will come. You should think about this world and not worry about that world outside of what you are told.

There are all kinds of views in non-halachic rabbinic literature about what the end will be. One view, probably the dominant one, can be explained by the following analogy.

Different universes have different natural law. The law of gravity holds in this universe, but it does not hold in other universes. Other universes can have other laws. Think of an arithmetic system in a single base as a universe. 1+1=2 in a base 10 system, but in a base 2 system 1+1=10. Both equations are true, but they are true in different universes. They are both absolutely true, but they are absolutely true relative to their respective universes. Similarly, the laws of morality and of nature are absolutely true for this sensible universe. For example, the law of gravity is an absolute truth for this universe, but only for this universe. Similarly, "Thou shalt not murder" is an absolute moral law for this universe, but different universes may have different laws. Different universes have different natural and moral laws. This last point becomes very important in much modern theology, especially in that of Friedrich Wilhelm Nietzsche (1844-1900).

A new man who introduces a new age brings with him a new morality. The new morality is not moral in the old universe, but the new man is not part of the old universe; he is part of the new universe. Similarly, the Frankist movement saw itself to be entering the messianic age, and consequently it practised a different morality. From the view point of this universe, its morality is immoral; but that is only this universe's viewpoint. Instead of the law of gravity of this universe, in the new one the rule might be that if you drop something it will rise. Similarly, in another universe to love your neighbor could be bad and to kill people could be good. The rules of this universe need not apply to another universe. As the laws of nature and morality are true only of this universe, so Judaism, defined as the system of Torah, is true for this universe; but it need not apply to any other universe.

Those who speculate about the messianic universe vary a great deal on how different that world will be from this one. Some make it only a little different, and others suggest great variances. There are certain obvious alterations. For example, presumably people will not die there. This is not a little difference. Assume that you will not die. Do you continue to age? What kind of world is it where there is no way to die but the aging process goes on without ever ending? It is a nightmare, and not a pleasant prospect. Then let us assume that the aging process also ceases. Now we have introduced enormous changes that make the messianic universe radically different from our own.

Consider a second example. It is a given that the temple will be rebuilt. Will there be animal sacrifices in the messianic age? If there is no death, then how do you carry out animal sacrifices? Note, the slightest change in a system has consequences that require enormous changes.

Whether or not there is Judaism in the messianic age, it will not be the same Judaism. There is no way that a messianic Judaism could be the same as the Judaism of this world.

The Unity at the End

How can God be free? Rosenzweig's answer was, God is free only when everything has become God. In the end these three things—God, man, and world—become the same thing. The world becomes fulfilled when it becomes a living world. Man strives to become God, and God is only redeemed when the world becomes alive and man becomes God. Then God, man, and world are a single thing. This unity is the end of the universe, the goal towards which the dialectic of the universe moves.

A hidden assumption in this description of the end of days is that, given a variety of values, there is ultimately a best one. Contrary to this assumption, it is possible that upon final analysis Rosenzweig might claim that there are multiple choices, all of which are equally valuable.

Liturgy

Remember that at each stage of the dialectic you pass on to a higher language. The language of philosophy and science was useful only at the level of the elements. Once we moved to the level of things in relationship, we used the language of poetry. Now, at the next level, our final stage, even poetry ceases to be adequate.

The end of the world cannot be dealt with in terms of poetry, because the end has not yet happened. If the elements are the past and the course is the present (the world we are in now), the configuration is the future. The future goes beyond what even the poet knows. Poets are still tied to the world they perceive. The scientist has to deal with the dead past. Poets can work with the living present, but they know nothing of the future.

Those who know the future are the prophets. Their language is the language of liturgy. Consequently, the language that Rosenzweig used to talk about the future is liturgical language. The logic of the third part consists of the analysis of liturgy.[41]

Look again at the outline of Part III.[42] Notice the parallelism between Judaism and Christianity form the titles of the paragraphs.[43] In the book on Judaism, Rosenzweig spoke about the rays—the eternal way; and in the final book he discussed the star—the eternal truth. Note the parallelism of "the promise of eternity," "eternal realization," and "eternity of truth." Remember that "eternal people—the Jewish fate" parallels "the way through time—Christianity," which leads to "truth—cosmology." Again, this parallelism runs throughout Part III. The language that *The Star* uses in all of these cases is built around festivals. Its analysis of Judaism concentrates on the High Holy Days and The Three Pilgrim Festivals.

Corresponding to the Jewish festivals in Christianity is the Christian liturgical year. When *The Star* deals with the promise of the future, the concentration focuses on the meal in Judaism. For Rosenzweig, the meal was the ultimate Jewish religious expression. In the case of Christianity, the counterpart to the meal is church architecture. As the meal becomes the ultimate expression of Jewish life, the architectural structure of the church becomes the ultimate expression of Christianity.

Rosenzweig did not tell us why he made the meal so central to Judaism, but I can construct an argument to explain it. The high point of the rabbinic worship service is the *AMIDAH*, which the traditional rabbis intended to function as a substitute for the sacrifices in the temple service. The rabbinic prayer service contains everything that was in the temple sacrificial service except for the meal, because after the destruction of the temple there could no longer be sacrifices. There is a sense in which it could be said that in exile Jews eat air instead of doves, bullocks, and the like. Hence, given the centrality of the *AMIDAH*, the traditional worship service becomes a kind of meal, albeit a substitute meal. The only exception is at the Passover seder, when the ritual leads up to and away from a real meal. Consequently, it can be argued that the meal is the liturgical center of every Jewish worship service. I would speculate that Rosenzweig arrived at his conclusion through a similar kind of analysis.

As the meal in Judaism becomes the focal point, so in Christianity the focal point is the environment. The most important thing that you notice in a Christian worship service is the church building; it is the ultimate expression of the worship service. This may be the reason why Rosenzweig reached this conclusion about Christianity.

Implied in his judgments about the focal points of Judaism and Christianity are most of what Rosenzweig had to say about these two religions. Let us now spell out a few of these implications.

Judaism and Christianity

In Rosenzweig's primary imagery, out of the fire (= Judaism) come rays (=Christianity) into the darkness (=the pagan, unredeemed world). Note that his metaphor is taken from geometry. The business of the universe is to become God. Light is God. Besides God (=light) there is nothing but darkness. The movement of the universe consists of light that reaches out and spreads into the darkness until the darkness becomes full of light.

On this image, the Jews are an eternal core that are not subject to the universal movement of world history. They are not in history, i.e., the Jewish life cycle has nothing to do with history. The Jews continuously do the same thing over and over again without change. Jewish life moves from Rosh Hashana and Yom Kippur to Sukkot, Pesach, Shavuot and back again to Rosh Hashana. The Jewish year is a cycle, but it contains no events, nothing new ever happens. Similarly, the week moves to the Sabbath, and every Sabbath is the same. It is in this sense that the Jews are outside of time. They stand within a cycle, but they are not subject to time. Nothing new has happened to the Jew as a Jew since Sinai.

It must be remembered that Rosenzweig was speaking about the people, and not about individuals. Jews are discussed only as part of the Jewish people. Jews are Jews by birth. Nothing new happens even when they become Jews. The only thing that Jews as Jews can do is choose to observe not to observe the law (*HALACHAH*); but they must observe, for as Jews they have no free will.

The only people who act in history are the Christians. Being a Jew is not determined by the Jews, but by the community.[44] A Christian has to choose to be a Christian; no one can be born a Christian; and what a Christian does is make other people Christians. If one asks, what does a Jew do? The answer is, he observes Passover, Shavuot, and the other Holy Days. Similarly, what does a Christian do? He makes other people Christians. The business of the Christian is to make Christians.

If you ask, from where does the life of the Christian come? The answer is from Judaism. Judaism is the fire that gives light to the Christian as he spreads through history, turning pagans into Christians. At the level of the configuration, there are three entities in the universe—Jews, Christians, and pagans. It is the job of the Jew to give the Christian light to change the pagan into a Christian. Everything at the core of Christianity is Jewish; Christianity is totally dominated by what is Jewish. Almost every individual admired within Christianity is a Jew. Most of the people portrayed in art on the walls and windows of churches are Jews. There is no life in Christianity other than the light that comes from the Jew.

The reason why the meal becomes the ultimate expression in Judaism is that the meal is something very intimate. It is not something that can be shared with strangers; it is a family thing. Intercourse and eating are the two most intimate acts.[45]

In order to eat together, you must already be in community. In contrast, the church building is something that always reaches out to strangers. It says to the pagans outside, "This is a nice place, come in." Hence, the importance of the meal in Judaism is part of what Rosenzweig meant when he said that Judaism is totally self-enclosed.

The Jew and History

We can now explain how Rosenzweig' *Star* is a polemic against Christian efforts to convert Jews. Remember, Rosenzweig's friends sought his conversion to Christianity, believing that to become Christian is part of the ultimate development of history. Based on Hegel's dialectic, they could argue that Christianity is the most recent stage of history, and Judaism is a prior phase. His friends felt that one ought to identify with history at the most progressive level. Rosenzweig's response to this argument is that Judaism is not within history; Judaism already is where Christianity is striving to get. The advantage that Jews have over Christians is that they already are at the end; the advantage that Christians have over Jews is that they live in the world. Individual Jews, of course, are subject to the world; but Judaism is not. A Jew as a Jew is a participant in Judaism; hence the Jew as a Jew is not subject to the world. This then is the main polemical point of Rosenzweig's work—a proper understanding of the universe entails the conviction that a Jew ought not to become a Christian.

Rosenzweig's analysis of the relationship between Judaism and history entails the fact that he was not a Zionist, because Zionism's central theme is that Jews should reenter history.[46] Although he did not discuss this question overtly in *The Star*, Rosenzweig's objection to Zionism is clear. He would argue in this way: Why should a Jew enter the imperfections of history when he already is beyond history? Within the intimate circle of Judaism, the three elements have already achieved their unity.

How does it happen that God and the world become one? Rosenzweig said that it happens through history, and that this evolving unity is precisely the goal of history. More precisely, according to Rosenzweig, there was a Jew at one time in history named Paul, and he had his light. What Jews were doing all the time were sharing their light with each other. The fire kept going on, but there was no, so to speak, combustion. Paul started the combustion. He transformed himself into a gentile who had light. he ceased to be a Jew; He moved outside the inner core of the Jewish people and became the first ray. The process of having rays from the fire break out of the inner circle began with Paul. What Paul did was turn to an other gentile and set him afire with the divine light. In other words, the first gentile with light lights up another gentile.

To which gentile did Paul turn? To whomever was around. The first Christian turned to any gentile who was nearby. Similarly, every new Christian also turns to whomever happens to be around and transforms the chance neighbor into a fellow Christian. In this way, a chain reaction was set off of Christians turning pagans into Christians that will continue until all of the pagans will have become Christians.

In the end of days, there will no longer be pagans. However, this mission is exclusively the business of Christians and not of Jews. Hence, Christians who go around converting people are doing the right thing. At the same time, they should know that they should not try to convert Jews. In fact, if all Jews would be converted, that would bring about the end of Christianity; for, if all of the fire were transformed into rays of light, there would be no more fire; and then there would be no more light. Christian missionaries who spread their message to Jews endanger the universe. If they were successful, darkness and paganism would be victorious over the light of God.

Some Rosenzweig scholars debate this point: whether Judaism is superior the Christianity, Christianity is superior to Judaism, or they are co-equal. The question the be asked is: What does everyone become in the end—Jews, Christians, or something else? Rosenzweig did not tell us. Judaism could never fully reach redemption without Christianity, but neither could Christianity be redeemed without Judaism. I suspect that the answer is, "Something else." Judaism (Book I) and Christianity (Book II) are not ultimate, but penultimate. They are the final stage before the fulfillment (Book III), which transcends what we can know.

Dangers to the Kingdom

While Judaism is at the core of redemption and Christianity is on the way, neither grasps the whole of reality. Since we have not as yet reached the end of days, we cannot state the whole truth. We can only point out what leads to it and what inhibits it. Rosenzweig's concluding remarks on Judaism and Christianity turn to the dangers of both that can inhibit reaching the kingdom. This conclusion shows that for Rosenzweig there is nothing inevitable about his picture of a progressively-improving universe.

In Judaism's case, there are dangers that threaten individual Jews. They may deny, disdain, or mortify the world.[47] Since the Jewish people are already redeemed, these dangers are no threat to Judaism as such.

The real fear resides in Christianity, whose redeemed individuals remain individuals; so that in their fall they may hinder the kingdom. Christianity's God can deteriorate into a deification of spirit, rather than be a spiritualization of God; then, for the sake of spirit, God is forgotten. Christianity's man can deteriorate into a deification of man and a humanization of God, where God is again forsaken for the sake of the world. Rosenzweig had the Eastern Church in mind with the first danger, the Protestant Northern Church with the second, and the Roman Catholic southern Church with the third.

Finally, Rosenzweig noted that Christian anti-Semitism is an ever-present danger that can hinder the Christian mission of entreating the kingdom of God. The danger arises when the unredeemed Christian sees the redeemed Jew who, as redeemed, shames the Christian, whose shame produces a self-hatred that he turns against the Jew. The danger is that in closing himself to the Jew, the Christian shuts off his source of light, viz., the Jewish people. Then he can only see what is illuminated, viz., the secular world upon which Christianity shines; but without a source of light, the illumination fades. In other words, the danger of Christian anti-Semitism is that it may return the world to a pre-pagan darkness. A Christian mission to the Jews and Christian anti-Semitism have the same consequences.

It would be reading too much into Rosenzweig's words to suggest that this concluding warning about anti-Semitism is a premonition of the darkness that would shortly envelop his beloved Germany. His words do suggest a framework into which the Holocaust could fit into his schema. The Holocaust could not be, as some contemporary Jewish thinkers have debated,[48] an epoch-making event for the Jew. Such an event marks a turn in the course of history. As a redeemed people, they have nowhere to turn. However, the Holocaust could be an epoch-making event for the Christian.

Rosenzweig's picture of the universe is not a simplistic doctrine of inevitable progress. His redeemed Christian is not fully redeemed.

He is not a Jew. What separates him from the Jews is that he still contains within himself the pagan. In Rosenzweig's words, within each Christian there is an unresolved strife between a "Siegfried" and that Jew who is "the man of the cross."

> A Siegfried who, depending on the nation he comes from may be blond and blue-eyed, wrestles again and again with this stranger who resists the continued attempts to assimilate him to that nation's own idealization.[49]

The more mature Martin Buber spoke of an "eclipse of God,[50] whereas the youthful Rosenzweig of *The Star* (in 1919) seemed assured that the man of the cross would conquer Siegfried. The coming Holocaust might have shattered Rosenzweig's optimism, but in itself it does not alter his picture of reality.[51] Prayer affects redemption; but while it may be hindered, it cannot be rushed. Buber judged the movement from I-Thou to I-It to I-Thou to be a spiral in which each successive realization of the world as spirit leads to another successive corruption of the world as objects.[52] Each extreme swing leads to a greater extreme in the opposite direction. Buber's eclipse of God parallels Rosenzweig's danger of the victory of Siegfried; but at least on Buber's terms, Siegfried's victory cannot be total. The same may be true for Rosenzweig. He told us that there is a proper time for redemption, which means that there is God's time for it. Fanatics (those who try to hasten the kingdom), and sinners (those who try to prevent the kingdom), may hinder its coming, but perhaps they cannot prevent it. In the immediate future, there is at least the expectation that the on the cross can return, and the eclipse will pass for now. The Holocaust is no end to history; it is in its most pessimistic interpretation, only an event in history; and most hopefully, it is the beginning of an epoch-making turn in the direction of Christian redemption.

APPENDIX A
Diagram of Rosenzweig's Star

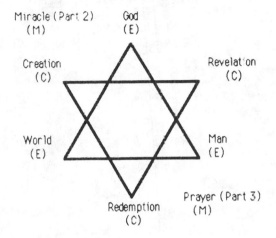

Note:

E = element (Part I)

C = course (Part II)

M = Mediation*

*   miracle mediates creation and revelation
prayer mediates revelation and redemption
? mediates redemption and creation

APPENDIX B
Diagram of Rosenzweig's Dialectic

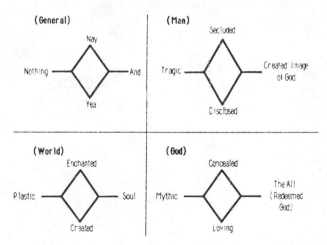

APPENDIX C

List of Rosenzweig's Logical Signs

(Part I, Book 1)

y=x	grammatical subject is predicative. Note that "is" is intransitive.
y=x	nay is yea
y=	freedom
A	God, divine power
A=	God, divine freedom
=A	God, divine essence

(Part I, Book 2)

=A	world-spirit, logos
B	individuality, peculiarity, character, plenitude, sensate world
B=A	world content is world form, particular is universal, activity is passivity, world is God

(Part I, Book 3)

B=	free will, ephemerality (man's permanent essence)
B=B	predicates about the self, self is self, Ding An Sich, one's own will, self, personality, multiplicity of sensuality, datum

(Part II, Book 1)

A=A	Ich An Sich, god as object of volition, absolute spirit
B=B	Dind An Sich, one's one will
A(=B)	world as emanated from God
A(=A)	God as source of emanation of world
A=A, A=B, B=B	idealist movement from Ich An Sich to Ding An Sich, generation
B=B, B=A, A=A	idealist movement from Ding An Sich to Ich An Sich, submission
B=A	principle of universal legislation
A=A	God as objection of volition

APPENDIX D

List of Rosenzweig's Grammatical Symbols (Part II)

Root Word	*Root Sentence*
	(Book 1)
Thus	he is good
good	adjective-attribute
a, the	article, substantive
	(Book 2)
I, I however	nominative: asserts subjectivity
I, not otherwise	accusative: asserts objectivity
I, not otherwise than everything	dative: unites subjectivity and objectivity
	(Book 3)
Thou	Where art Thou
	Here I am
	Love me, I the Lord
	I am thine, I have sinned
	Thou art mine
we, ye	Praise ye, thank ye,
	let us thank, thank God

APPENDIX E

List of Rosenzweig's Liturgical Expressions

Expression	*Symbol*	*Liturgy: Jewish*	*Liturgy: Christian Art Form*
listening	creation	Sabbath	Sunday—architecture
meal	revelation	pilgrim festivals	religious festivals—music
prayer (kneeling, greeting)	redemption	Days of Awe	secular festivals—poetry, dance

APPENDIX F

Detailed List of Paragraph Topics in The Star

Part I: The Elements or the Ever-Enduring Proto-Cosmos

Book 1	Book 2	Book 3
Introduction		
1. Possibility of Cognition of the All		
God,	World,	Man,
His being—Metaphysics	Its Meaning—Metalogic	His Self—Metaethics
Negative Theology	Negative Cosmology	Negative Psychology
Divine Nature	World Order	Human Idiosyncracy
Divine Freedom	World Plenitude	Human Volition
Vitality of the Gods	Reality of the World	Independence of Man
Olympus of Mythology	Plastic Cosmos	Heroic Ethos
Asia: Unmythical God	Asia: Nonplastic World	Asia: Nontragic Man
		Tragic Hero
	Esthetic 1st Principle: Inner Form	Esthetic 1st Principle: Content
Twilight of the Gods	Slumber of the World	Solitary Man

2. Death
3. Philosophy of the All
4. Man
5. World
6. God
7. Math & Symbols
8.
9.
10.

Transition: Retrospect: Chaos of the Elements
Prospect: Cosmic Day of the Lord

Part II: The Course or the Always-Renewed Cosmos

Book 1	Book 2	Book 3
Introduction		
1. The Possibility of Experiencing Miracle		
2. Concerning Belief		
3. Theology of Miracle		
Creation—Ever-Enduring	Revelation—Ever-Renewed	Redemption—Eternal
Base of Things	Birth of Soul	Future of Kingdom
Creator	Revealer	Act of Love
Islam: Religion of Intellect	Islam: Religion of Mankind	Islam: Religion of Obligation

NOTES

1. See chapter 2.

2. As a youth Rosenzweig studied Bible from Zunz's German translation.

3. Cf. his letter of July 9, 1916 (Nahum N. Glatzer, *Franz Rosenzweig: His Life & Thought.* New York: Schocken, 1961. Pp. 37-39) with his letters of this period (Ibid., pp. 73-76).

4. Henceforth referred to as *"The Star."*

5. See chapter 3.

6. Ibid., p. 286.

7. Letter to Richard Koch, September 2, 1928. Ibid., p. 164.

8. Pat I, Introduction.

9. See Appendix A at the end of this chapter.

10. Rosenzweig also stated that miracles "mediate," (i.e., link), creation and revelation, while prayer mediates revelation and redemption. Minimally, these two mediations suggest a third between redemption and creation, which in turn suggests three points which can be linked by three other points to form a larger, encompassing six-pointed star. These are inferences beyond anything that Rosenzweig explicitly stated.

What is at stake here is the following: Part I presents a picture of the elements; Part II of the course; and Part III gives the star; i.e., the configuration formed by connecting the six points of elements and their course. As is explained below, what is pictured in Part I is that from which present reality (in Rosenzweig's terms, "the Cosmos") comes to be, and Part III is that towards which present reality is directed. (Rosenzweig called the former "the Proto-Cosmos" and the latter "the Hyper-Cosmos.") Rosenzweig's cosmos is reality in flux, from which we can picture the origin and the purpose of the flux. But the origin need not be an ultimate origin, and the purpose need not be an ultimate purpose. What is our origin may be the conclusion of a prior flux, and what is our purpose may in turn become the origin of another reality. In other words, our universe may be one of a series of universes, and not the only universe; but such a question cannot be settled from within a cosmos. Hence, Rosenzweig does not discuss the issue. Yet, his discussion of miracles and prayer suggests a certain possibility beyond what Rosenzweig would call the limits of knowledge.

11. See Appendix F at the end of this chapter.

12. See Appendix B at the end of this chapter.

13. *The Star* I, Introduction.

14. That P is not Q.

15. That P is non-Q.

16. I.e., each conjoining of the yea and the nay.

17. Franz Rosenzweig, *The Star of Redemption*. Translated into English by William W. Hallo. Boston; Beacon Press, 1964. P. 3. All subsequent quotations from *The Star* are taken from this translation.

18. Ibid., 424.

19. Ibid., 3-4.

20. Remember that Buber's starting point was that there are no things; there are only relations. (See chapter 10) In terms of Rosenzweig's structure, Buber began at the final negation of Book I that leads into Book II.

21. What Rosenzweig called a negation of the "aught."

22. See Appendix C at the end of this chapter.

23. Finitude is what Rosenzweig calls "ephemerality."

24. See Appendix C at the end of this chapter.

25. Rosenzweig's term for cosmology.

26. Rosenzweig considered poetry to be the supreme art, and the rules to which poetry is subject are the rules of grammar. His ideal poet is Goethe.

27. Note that of the three courses only redemption is called eternal; for when it comes, time will end. It is the expectation of redemption that is not eternal but like creation and revelation, is endless.

28. "The Great Hallel" that is recited on the festivals.

29. Cf. chapter 10. According to Buber, the theophany at Sinai consists solely of God's presence; it does not include any content. In other words, the content of the Torah was not given in the theophany;

rather, the content is Israel's response to God's presence.

30. See Appendix D at the end of this chapter.

31. Gen. 1:31.

32. Exod. 20:2 and Deut 5:6.

33. Gen. 3:8.

34. Deut. 6:5.

35. Lev. 19:18.

36. Again, this was Buber's starting point. See chapter 10.

37. Do not take Rosenzweig's Islam to be real Islam. We are not talking about any historical religions. There is a difference between Rosenzweig's Asian and Greek religions and the Asian and Greek religions. Similarly, we are discussing Rosenzweig's understanding of Islam. We are not summarizing Islam. In those cases where Rosenzweig said something about any religion (e.g. Islam) that we know historically not the be true, we could say that Rosenzweig did not understand the religion; but that judgment is not as obvious as it might appear to be. The problem will become apparent when we turn to his discussion of Judaism and Christianity. What he said about these religions also does not always agree with historical truth. Some of his claims are sufficiently strange that we could say that his Judaism and Christianity are no more recognizably Judaism and Christianity than are his Asian and Greek religions and Islam what they seem to be. In the case of Judaism and Christianity, though, he ought to know what he is talking about.

This problem suggests that his views about religions are not attributable simply to a lack of information. In fact, what he is doing is presenting a transformation of these religions. Whatever his reasons for this transformation, it is not because he was ignorant of their histories.

38. Humans in man and objects in the world.

39. In this way, Rosenzweig restated the prophecy given to the king in Judah Halevi's *KHUZARI* who has proper belief but, before conversion, lacks proper action. For Rosenzweig the only proper action is prayer. Halevi believed that only the Jew knows how to pray for redemption. In his words, the messiah will be a Jew and only Jews can prophesy. Rosenzweig extended this claim to the Christians as well.

40. Hence they are "rays" and not a ray.

41. See Appendix E.

42. Appendix F.

43. Just as there is a correspondence between all of the books of the whole work, so within each book every paragraph has a corresponding paragraph in each section of each book.

44. Your mother makes you a Jew; whether you like it or not, you are still a Jew.

45. Eating may be even more intimate than intercourse. It is only social taboo that makes six seem to be more intimate. Eating with someone may be more personal.

46. See chapter 6.

47. The very fact that Rosenzweig notes this as a danger indicates that whatever it means for the Jewish people as a people to be outside of history, it does not mean that Jews are outside of history.

48. See chapter 13.

49. *The Star* III, 1, p. 329.

50. See chapter 10.

51. That Rosenzweig had no simplistic belief that the kingdom of God was at hand is apparent in the following quotation from a note that he wrote to a poem by Judah Halevi entitled, "The True and the False Messiah":

> Hermann Cohen once said to me—he was over seventy at the time: "I am still hoping to see the dawn of the messianic era." What Cohen, who believed in the false Messiah of the nineteenth century, meant by that was the conversion of Christians to the "pure monotheism" of his Judaism, a conversion which he thought the liberal Protestant theology of his day was initiating. I was startled by the vigor of his belief that it would happen "speedily in our days," and did not dare tell him that I did not think these indications were true signs. All I said was that I did not believe I should live to see it. At that he asked: "But when do you think it will be?" I did not have the heart not to mention any date at all, and so I answered: "Perhaps in hundreds of years." But he understood me to say: "Perhaps in a hundred years," and cried: "Oh, please say in fifty!"

Judah Ha-Levi, p. 239; Glatzer, p. 351.

52. See chapter 10.

KEY NAMES

amyotrophic lateral sclerosis, Asian religion, Christianity, Rene Descartes, Hans and Rudolf Ehrenberg, Genesis, Edith Hahn, Georg Wilhelm Friedrich Hegel, Heraclitus, Islam, Judaism, Immanuel Kant, Moses Maimonides, Friedrich Wilhelm Nietzsche, Nehemiah A. Nobel, Parmenides, Psalms, Eugen Rosenstock, The Song of Song, *The Star of Redemption*.

KEY TERMS

Christian/Jew/Pagan, configuration, cosmos (hyper- & proto-), course creation, death/life, dialectic, element, freedom, God (concealed, loving, mythical, & physics), nothing/being, redemption, revelation, soul, world (created, enchanted, plastic).

KEY QUESTIONS

1. Describe the major events in Rosenzweig's discovery of his Jewish identity. What kind of education did he have? What happened to Rosenzweig on the eve of Yom Kippur, October 11, 1913? What did he discover in 1918 in Rembertow, Poland? What did he do after he was released from the army? How did Rosenzweig lead a "spiritual" existence in the last six years of his life?

2. Discuss the influences on Rosenzweig's *The Star of Redemption*. In what sense can he be said to have been a highly original author?

3. What are the main polemical and philosophical purposes of *The Star*?

4. How and why do Rosenzweig's and Hegel's philosophies differ? Describe Rosenzweig's dialectic. How does it differ from Hegel's? With what does each main book of *The Star* begin and end? How does each stage logically develop out of the preceeding stage in Rosenzweig's argument?

5. Outline Rosenzweig's dialectic with each of the three ele-

ments. Why does science provide the tools for understanding the elements of reality but not for anything else? Why is art appropriate for grasping the course of reality but not for what is beyond the course? Why is liturgy the means through which the configuration of reality can be comprehended?

6. What assumptions does Rosenzweig make about the basic structure of reality and what impact do these assumptions have on his philosophy?

7. According to Rosenzweig what are the values and the limitations of the different world religions—Greek, polytheism, Buddhism, Confucianism, Islam, Judaism and Christianity? Discuss the role of the meal in Judaism and architecture in Christianity. Why is there no Christian counterpart to the Days of Awe? What role do the arts play in Christianity? What role does the meal play in Judaism?

8. Would you say that Rosenzweig considers Judaism to be equal, superior, or inferior to Christianity? Give reasons for your judgment. Why are Christians not redeemed? Why are Jews not in history? What would Rosenzweig think of Zionism and the state of Israel?

9. What is the goal of history and how is it achieved? What could prevent the anticipated fulfillment at the end of days? According to Rosenzweig, why should Christians missionize everyone but Jews? Why should Jews be Jews? Why would a Christian be anti-Semitic? Why is anti-Semitism important for the world in general and not just for Jews?

10. Compare and contrast Rosenzweig and Buber on their respective views on the end of days.

RECOMMENDED READINGS

General

Robert M. Seltzer, *Jewish People, Jewish Thought: The Jewish Experience in History*. New York: Macmillan, 1980. Chpt. 16, "The Emergence of Jewish Existentialism," pp. 736-742.
Eugene R. Borowitz, *Choice in Modern Jewish Thought: A Partisan Guide*. New York: Behrman House, 1983. Chpt. 6.

Primary

Eugene Rosenstock-Huessy, and Franz Rosenzweig, *Judaism Despite*

Christianity. New York: Schocken, 1969.

Franz Rosenzweig, *Das Buechlein vom Gesunden und Kranken Menschenverstand*. Translated into English by N. N. Glatzer in *Understanding the Sick and the Healthy: A View of the World, Man, and God*. New York: Noonday Press, 1953.

——*Kleinere Schriften*. Berlin: Schocken, 1937.

——*Franz Rosenzweig: Der Mensch und Sein Werk, Gesamelte Schriften*. The Hague: Martinus Nijhoff, 1976-1979.

——*NAHARAYIM*. Jerusalem: Bialik Institute, 1977.

——*On Jewish Learning*. Edited by Nahum N. Glatzer. New York: Schocken, 1955.

——*Der Stern der Erlösung*. Frankfurt a.M.: J. Kauffmann, 1921.

——*The Star of Redemption*. Translated into English by William W. Hallo. Boston: Beacon Press, 1971.

——*KOKHAV HA-GEULAH*. Translated into Hebrew by Yehoshua Amir. Jerusalem: Bialik Institute, 1970.

Secondary

Bernhard Casper, *Das Dialogishe Denken: Eine Untersuchung der Religionsphilosophischen Bedeutung Franz Rosenzweigs, Ferdinand Ebners und Martin Bubers*. Freiburg: Herder Verlag, 1967.

Else Freund, *Die Existenzphilosophie Franz Rosenzweigs*. Leipzig: Meiner, 1933.

Nahum Glatzer, *Franz Rosenzeig: His Life and Thought*. Philadelphia: Jewish Publication Society of America, 1953.

Hermann-Josef Heckelei, *Erfahrung und Denken: Franz Rosenzweigs Theologish-Philosophischer Entwurf eines 'Neuen Denkens'*. Bad Honnef: Bock und Herchen, 1980.

Reinhold Mayer, *Franz Rosenzweig Eine Philosophe der dialogischen Erfahrung*. Munich: Kaiser, 1973.

Else Rahel-Freud, *Franz Rosenzweig's Philosophy of Existence: An Analysis of The Star of Redemption*. The Hague: Martinus Nijhoff, 1979.

Richard Schaeffler, Bernhard Kasper, Shemaryahu Talmon and Yehoshua Amir, *Offenbarung im Denken Franz Rosenzweigs*. Essen: Ludgerus, 1979.

Jacob Tewes, *Zum Existenzbegriff Franz Rosenzweigs* Meisenheim a. Glan: Anto Hain, 1970.

12

MORDECAI KAPLAN

Mordecai Kaplan (1881-1984) is commonly recognized as a major figure in Jewish thought who made a major contribution to what American Judaism became after World War II, but continued interest in Kaplan was justified only as a phenomenon in modern Jewish intellectual history. However, the degree of interest that contemporary Jewish college students have exhibited in the writings of Kaplan and in the recently formed Reconstructionist Rabbinical College suggest that this view underestimates Kaplan's importance. The thought of Kaplan is as vital a source for the thought of American Jews today as it was in the 1930s and 40s.

While Kaplan has written many books, none has had the influence and none is as important as his *Judaism as a Civilization*,[1] published in 1934. In this work, Kaplan stated his then unique understanding of what it means to be a Jew and the people Israel, and he spelled out the implications of that thought with a breadth unequaled in any of his subsequent monographs. In later studies, he elucidated the multiple implications of his basic conception and, in some cases, modified his claims. Still, Kaplan's fundamental understanding of Judaism never changed. Hence, to focus on *Judaism as a Civilization* is to focus, through a single work, on Kaplan's total philosophy of Judaism.

THE PROBLEM

Kaplan attempted to isolate factors that tend to disintegrate and to conserve the Jewish people. Disintegrating factors must either be overcome or diminished in a proposed model for future Jewish civilization. Conversely, conserving factors must be perpetuated or enhanced in any acceptable reconstruction of Jewry. Kaplan stated that the factors of disintegration in contemporary Judaism fall under three general categories of modern beliefs in the Western world. First, there is what Kaplan called the modern political order, which is some form of democratic nationalism. At the level of theory, this political doctrine challenges the Jew's belief in being a chosen people. It claims that nations should be based on geographic continuity over and against any other criteria, including religious or cultural groupings. Practically, this doctrine militates against the Jew's prohibition against mixed marriages, commitment to the primacy of the law of the Torah, and continued obedience to autonomous Jewish civil ordinances. Furthermore, democratic nationalism seems to be in conflict with the Jew's aspirations to create and preserve a distinct Jewish political state and with the apparent need for separate institutions of education.

Second is what Kaplan called the modern economic order that can be identified with some form of capitalism. Kaplan argued that this economic order threatens the Jew's belief in the traditional system of other-worldly salvation. Class mobility has the consequence that an individual must dedicate a greater amount of time and energy to an occupation than generally would be the case in a static class society such as feudalism. The more time and energy given to economic concerns, the less is available for other pursuits, including most of the activities upon which Judaism has traditionally placed value. Furthermore, capitalism implicitly contains judgments about the sorts of accomplishments that are valuable for human existence, all of which are independent of the kinds of values that can be derived from a life committed to observing *MITZVOT*. Kaplan argued that the traditional Jewish value system was tied to other-worldly salvation, whereas capitalism implies a value system that threatens Judaism in the sense that the achievement of the new values is entirely independent of participation in the life of the Jewish people. Kaplan also argued that capitalism, in effect, makes class identity a more basic grouping than religious or cultural identity. Finally, he noted that in a capitalist world there is a high economic cost for asserting Jewish identity, and this cost militates against that identity.

Third is what Kaplan called modern ideology, which is scientific humanism. Kaplan subdivided the category of modern conceptual commitment into beliefs about what is true, what is good, and what is beautiful. He argued that modern scientific thinking produced biblical criticism, which in turn raised doubts about any acceptance of the Torah on traditional terms. For him the real conflict of science and religion is with human sciences, most notably with history, rather than with the physical sciences. Kaplan asserted that the specific challenge of modern interpretations of history to Judaism lies in the fact that so-called scientific history excludes the categories of both miracles and revelation from being legitimate causal factors in human events. Its method implies an epistemology that structurally in its very premises rules out the legitimacy of the existence of any deity who functions in human history. This denial threatens continued acceptance of the authority of the Torah.

Kaplan discussed the affirmed conflict between his understanding of modern ethics and Judaism in terms of a contrast between what he called "humanist" and "theocentric" interpretations of the good. He also argued that the Jewish people have ignored the area of the beautiful and in so doing have contributed to the disintegration of Judaism.

Kaplan listed his factors of conservation under two headings, which he labeled "inherent" and "environmental." He listed nine inherent factors in Jewish life, along with anti-semitism and American Roman Catholicism as external factors that help conserve Judaism. The nine internal conserving factors are (1) the tendency to aggregate in large cities and within specific neighborhoods in these cities, (2) a tendency against intermarriage, (3) Jewish communal centers, (4) fraternal organizations such as *landsmannschaften*, (5) religious activities, (6) Jewish education, (7) cultural activities, (8) philanthropic activities, and (9) Zionism. Kaplan argued that, with regard to the past, Judaism never ceased to be a nation. As such, it exhibited a unified ideology and system of practice that was a highly viable form of collective and individual life. Kaplan claimed that, in spite of all of the factors of disintegration, Judaism's communal system continues to contribute to Jewish life. Furthermore, as a nation rabbinic Judaism has been most extraordinary in terms of both preservation and applied morality. However, to remain viable, Kaplan argued, certain changes need to be instituted into the system of Torah. The main problem for Torah's continued real application to the life of more than a small handful of Jews is that the ideology for that system must be reconstructed. Kaplan saw the issue primarily in terms of problems with the doctrine of other-worldly salvation.

THE SOLUTION

Kaplan discussed in detail what he considered to be the major interpretations of Judaism current in the 1930s. Generally, he rejected all of them on the grounds that in different ways they emphasized one aspect of what Judaism is, but either failed to integrate all its essential features into their programs or lacked a conceptual outlook that could satisfactorily account for those different aspects. On one hand, there are a series of Jewish religious movements which fail to incorporate adequately the cultural dimensions of Judaism. On the other hand, there are a number of Jewish cultural movements which fail to incorporate adequately the religious dimensions of Judaism. In contrast, Kaplan maintained that his understanding of Judaism as a civilization offers an organic, rather than an aimless, approach to solving the current crisis in Judaism by integrating the totality of Jewish experience based on what he called an "affirmative and realistic philosophy of Jewish life."[2] By "affirmative" he meant simply that it is a philosophy that promotes active Jewish identity. By "realistic" he meant that it is a philosophy that can be believed by a large number of Jews including a program that practically can be carried out. He assumed that "Jewish civilization can function in varying degrees in the diaspora, provided it have its home in Palestine and retain both its Hebraic and religious character."[3] Judaism as a civilization, therefore, is conceived to be a philosophy to justify and to promote a conception of Judaism that posits both its cultural and religious aspects as essential, while affirming both a diaspora and a homeland as necessary for Judaism to preserve in the modern world.

Civilization

Kaplan says that a civilization is

> the accumulation of knowledge, skills, tools, arts, literatures, laws, religions and philosophies which stand between man and external nature and which serves as a bulwark against the hostility of forces that would otherwise destroy him.[4]

Any activity or product of activity of a person or a group of people which promotes the continued existence of a particular group is a constituent of that group's civilization. Furthermore, any group that has a civilization is a nation. However, a nation is not merely on Kaplan's terms an *ad hoc* collection of artifacts. To count as a civilization this composite in some sense must constitute a complete, self-contained entity.

One of Kaplan's main contentions was that for a given collection of people to be a distinct civilization, they must have a number of distinct features. In chapter 14, Kaplan enumerated these features as history, literature, language, social organization, folk sanctions, standards of conduct, esthetic values, and social and spiritual ideals.[5] He presented a slightly different list in chapter 15. There the enumerated elements are land, language, literature, mores, laws, folkways, folk sanctions, folk arts, and social structure. Kaplan claimed that every collection of people who are distinct in these ways is a civilization, and as such its existence is an end in itself. The existence of a civilization is of value even if it serves no other purpose than its own existence, in the same way that it is true that the existence of a human being is of value in and of itself.[6]

Folk sanctions are a means that a people uses to impose its values and ideals on its individual constituents. Kaplan defined values as "ideas which validate customs, usages, laws and standards,"[7] and stated that their main purpose is to serve as "judgments as to the importance of the social habits and attitudes to which they refer and the reasons for such importance."[8] Such values are folk, rather than individual, values when they apply to a collective. Similarly, a folk ideology is defined as "ideas which are not only subscribed to by the entire folk, but refer to the interests and the welfare of the entire folk."— Note that both values and ideology are understood in psychological rather than objective terms. A value is in no way defined as what is right or true, and neither of these values have any application to an ideology as Kaplan used the word. Values are what people judge to be important, and an ideology is what promotes values that are in the interest and welfare of the collective.

Kaplan defined religion as well as truth and morality in such a way that they are subordinate to the interests of the civilization. While arguing that religion is not separable from a civilization, he said that today creeds, rituals, and ceremonies in all of the historical religions have lost their value by becoming "detached from the basic interest of the life of the individual."[10] Given his definition of value, what ought to be of value for the individual is more a question of what is in the interest of the collective than of the individual's own interests. In any case, note that Kaplan's emphasis on the value of religion as part of a civilization is solely in terms of its relevance to human (collective or individual) interests. In this connection, it is noteworthy that, rather than using this term to express that which in some sense belongs to God, we are told that the word *sacred* merely means *important*.[11] In other words, something in a civilization is sacred if it is valuable, where value is understood to refer to what validates the accepted social practices of a civilization. Thus, something may be sacred that has nothing to do with God.

Kaplan called the philosophies of Judaism he discussed "spiritual movements." His term *spiritual* simply refers to any kind of conceptual activity. A Jewish spiritual movement is a synonym for a philosophy of Judaism. We need not concern ourselves here with Kaplan's critique of the other modern versions of Judaism. However, in the course of stating his critique, Kaplan stipulated a number of criteria by which a spiritual movement should be judged. Kaplan stated five criteria: (1) A spiritual movement should be judged by the extent of success it achieves in formulating a program that can "bring order into men's inner life" that is "spiritually compelling" and "socially practical,"[12] and (2) the "degree to which its adherents live up to its professed ideas and ideals."[13] (3) The "theoretical background" of a successful Jewish spiritual movement will include the "most vital issues" confronting contemporary Jews.[14] Kaplan enumerated these issues as Zionism, diversity in outlook and life style, anti-Semitism, disunity of the diverse organizations in local Jewish communities, and Jewish education for both children and adults. (4) A spiritual movement will be judged by its "ability to adjust to changes in the environment of Jewish civilization."[15] Furthermore, this adjustment must (a) proceed from the "essential nature of Judaism," (b) lead to "enrichment of the content of Judaism," and (c) be "inherently interesting." Kaplan meant that the philosophy is such that any individual will "so identify himself with every facet of Jewish life that all aspects of it find their reflection in him."[16] (5) An adequate spiritual movement must formulate "the proper type of social structure which would animate the form and content of Jewish civilization" and would "integrate this structure within the life of the various nations with whom Jews have come to identify themselves."[17]

With respect to the first criterion, the only modern version of Judaism that meets the standard of presenting an all-encompassing, consistent orientation to the plenitude of on-going human activities is that offered by traditional rabbinic Judaism. That is the strength of Orthodoxy. However, its philosophy is at the same time the least believable of modern versions of Judaism for most Jews. In this sense, we may characterize Kaplan's reconstruction of Judaism as an attempt to save the virtue of the traditional system of the Torah by substituting a new, hopefully more believable ideology to sustain that system. This is also the reason why Kaplan claimed that Orthodoxy failed the test of the second criterion; a philosophy that most people cannot believe is not practical.

Kaplan believed that his understanding of Judaism as a civilization passed all of these tests. His arguments for this contention were separated into three topics, which Kaplan labeled "The Israel Idea," "The God Idea," and "The Torah Idea." Under each subject, Kaplan proposed a theoretical model for understanding each concept as a constituent of a reconstructed Judaism. He formulated an outline of the consequences that this model would have in a viable Jewish civilization.

Israel

What Kaplan called "The Israel Idea" consists of a description of what the Jewish people are and a *raison d'etre* for the Jewish people continuing to be what they are. In biblical terms, a people is a nation when it is related to a deity who protects and preserves it. In this sense, the Jewish people is a nation because it stands in a covenant relationship with a particular deity who comes to be known as the only effective God in the universe. It is this understanding of Israel that Kaplan argued is threatened by scientific humanism. What makes this conception of the national status of Israel unacceptable to many modern Jews is that this *raison d'etre* conceptually presupposes the existence of a deity, and the crucial feature of modern scientific explanation is that appeals to superhuman persons in principle are inadmissible.

Kaplan claimed that his understanding of Judaism as a civilization escapes these disadvantages. He asserted that any group of people is a nation once it has achieved a sufficient degree of collective consciousness to have a "will to civilize."[18] Having achieved nationhood, the people's right to distinct existence is ineradicable and inviolable.

The source of Kaplan's understanding of Judaism as a nation is Ahad Ha-Am (1856-1927).[19] He defined nation in cultural rather than political terms. Any collective so defined has an inalienable right to separate existence. On this basis, we may assume the right of the Jewish people to continue to exist independent of any appeal to deity or superiority of any kind.

Kaplan also presented a sketch of what a nation ideally ought to be. He argued in chapter 17 that it should be an instrument by which citizens can maximize personal freedom for all people against any form of tyranny. Also, any particular nation's interests ideally must be disciplined for the benefit of all mankind. Although he did not say so explicitly, it is clear that Kaplan was responding to those modern Jews who objected to any form of nationalism. Those people believed that nations can be and often are instruments of tyranny, which invariably serve their own interests over against all others. Kaplan's response was that this state of affairs need not be true of any nation, including that of the Jewish people. Kaplan argued from Jewish history that cultural nationalism is superior to political nationalism precisely because it can overcome the disadvantages of the nation state. While a nation is morally absolute, a state is not. By promoting states that are multi-national, we can avoid the threat of chauvinism and the danger of raising the state to the level of a religion.[20] Kaplan strongly advocated the creation of a Jewish state in Palestine, but he opposed the notion that all Jews should settle in that state. He argued that the Jewish nation must continue to be a universal people.

In chapter 21, Kaplan reasoned that particularly in the diaspora the Jewish community must be so structured that the community as a whole and its individual constituents are connected organically. The model for organic connection in this instance is the relationship of a body to its parts. While each part of a body is in itself a substance and, in this sense, is distinct from the substance of the body; nevertheless, these two kinds of substances are so connected that the body can be healthy, i.e., survive, only if its parts are healthy. Conversely, any part can remain healthy only if the body as a whole is healthy. In this way, the body is essentially connected to its parts, and the parts are essentially connected to the body. If we cannot assume that citizens in a nation will be loyal because they believe that loyalty is an ultimate obligation, then a nation may command such primary allegiance only if it serves the best interests of each of its constituents. The nation will consistently serve it constituents' individual needs only if the structural relationship between the two is organic. If the two are connected organically, then in principle there can be no conflict of interest between the healthy collective and its healthy parts. Consequently, Kaplan advocated a doctrine of this-worldly rather than other-worldly salvation. With reference to the community, this-worldly salvation is understood in terms of the social and economic welfare of its members.

As interpreted by Kaplan, the nation is obligated out of its own interest to each of its constituents in the following three ways: (1) It must assist them to find "a place in the sun"[21'] i.e., the individual should have some form of on-going activity in which he or she may achieve some degree of success that is useful within and to the community. (2) It must assist them to make the necessary "social and economic adjustments" to their environment.[22] (3) It must impart to them the "cultural values and habits which make (their) life significant."[23]

At present, in most diaspora Jewish communities, the basic institution through which most Jews are actively identified with the Jewish people is the synagogue. Given the above objectives, Kaplan argued in chapter 21 that there are a number of reasons why it is not desirable for the synagogue to have this position. He believed the synagogue failed to be responsible to its congregants in any of the ways listed above and therefore has no real claim on their allegiance.

It could be argued that the synagogue should expand its functions to include the above proposals, thereby overcoming this objection. Many of the young rabbis who read *Judaism as a Civilization* in the 1930s did just that when they assumed the leadership of new synagogues in America's suburbs after World War II. However, Kaplan claimed that the problem was more fundamental than merely the fact that the synagogue has not been used in ways that it could be. Rather, his claim was that the very structure of the synagogue as an institution renders it ineffective in the desired ways.

Kaplan enumerated three objections to the synagogue.[24] The synagogue functions as "an exclusive clubhouse for a homogeneous group." Its main professional—the rabbi— is "monopolized by those who can pay his salary." Finally, even if these problems could be overcome, the synagogue is too small a unit to provide the communal authority to pressure individuals into becoming members of the Jewish nation. In Kaplan's words,

A person is a member of a nation not by choice, but by virtue of the pressure of the cultural group into which he is born....If, then, Jewish nationhood is to function in the diaspora its principal manifestation must be this very element of involuntarism characteristic of national life. The congregation cannot supply it because it is too small, intimate and transient to be authoritative.[25]

Kaplan's alternative to the synagogue is the *kehillah*. He modeled his conception on the plan for the kehillah of New York City in the 1910s[26] and a number of proposed models for restructuring and unifying multiple Jewish service and philanthropic agencies in American cities, most notably Israel A. Abraham's 1933 plan for a Jewish Community Council in Pittsburgh.[27] Kaplan's kehillah model has the following features: It is a civic rather than a religious organization. It encompasses all types of Jews. It is organized by districts within the metropolitan area, including all kinds of Jewish organizations that serve the special interests federated under it. Finally, authority is vested in a legislative body than can express all of the interests of the multiple agencies within the district. In Abraham's plan, each special-interest activity within the community would have at least one and at most four representatives, depending on the size of the agency's budget, in the General Assembly. The General Assembly would elect one fourth of its membership to constitute an Administrative Council. The Administrative Council would elect an Executive Council that would carry out the actual work of the community. The Executive Council would finance and coordinate the multiple religious, educational, welfare, and professional agencies that constitute the membership of the whole.

Kaplan argued that a kehillah is preferable to a synagogue communal structure, since it encompasses all types of Jews, which gives the kehillah the variety lacking in synagogues. For this reason, the kehillah should be secular rather than religious. Since most Jews are not religious, an institution that by definition is religious could not encompass all Jews. Furthermore, since the rules for decision-making in a kehillah are democratic, it could not serve exclusively the special interests of the few Jews who are wealthy enough to pay for its services.

Kaplan was aware that the proposed kehillah in New York City failed. He related that no matter how desirable a proposal may be in theory, if it cannot be put into effect and persevere, it is ultimately not desirable because it is not practical. Kaplan attributed the failure of the New York kehillah to the fact that it tried to unify the entire metropolitan area of the city. A functional kehillah presupposes a unified community. While Jews live in community within districts of the city, they do not live within the entire city itself. Hence, while a kehillah for all of New York City could not work, Kaplan claimed that a kehillah organized along districts could succeed.[28]

God and Torah

We will now deal briefly with Kaplan's God Idea. What Kaplan has to say about God at any particular time in his life and in any one book on the subject is of little importance for Kaplan's major thought, because no single conception of deity can properly be pointed to as his understanding of God. Kaplan's writings subsequent to *Judaism as a Civilization* show considerable flexibility on this question. While Kaplan believed that it is of benefit to Jewish civilization for Jews to believe in something that would enable them to affirm that God exists, it does not seem that he had any real vested interest in any particular conception. This peculiarity of Kaplan's thought is a consequence of his understanding of pragmatism, viz., that concepts are judged more often by how useful they are rather than by whether or not they are true.

Kaplan's idea of God is not primary to his program of Jewish civilization beyond the fact that no viable civilization will exclude folk religion. His idea of Torah is a vital element upon which his basic conception of the Israel Idea rests. Torah is the name that Kaplan applied to those means by which his program of Jewish civilization is to be embodied. So understood, Kaplan's Torah is not the same thing as what biblical or rabbinic Judaism called Torah. It is legitimate to call both by this single word. Both are intended to be detailed accounts of the procedural rules or institutions of the Jewish people, by which all individuals within the community relate to the community and the world. Also, both detail how the community relates to its constituents and the world. Furthermore, the institutions or rules in Kaplan's Torah are influenced and often based on the rabbis' Torah. But clearly the two uses of the term do not completely coincide.

Folkways

Kaplan divided the content of his Torah into two categories. The first—folkways—appears to be an approximation of the traditional rabbinic list of *MITZVOT* and *MINHAGIM*.[29] The second—ethics—is a general account of conditions for economic and social justice in a Jewish civilization. Folkways are further subdivided into two kinds—the religious and the cultural. One might think that Kaplan used these terms to distinguish between practices that are prescribed by Jewish law (HALACHAH) and those that distinctly characterize Jewish behavior but do not have the status of law (*MINHAGIM*); but this distinction would not fit Kaplan's use. For instance, the Jewish calendar is as much a matter of Jewish law as are questions of *KASHRUT*. Yet, Kaplan listed the former as a cultural folkway and the latter as a religious folkway. The adjective religious in this context must be understood with reference to Kaplan's description of folk religion.

Kaplan stated that Jewish religion is the "cluster of concrete elements within the civilization which figure in the consciousness of the

Jew as indispensable to his self-fulfillment or salvation."[31] Based on this definition, a religion, as opposed to a religious philosophy, consists of concrete practices rather than a set of beliefs. The term *indispensable* expresses the criterion by which communal practices or folkways are to be distinguished as cultural or religious. Kaplan stated that religious folkways are most important than cultural folkways.[32] He noted the observance of the Sabbath, the festivals, and *KASHRUT* as examples of religious folkways; and he listed the Hebrew language, Jewish names, the Jewish calendar, and Jewish art as examples of cultural folkways. Kaplan maintained that there is no single aspect of Jewish practice or single doctrine of Jewish belief which, no matter how desirable, is so essential that, if it were discontinued, Judaism would disappear. Rather, Judaism is defined as an organic unity, composed of a cluster of characteristics, ideological and practical, the elements of which are such that any one of them may be replaced by some other element but all of which cannot be altered at any one time. In other words, while no single example of a religious folkway is indispensable, the cluster itself is. Yet, while Judaism could survive without any one of these religious elements at any one time, if none of them survived Judaism would die. On the other hand, if all of the cluster of cultural elements ceased to function in a Jewish community, while the community would be seriously bankrupt, it would remain a Jewish community.

The Jewish Milieu

Kaplan delegated to two institutions—the family and the synagogue—the responsibility to indoctrinate or promote among individual Jews the content values and practices of Judaism. In Kaplan's terminology, these two organizations constitute the Jewish milieu.[33]

We noted above that Kaplan had reservations about the efficacy of the synagogue serving as the basic unit of Jewish identity beyond the family. However, he recognized that, in fact, the synagogue has this exalted position. Consequently, any change in Jewish communal institutions could more readily come about through a reconstruction of this unit than through fostering separate, new institutions. Hence, Kaplan argued that contemporary, independent congregations should expand into a multi-functional Jewish neighborhood, which he called a *BET AM*. Kaplan proposed that each Jewish neighborhood eventually should have a single congregation which would continue at least all of the existing functions presently taking place in multiple synagogues in a given neighborhood. These new basic units will be constituents of Kaplan's proposed inter-neighborhood kehillah. The functions of the *BET AM* would include multiple welfare, social, cultural, and educational activities, as well as worship.

Kaplan's conception of the *BET AM* had considerable influence on the way that suburban congregations developed after World War II, when Jewish life relocated in metropolitan suburbs.[34] While many congregational rabbis and lay leaders hoped that their synagogues would be total Jewish neighborhood or village associations, in fact this did not happen. In the course of a decade, the kind of organizational fragmentation that had existed within the city limits was transposed to the suburbs. The synagogue became a secular as well as a religious Jewish institution. Interaction between different kinds of committed Jews increased. Unfortunately, neighborhoods continue to have separate Reform, Orthodox, Conservative and sometimes even Reconstructionist synagogues as well as independent Jewish welfare, social, and educational organizations.

CONCLUSION

Judaism as a Civilization is a unique composition in Jewish thought. Let me explain this claim in the following way: Judaism always has been the expression of a relationship between a specific deity and a specific people. This two-term relationship traditionally has been expressed in the tri-partite dogma of God, Torah, and Israel. The terms *God* and *Israel* represent the two entities that stand in the relationship, and the term *Torah* expresses its nature and content. No Jewish thinker has conceived Judaism without these three elements. However, no Jewish thinker since biblical times has ever given a detailed account of all parts of the relation. Rather, different Jewish thinkers at different times have focused on one or the other of these factors. In the classical rabbinic period (200 B.C.E.—500 C.E.), the emphasis was on the nature of Torah. In medieval Jewish philosophy the emphasis was on the nature of God. Since emancipation the emphasis has been on the nature of the Jewish people, Israel. In developing a philosophy of the Jewish people, the nineteenth-century, liberal-religious Jewish thinkers and their twentieth-century American-liberal followers focused their attention primarily on medieval and modern Germanic conceptions of God. Most Jewish thinkers who laid the groundwork for Zionism attempted to develop a philosophy of the Jewish people largely independent of both God and Torah. Kaplan is distinct among these Jewish thinkers in recognizing that any successful account of any single fundamental tenet of Jewish commitment—be it God, Torah, or Israel—must be understood not independently but in relationship to the other two basic elements.

Kaplan's work is unique in yet another way. The philosophy of Judaism as an enterprise can be understood in the following terms: The Hebrew Scriptures tell of the birth and initial development of the Jewish people in relationship to God. Taken as a whole, the Scriptures are not only a record of Jewish origins. They also function for Israel as a constitution containing implicitly as well as explicitly the fundamental commitments of the Jew. If the Jew had never left the world of the ancient Near East and if it had never changed, presumably there would not have been a need for another work to express what consitutes Judaism. Each fundamental change in the life of the Jewish people brought about changes in practice and mental perspective that raised at least possible doubt about the viability of the program of personal and communal life and thought affirmed in the Scriptures. The topic of all subsequent Jewish thought is the resolution of these areas of doubt.

Let me state the same point in a different way. To write a philosophy of Judaism implies the following presuppositions: In some sense, Judaism is true; there seem to be sources of truth independent of Judaism; and there seem to be areas of conflict between Judaism and the independent sources. In the late middle ages, for example, the seemingly independent source of truth was the philosophy of Aristotle as understood by his Greek and Muslim commentators; and the area of apparent conflict with Judaism was in what they called metaphysics and we call theoretical physics, focusing attention most specifically on the nature (but not the existence) of God and the origins, if any, of the physical universe. Now, however, modern metaphysics, be it British or Continental let alone Aristotelian, is viewed by few people in general and by practically no Jews in particular to be a source of truth. Insofar as there is a need for a philosophy of Judaism, it is on entirely different terms than those of medieval Jewish philosophy. Kaplan is among the few major Jewish thinkers in the modern world to change the focus of attention of Jewish philosophy in this respect.[35]

There is considerable justification for contemporary Jewish philosophy shifting the concentration of its defense from issues in science to challenges in political theory. In the nineteenth century, most German intellectuals still believed that what they thought to be the new empirical science[36] provided the key for people to know all that was worthy of knowing and to solve all human problems in a rational, objective manner. What was called "science" constitued a mass religion of the intelligentsia. They were totally committed to a methodology in which they had complete faith as a source for human salvation, i.e., as the way for humanity to fulfill all of its aspirations in this world. Indeed, they not only believed that the so-called scientific method could solve problems, but that, in fact, it already had solved many of them. They believed that Euclid (4th century B.C.E.) completed mathematics in the sense that human beings knew all that there was to know about mathematical truths, which were eternal. Later, Isaac Newton (1647-1727) contributed an eternally true conception of the nature of the physical universe. Recently, German intellectuals, Sigmund Freud (1856-1939) and Karl Marx (1818-1883) being the most important among them, thought that they could extend this purported certainty in the physical sciences to so-called human sciences such as psychology, sociology, economics, and political theory. This faith was rooted in the broad area of common consent in mathematics and the physical sciences. Hence, in the last century it was reasonable that Jewish philosophy concentrated on issues of apparent conflict between Judaism and science, but in the twentieth century this foundation for faith in science has been shattered.

Today Euclidean geometry is recognized to be one special kind of geometry. No mathematician can claim that his mental labor bears anything but merely formal or linguistic truth. Similarly, Newtonian physics is no longer considered by physicists to be the true picture of the universe. It is, at most, the best single hypothetical model that is convenient for solving some problems. There are other models, even contradictory ones, that are more applicable to other problems, such as the four dimensional space/time model for astronomy in the relativity theory of Albert Einstein (1879-1955) and the indeterminacy principle in the Copenhagen Interpretation of Werner Heisenberg (b. 1901) for quantum physics. Theories of the universe are in principle nothing but theories which can be said to be true only in the highly restricted sense that they enable us with varying degrees of probability to make predictions. Even this highly limited degree of truth-claim greatly exceeds any affirmation of knowledge that a human or social scientist can make.

The predominant view of most American philosophers is that their talents are useful in clarifying the conceptions and exhibiting the logic of the language of truth-claims that others legitimately or illegitimately make, but philosophy in itself offers no methodology by which any truth-claims can be made about the empirical world. What was viewed in the nineteenth century as an independent source or tradition of truth, that could, at least in principle, raise doubts about the truth-claims of any version of modern or classical Judaism, can no longer be seriously considered a threat in itself by any informed individual.

Nevertheless, twentieth-century American Jews have reasonable commitments that are independent of Jewish sources and that are, at least in principle, a possible threat to rationally affirming Jewish commitment. Most American Jews believe in nationalism and are committed in some sense of the word to democracy as the ideal form of national government. Similarly, most Jews are not cognizant that this belief is independent of Judaism and may even be in conflict with it. As the seeming conflict between Aristotelian philosophy and Judaism called for a Jewish theology that expressed itself in terms of metaphysics and physics, so the seeming conflict between democratic nationalism and Judaism today calls for a Jewish theology that expresses itself in terms of moral and political philosophy. Yet, with the possible exception of some of the Zionist theoreticians such as Ber Borochov (1881-1917), few Jewish thinkers have been cognizant of political and moral theory as a modern need for Jewish theology. The most important exception to this negative generalization is Mordecai Kaplan, who, in *Judaism as a Civilization*, offered a Jewish theology in terms of a political theory of democratic nationalism. Kaplan may be the only serious American-Jewish thinker to deal with Judaism in the light of what were important intellectual commitments of Westernized Jewish intelligentsia in the first third of the twentieth century. This fact may be the reason why Kaplan's influence has been so much greater than that of any other American Jewish thinker; i.e., no matter what we might think of his answer, he asked the right questions.

As was stated above, every philosophy of Judaism presupposes, beyond a commitment to some understanding of Judaism, the affirmation of some set of beliefs that are external to or independent of Judaism. In Kaplan's case, the range of Jewish commitment included a liberal understanding of rabbinic Judaism, as well as some form of modern Zionism, affirming the necessity and desirability of both a Jewish state and the Jewish nation extending beyond the borders of that single political entity. In addition, the author of *Judaism as a Civilization* appears to have been committed to utilitarianism in ethics, to what Willian James (1842-1910) called "radical empiricism" (but what today is more commonly called "American pragmatism") in theory of knowledge, and to the moral desirability of some form of democratic nationalism in political theory. Maimonides' *Guide of the Perplexed* can legitimately be characterized as what an intelligent Aristotelian might say if he were a traditional rabbinic Jew with definite sympathies for the Kabbalah. In this way, Kaplan's *Judaism as a Civilization* is what an intelligent, utilitarian, pragmatic, social democratic nationalist would say if he were a liberal, neo-rabbinic, utopian Zionist. In this sense also, Kaplan's work is unique. Kaplan is a distinctly American Jewish theologian, for no set of beliefs is more characteristically American in the first half of the twentieth century than the conjunction of pragmatism with utilitarianism and democratic nationalism.

NOTES

1. Mordecai M. Kaplan, *Judaism as a Civilization*. New York, Macmillan, 1934. Henceforth to be identified as "Kaplan."

2. Kaplan, p. 80.

3. Kaplan, p. 86.

4. Kaplan, p. 179.

5. Kaplan, p. 178.

6. For example, see Kaplan, p. 246, where he says,

Once a group has reached the degree of collective consciousness when it possesses the *will to civilize*, it has established a right to existence which no one can question any more than one can question the right of a human being to live once he has come into the world.

7. Kaplan, p. 197.

8. Kaplan, p. 197.

9. Kaplan, p. 198.

10. Kaplan, p. 200.

11. Kaplan, p. 200.

12. Kaplan, p. 92.

13. Kaplan, p. 92.

14. Kaplan, p. 174.

15. Kaplan, p. 184.

16. Kaplan, p. 184.

17. Kaplan, p. 208.

18. Kaplan, p. 179.

19. See chapter 6.

20. Kaplan, chapter 18.

21. Kaplan, p. 284.

22. Kaplan, p. 284.

23. Kaplan, p. 284.

24. Kaplan, p. 291-293.

25. Kaplan, p. 292-293.

26. Kaplan, p. 294-296.

27. Kaplan, p. 541-544.

28. Kaplan, p. 295.

29. Kaplan, chapter 29.

30. Kaplan, chapter 30.

31. Kaplan, p. 323.

32. Kaplan, p. 433.

33. Kaplan, chapter 28.

34. See chapter 3.

35. The only other clear example is Spinoza. See chapter 7.

36. Which was really the old material atomism of the Mutakallimun

KEY NAMES

Ahad Ha-Am, Israel A. Abrams, Ber Borochov, William James, *Judaism as a Civilization*, Reconstructionist Rabbinical College.

KEY TERMS

administrative council, *BET AM*, civilization, democratic nationalism, executive council, folkway, general assembly, Jewish milieu, *KEHILLAH*, nation, organic, people, pragmatism, sacred, salvation, sanction, spiritual, this-wordly salvation, utilitarianism, will-to-civilize.

KEY QUESTIONS

1. What are the three ways that *Judaism as a Civilization* is a unique work in Jewish thought? What presuppositions are necessary to write a philosophy of Judaism? Why does the content for contemporary Jewish philosophy differ from that of classical Jewish philosophy?

2. According to Kaplan, on what five criteria are Jewish spiritual movements to be judged? Why did he think that Reform, Orthodox, Conservative Judaism and secular Zionism cannot save Judaism? What is wrong with modern Judaism? What are the three general categories of contemporary Jewish disintegration? How does each threaten Jewish survival? Why is modern history singled out as a threat over the other academic disciplines?

3. According to Kaplan, what are the two general categories of contemporary Jewish conservation? How does each function to preserve the Jewish people?

4. According to Kaplan, why ought the Jewish people to survive? What is a civilization? What are its distinct features?

5. How did Kaplan defend his belief in nationalism? How can a modern nation command the loyalty of its constituents? What obligations does the nation have to them?

6. How did Kaplan propose to reconstruct Judaism? Describe Kaplan's kehillah model. How does it differ from the New York City kehillah of the 1930s? What is religion and why is it important? Why shouldn't the synagogue be the primary public institution of Jewish identity? What is Kaplan's alternative? What function should be synagogue have?

7. What are the two main divisions in Kaplan's understanding of Torah? What are the two main divisions of folkways? How do they differ from each other? What are examples of each kind of folkway?

8. How is Kaplan's idea of God based on pragmatism? Why is

it of secondary importance in his general philosophy of Judaism?

RECOMMENDED READINGS

General

Robert M. Seltzer, *Jewish People. Jewish Thought: The Jewish Experience in History.* New York: Macmillan, 1980. Chpt 16, "Two Styles of Jewish Religious Thought in America," pp. 748-752.
Eugene R. Borowitz, *Choices in Modern Jewish Thought: A Partisan Guide.* New York: Behrman House, 1983. Chpt. 5.

Specific

Ira Eisenstein and Eugene Kohr., *Mordecai M. Kaplan: An Evaluation.* New York: Jewish Reconstructionist Foundation, 1952.
Mordecai M. Kaplan, *A New Approach to Jewish Life.* New York: Society for the Advancement of Judaism, 1924.
———*The Future of the American Jew.* New York: Reconstructionist Press, 1967.
———*The Greater Judaism in the Making.* New York: Reconstructionist Press, 1960.
———and Arthur Cohen, *If Not Now, When?* New York: Reconstructionist Press, 1967.
———*Judaism as a Civilization.* New York: Macmillan, 1934.
———*Judaism Without Supernaturalism: The Only Alternative to Orthodoxy and Secularism.* New York: Reconstructionist Press, 1958.
———*The Meaning of God in Modern Jewish Religion.* New York: Behrman, 1937.
———*The Purpose and Meaning of Jewish Existence.* Philadelphia: Jewish Publication Society of America, 1964.
———*Questions Jews Ask.* New York: Reconstructionist Press, 1956.
———*The Religion of Ethical Nationhood: Judaism's Contribution to World Peace.* New York: Macmillan, 1970.
Norbert M. Samuelson, "Can Democracy and Capitalism Be Jewish Values? Mordecai Kaplan's Political Philosophy," *Modern Judaism* (May, 1983): 189-215.
Mel Scult. "The Sociologist as Theologian: The Fundamental Assumptions of Mordecai Kaplan's Thought," *Judaism* 99 (Summer, 1976): 345-352.
Mel Scult. "Mordecai Kaplan: Challenges and Conflicts of the Twen-

ties," *American Jewish Historical Quarterly* LXVI, 3 (March, 1977): 401-417.

Mel Scult. "Kaplan's Reinterpretation of Torah," *Conservative Judaism* 33, 1 (1979): 63-68.

13

EMIL FACKENHEIM AND CONTEMPORARY JEWISH PHILOSOPHY

Religious philosophy necessarily is polemical. If there was no challenge to Judaism from the outside—if there was no system of thought outside of Judaism that was taken seriously—then there would be nothing to talk about in Jewish philosophy. It is the external challenge that determines the agenda. For example, if you are an early twentieth-century neo-Hegelian who wants to be a Jew, but you can only be a Jew if you come to terms with reality as presented in neo-Hegelian terms, then you will develop a philosophy of Judaism similar to the philosophies of Buber and Rosenzweig. Similarly, if you are a twelfth-century neo-Aristotelian who wants to make sense out of your commitment to rabbinic Judaism in terms of the religious/scientific world view of someone like Ibn Sina, then you will develop a philosophy of Judaism similar to the philosophies of Abraham Ibn Daud and Maimonides.

In this author's judgment, there are two major periods of Jewish thought. One is the medieval period, under Platonic/Aristotelian and Muslim influences, which lasted from the tenth through the fourteenth centuries. In this period, the giants were Saadia, Abraham Ibn Daud, Maimonides, Gersonides and Crescas. Of these four, the best known is Maimonides; but the most rigorous were Gersonides and Crescas. The next period is the one dealt with in this text. Its greatest achievements as philosophy were in the first third of the twentieth century, when the external source for the polemic was German-Christian, Kantian/Hegelian philosophy. The three major voices of this period were Hermann Cohen, Martin Buber, and Franz Rosenzweig.

Some Jewish philosophers who do Jewish philosophy today find the best model for their work in the medieval period. They base their modern Jewish thought on classical Jewish thought. Others base their modern Jewish thought on Rosenzweig and Buber. The members of these two groups make the following choice. If they base their work on the medieval model, they do so because they judge medieval Aristotelian science to be better than modern philosophy. Conversely, those basing their work on a Hegelian model accept the worth of the Hegelians. If you do not believe that some form of Aristotelian or Hegelian philosophy is best, then the teachings of the classical and modern Jewish philosophers will have a restricted relevance to your own contemporary Jewish thought. However, these negative judgments do not lessen the importance of studying these philosophers. Their value can be explained in the following way.

If you want to play chess well, the way to become a good player is to study every major game a chess master played. That does not mean you are going to make the same moves he made. No two chess games are the same. Besides, your opponent might also know what your master did. The master's moves solved chess problems in his day and motivated others to develop counter moves. What was a winning choice in his time would probably lead to a loss against a good tournament chess player today. Consequently, your moves will differ from those of your teacher. However, you will not be able to move like a master until you have developed the ability to think like a master, which you can only do by mastering masters. All of the Jewish philosophers mentioned above are masters of Jewish thought. You study these people not to defend their conclusions, but to grow as a thinker yourself in order to make new thought-moves in solving new problems.

At this point, it should be clear that no one can do serious work in Jewish philosophy unless he/she has an appropriate background in Jewish sources and professional training in the discipline of philosophy. How skilled he/she becomes in the enterprise largely depends on the scope of his/her background in Judaism and the degree of his/her excellence as a philosopher. Many committed Jews have backgrounds in Judaism, but few of them have attained the skills of the philosopher. Among those who are so skilled, few have exhibited the talent of Emil Fackenheim (b. 1916) in his *The Religious Dimension of Hegel's Thought*.[1] This book is generally recognized as one of the most important expositions of one of the premier philosophers of Western civilization. Fackenheim is the most recent major exponent of a form of Jewish philosophy known as "biblical faith," whose origins are in the modern German-Jewish theology of Martin Buber and Franz Rosenzweig.[2] As such, all of Fackenheim's work is important because it belongs to the corpus of Jewish religious philosophy initiated by Hermann Cohen,[3] whose historic importance is second only to the tradition of medieval Jewish philosophy.

Fackenheim's major books on Jewish philosophy are *Quest for Past and Future*,[4] *God's Presence in History*,[5] *Encounters Between Judaism and Modern Philosophy*,[6] *The Jewish Return into History: Reflections in the Age of Auschwitz and A New Jerusalem*,[7] and *To Mend the World*.[8] In *Quest*, Fackenheim gave his reasons for rejecting classical Jewish liberalism, which largely had to do with issues of authority; but we are left wondering where authority can come from if not from reason or Sinai as understood by the Orthodox. In *Presence* and *Encounters*, we are told that the new authorities are new epoch-making events expressed through new Midrash, that the new religious epochs include the Holocaust, and the new Midrash includes the stories of Elie Wiesel.[9] Fackenheim does not give a clear statement of what an epoch making event is, why the Holocaust counts as one, what else counts as one, and what is his understanding of Midrash as he formulates modern Jewish thought from the tales of Wiesel. Furthermore, as Fackenheim spells out his rejection of the authority of reason from *Quest* in *Encounters*, he tells us that as philosophy used logic in the past to judge all religions, including Judaism, so now after the Holocaust Judaism may use Midrash to judge all philosophy. But we are not told what this Midrash is. Fackenheim attempts to answer these questions in *Return*. There, he explains that the Holocaust is epoch-making because it is a unique event that makes new moral demands on all of mankind and alters the way that human beings must perceive the past and the future. Based on his discussion of the Holocaust, Fackenheim extends his claim about the meaning of history to include the creation of the modern State of Israel as an epoch-making event.

In *To Mend the World*, the conclusions from all of Fackenheim's previous collected essays are brought together for the first time as a unified, systematic whole. In essence, Fackenheim makes the following claims. (1) Baruch Spinoza[10] and Franz Rosenzweig,[11] whom Fackenheim identifies as the greatest Jewish philosophers, present the two, possible, diametrically-opposed responses to modernity that were available to the Jews before the Holocaust. Based on Spinoza's philosophy, the Jew could opt out of Judaism by becoming a "free-man-in-general." Based on Rosenzweig's theology, the Jew could opt into Judaism by becoming a "free-Jew-in-particular," at the price of making the Jewish people an entity outside of history. (2) After the Holocaust, neither alternative remains viable. Spinoza's assimilation from Jewish particularism and Rosenzweig's divorce of Jewish life from the realities of political power both resulted in (in the recent past) and can bring about again (in the future) the extinction of the Jewish people. After the Holocaust, the Jew must return as a Jew into the realm of lived history. The problem is how such a return is possible.

Underlying Fackenheim's philosophy is his commitment to a biblically-based faith, affirming that there is a perfect being who is the God of Israel and who acts in history in special ways. God's special manifestations in history are called "epoch-making events." These epochs include the exodus from Egypt, the theophany at Sinai, and the fall of the first two Temples of ancient Israel. To these presuppositions, Fackenheim adds the claim that epochs in Jewish history serve to distinguish authentic from inauthentic Judaism, and Midrash is the most authentic expression of Jewish theology. Against this background, the central thesis of *Return* is that the Holocaust and the establishment of the modern State of Israel are epoch-making Jewish events. These two events and emancipation are the only epoch-making events since the destruction of the Second Temple. These three events are intimately tied together and have produced a new age of Midrash. In order to be a epoch-making Jewish event, the historical phenomenon must be unique, must alter the way that subsequent history is to be understood, and must make special and new demands on the Jewish people as well as on all mankind. Fackenheim argued at length for the uniqueness of the Holocaust as well as the State of Israel. He asserted that these two events require a new way for both Jews and Christians in particular and all mankind in general to perceive the present and the future. He claimed that each event creates a new divine-moral demand. The demand from the Holocaust is called "the 614th Commandment," and the demand from the rise of the State of Israel is labeled, *AM YISRAEL CHAI.*

MIDRASH

In *Encounters,* Fackenheim argued that as philosophy used the tool
of logic in the past to judge all religions, including Judaism, so now
Judaism may use the tool of Midrash to judge all philosophy. This is
claimed by Fackenheim to be one of the monumental consequences
of the Holocaust. Philosophy lost its superior state, because philosophy in its own way contributed to the rise of Nazi Germany and
because it could continue to function in Nazi Germany. Hence, Judaism has gained the right to judge philosophy.

At one level, Fackenheim's claim against philosophy can be
understood as follows. Philosophers legitimately are involved in making precise formulations of general claims. When no precise formulation is possible, they tend to make negative judgments about the general claims. Historically, philosophers have been interested in the
truth-claims of various religions, including Judaism. Many European
Christian philosophers have reached negative judgments about Judaism. Furthermore, given that an argument is logically valid, the
premises entail certain conclusions, which means that the conclusions of valid arguments can be denied only if the premises are
denied. Fackenheim may assert that if the claims of Judaism are not
consistent with the claims of logic, just as it is possible to affirm logic
and deny Judaism, so it is possible to affirm Judaism and deny
logic.

It is not clear how Fackenheim intended to use Midrash to judge
philosophy. *Prima facie,* Midrash and logic are in no sense comparable. Midrash is not a formal tool for expressing truth-claims. It is a
specific set of claims made by rabbis through the use of parables and/
or stories. One could compare philosophic claims with Midrashic
claims, although that hardly seems to be appropriate. Conversely, one
might compare philosophic claims in logical forms with philosophic
or other truth-claims in alternate forms such as poetry, sculpture, etc.
We must still ask, how are we to compare logic and Midrash?

In *Return,* Fackenheim suggested the following answer: Discursive language is limited in expressing truth-claims. It can only formulate what human beings can precisely comprehend, which necessarily
is limited, but what people can experience is broader. Much that is
experienced is beyond the powers of discursive language. Now, the
powers of logic are limited only to discursive language, and they have
no authority over what human beings express beyond this limitation

in other forms of language. One such language is story-telling, and Midrash is a specific example of story telling.

Midrash is not merely stories told by Jews. It is the mode of a certain set of stories told by Jews. Epoch-making events are special encounters in human, finite history with an infinite God. At such moments, the Infinite is inescapably part of the history to be described; but because He is infinite, He cannot adequately be expressed. Midrash is story-telling that struggles to express the inexpressible, because it must be expressed. Again, it is inexpressible because it involves an infinite God, and it must be expressed because the subject matter is momentous, i.e., it alters the perception of subsequent history and makes special moral demands. The technical term used in the Midrash to indicate that the rabbis know that what they are trying to express as well as they can cannot precisely or adequately be expressed is *K'B'YACHOL*.

Based on the above analysis, Fackenheim explains his statement about the judgmental role of Midrash. In one sense, Midrash does not make truth-claims. No clear statements are formulated in Midrash that can simply be said to be true or false. Yet Midrash is as much committed to the expression of truth as is logic, because its method encompasses a broader category of truth-claims than is accessible to logic.

AUTHENTIC JEWS

Fackenheim asserted that Midrash is the response of authentic Jews to epoch-making Jewish events. It is not an answer, because what is inexpressible cannot be answered; but it cannot be ignored. A response is called for. We are told that those who respond are authentic Jews and those who fail to respond are inauthentic.

For Fackenheim, these two categories of Jews made the old distinctions between secular and religious, liberal and traditional Jews obsolete. It is no longer of primary importance whether a Jew explicitly believes in the God of Israel or implicitly affirms any of the previous 613 commandments. These issues mattered in the past because they were appropriate responses to the epochs of the Exodus, Sinai, and the destruction of the Temples. Now, Jews are to be judged by how they respond to the Holocaust and the State of Israel. The problem is, no one can be sure what is an epoch-making event when it occurs; yet there is no choice but to respond to it either by affirmation or negation. Today, we cannot be sure if these two contemporary events are epoch-making. If they are, then those Jews who respond are authentic, and those who do not are inauthentic.

For Fackenheim the two major claimants as modern epoch-making events are the Holocaust and the rise of the modern State of Israel. These are not just very important events. Fackenheim made a far stronger claim. For him they are comparable to the Exodus, the theophany at Sinai, and the destruction of the two Temples. Consequently, Fackenheim claimed that how Jews respond to these two events is how we are to distinguish between authentic and inauthentic Jews.

THE HOLOCAUST AS AN EPOCH-MAKING EVENT

Fackenheim claimed that the Holocaust is an epoch-making event because it is unique, makes new moral demands, and alters the perception of consequent history. He argued that every other possible goal of the Nazis, including winning the war, was secondary to their commitment to murder Jews. The proof is that in situations where the interests of the concentration camps conflicted with other German interests, the interests of the concentration camps took precedence. Furthermore, the Jews were murdered no other reason than the fact that they were Jews. They were not murdered for what they believed or did, since that had nothing to do with being Jewish. They were not murdered for belonging to an inferior race. The Nazi view of the Jew was the basis for their definition of races rather than the opposite being the case. Hence, the Nazi state ultimately existed for one purpose, to kill Jews for no reason other than the fact that they were Jews. The Holocaust was evil for evil's sake. Such evil has no equal anywhere else in history. Hiroshima, for example, was not comparable, because the Japanese were murdered presumably in order to end the war and to save American lives. The murder of Japanese was a secondary end, if it was a goal at all, to the primary, otherwise rational goal of winning the war. Only the Nazi extermination of the gypsies holds any possible counterpart to the extermination of the Jews.

The new moral demand of the Holocaust is Fackenheim's 614th commandment. It states that an "authentic Jew of today is forbidden to hand Hitler yet another, posthumous victory."[12] Fackenheim grants that this formulation is inadequate, so he spelled out a number of consequences that he intended for us to draw from the commandment. We must not forget the victims of the Holocaust. We must affirm the sacredness of life over death with the further consequence that we must reject collective and individual suicide; we must have hope for the world, which entails that we may not allow a second Holocaust to occur to anyone anywhere again. We must not despair of God. Finally, Jews must survive, raising Jewish children. For him, secular Jews who fight to survive as Jews are authentically Jewish.

In an essay entitled "Sachsenhausen 1938: Groundwork for Auschwitz," Fackenheim provided a dramatic example from his own experience about how he intended to apply his new commandment. At the beginning of their internment, he and other inmates were seduced into seemingly insignificant compromises that significantly contributed to the ultimate mass murder of the Jews by the Nazis. In the first days at the camp, an S.S. officer would ask a Jew what his profession was; and if the Jew did not give an acceptable answer, he would be beaten. A rabbinic student learned to say: "I am a public school teacher." Through this white lie he avoided a beating. It would seem that it is morally justifiable as well as pragmatically reasonable to commit such a minor sin (telling a white lie) in order to avoid a senseless negative consequence (a beating). However, Fackenheim told us that in so acting

> we (the Jews) fell into their (the Nazi's) trap... we protect ourselves, but at the same time we also lost some of our dignity... until finally a sliding scale is reached where it becomes more and more difficult to escape from the system.[13]

In this case, Fackenheim's application of his 614th commandment yields the obligation to resist and not compromise with evil. His example of observing this dictate is the Warsaw Ghetto uprising. then Fackenheim made a strong case for the moral duty to resist evil no matter how insignificant.

Fackenheim argued that any attempt to rob the Holocaust of its uniqueness, by reducing it to an instance of some universal, comprehensible human phenomenon, is a form of escapism that constitutes inauthentic existence. The Holocaust defies any form of rational explanation. It can be overcome in action, but not by rational thought. In Fackenheim's language, the Holocaust ruptures all continuity with the past. This rupture cannot be overcome by comprehension. Only through the example of the resistance of the few during the Holocaust can continuity with the past undergo *TIKKUN* (healing).

All Christian thought is inauthentic if it does not begin from the trauma that these questions arouse: Would Jesus have been sent to a concentration camp? Did the good news of Easter come too late, so that it is overwhelmed by Good Friday? Could Jesus have been made into a *muselmanner*—a mere shadow of a human being, a living dead, a man without freedom of choice? And, if it happened again, would you resist?

Finally, Jewish thought and life that is not rooted in the experience of the Holocaust also is inauthentic. In *To Mend the World*, Fackenheim presented the Jewish people with two focal expressions of this judgement. Again, the first was his 614th commandment. The second was his new definition of a Jew. "A Jew today is one who, except for an historical accident— Hitler's loss of the war—would have either been murdered or never been born."[14]

THE RISE OF THE MODERN JEWISH STATE AS AN EPOCH-MAKING EVENT

The meaning of the Holocaust in history is tied in Fackenheim's thought to the preceding emancipation and the subsequent creation of the State of Israel. That political emancipation has changed Jewish history is, from the standpoint of the mid-twentieth century, unquestionable; and as such, it qualifies as a Fackenheim epoch. However, it is not yet clear how emancipation has changed Jewish history. At one time, many Jews thought that emancipation initiated an age of humanism and enlightenment that marked the dawning of the messianic age.[15] Since the Holocaust, that belief is less credible.[16] Still other Jews[17] maintained that it marked the dawning of the messianic age for a diametrically-opposed reason. It began the age of total evil that would precede the coming of the Messiah. Certainly the Holocaust could be understood as epoch-making in this way, but it is not the sense that Fackenheim affirmed. For him, the Holocaust marks the low point in a struggle for Jewish self-liberation that began with emancipation and will not be concluded until the independent Jewish state becomes safe from all external threats.

Fackenheim understood the main import of the 614th commandment to be the demand for Jewish self-liberation. That demand began when emancipation granted freedom to the Jews as individuals and will end only when the Jewish people win for themselves collective freedom in an emancipated, i.e., safe and secure, Jewish state, which, because it is liberated, is religious. For Fackenheim, the clearest expression of authentic Jewish life is that Jews should unconditionally support and promote the welfare of the modern State of Israel. For Jews, this act of support is the ultimate Jewish expression of world-healing resistance.

CONCLUSION

While this text is being written, Jewish philosophers are absorbing Fackenheim's theses. Almost every original claim by Fackenheim is controversial. For example, there are obvious objections to Fackenheim's proposed post-Holocaust definition of Jews. It both includes people who should be excluded and excludes people who should be included.

Assume that the Allies had failed to defeat Hitler. It is not unreasonable to assume that, at some time after Hitler's defeat of the Allies, he would have turned against Japan. In the ensuing war, hundreds of thousands of Japanese would have been killed. Consequently, by Fackenheim's stated definition, the Japanese are Jewish.

Conversely, there is a significantly large number of children whom American Jews have adopted and raised as committed Jews whose natural parents are not Jewish. If Hitler had conquered America, these children would not have been raised as Jews, nor would they have been put to death. Consequently, by Fackenheim's definition, children adopted and raised to be committed Jews are not Jews.

Both of these are obvious, common-sense objections. There are theological objections as well. For example, Adolph Hitler, a gentile, not to mention an anti-Semite, is allowed to legislate for the Jewish people who is and is not a Jew.

While many contemporary Jewish philosophers will find Fackenheim's most fundamental theses about authenticity, reason, philosophy, and the future direction of Judaism to be wrong, none find them to be foolish. On the contrary, Fackenheim's writings are the work of a committed Jew who is a first-rate philosopher. Readers of any of the books discussed in this text will have to judge for themselves the diverse claims of modern Jewish philosophy on the basis of their own common sense, their philosophical sophistication, and their Jewish commitment. They should resist name-calling, and not judge anyone who disagrees with them to be inauthentic. They should not be overpowered by any author's prestige or aesthetic use of language. But whatever their conclusions about the truth of the claims of any of the Jewish philosophers discussed in this text, they should remain aware that they are reading first-rate books of Jewish thought by some of the most gifted philosophers in history.

NOTES

1. Emil L. Fackenheim, *The Religious Dimension in Hegel's*

Thought, Boston: Beacon Press, 1970

2. See chapters 5, 15 and 16. Fackenheim calls biblical faith "neo-orthodoxy" after the common title of the Christian religious thought of Karl Barth and Reinhold Niebhur. The parallels between the work of Buber-Rosenzweig and Barth-Niebhur are obvious. All of them are deeply influenced by the language and logic of Hegel's philosophy even in the way that they reject Hegel; and they are profoundly influenced by German biblical criticism, even in the way that they reject that criticism, opting for a form of biblical faith.

3. See chapter 10.

Bloomington: Indiana University Press, 1968. Henceforth called *Quest*.

5. New York: New York University Press, 1970. Henceforth called *Presence*.

6. New York: Basic Books, 1973. Henceforth called *Encounters*.

7. New York: Schocken, 1978. Henceforth called *Return*.

8. New York: Schocken, 1982.

9. See chapter 4.

10. See chapter 7.

11. See chapter 11.

12. *Judaism*, 16, 3 (Summer 1967): 269-273.

13. *Return*, pg. 63.

14. *To Mend The World*, p. 295.

15. See chapter 2.

16. See chapter 4.

17. For example, Rabbi Naḥman of Bratslav. Cf. Arthur Green, *The Tormented Master*. University, Al: University of Alabama Press, 1979.

KEY NAMES

Auschwitz, Hiroshima, Adolph Hitler, Nazi, Franz Rosenzweig, Sachsenhausen, Sinai, Baruch Spinoza, Eli Wiesel.

KEY TERMS

AM YISRAEL CHAI, authentic/inauthentic, Biblical faith, emancipation, epoch-making event, free-Jew in particular/free-man in general, The Holocaust, The inexpressible, K'B'YACHOL, MIDRASH, momentous, MUSELMANNER, neo-orthodoxy, resistance, response, rupture, self-liberation, The 614th Commandment, theophany, TIKKUN.

KEY QUESTIONS

1. Independent of what you think about Fackenheim's claims, why is he a major contemporary Jewish philosopher?

2. What does Fackenheim say about the Holocaust and the State of Israel?

3. According to Fackenheim, how can MIDRASH be used to judge philosophy?

4. How would Fackenheim distinguish between different kinds of Jews? What is his definition of a Jew? Why does he think that the categories liberal, traditional, religious and secular are now obsolete?

5. Why does Fackenheim claim that the Holocaust is an epoch-making event? What new moral demand does it make?

6. Why does Fackenheim claim that the creation of the State of Israel is an epoch-making event?

RECOMMENDED READINGS

General

Robert M. Seltzer, *Jewish People, Jewish Thought: The Jewish Experience in History.* New York: Macmillan, 1980. Chpt. 16, "Diverse Tendencies and Representative Figures: An Overview," pp. 720-728, and "Concluding Remarks," pp. 757-766.

Eugene B. Borowitz, *Choices in Modern Jewish Thought: A Partisan Guide.* New York: Behrman House, 1983. Chpts. 3, 8-12.

Raphael Mahler, *A History of Modern Jewry.* London: Valentine, Mitchell, 1971.

Jewish Philosophy: Primary

Jacques Derrida, *The Archeology of the Frivolous: Reading Condillac.* Translated into English by John P. Leavey, Jr. Pittsburgh: Duquesne University Press, 1980.

———*Edmund Husserl's Origin of Geometry: An Introduction.* Translated into English by David B. Allison. Stony Brook, NY: Nicolas Hays Ltd., 1978.

———*Dissemination.* Translated into English by Barbara Johnson. Chicago: University of Chicago Press, 1981.

———*Eperons: Les styles de Nietzsche.* Translated into English by Barbara Harlow in *Spurs: Nietzsche's Styles.* Chicago: University of Chicago Press, 1979.

———*L'ecriture et la difference.* Paris: Editions du Seuil, 1967.

———*L'ecriture et la difference.* Translated into English by Alan Bass. Chicago: University of Chicago Press, 1978.

———*Margins of Philosophy.* Translated into English by Alan Bass. Chicago: University of Chicago Press, 1982.

———*Of Grammatology.* Translated into English by Gayatri Chakravorty Spivak. Baltimore: John Hopkins University Press, 1976.

———*Positions.* Translated into English by Alan Bass. Chicago: University of Chicago Press, 1981.

———*La voix et le phenomene. Paris: Presses universitaires de France, 1967.* Translated into English by David Allison in *Speech and Phenomena and Other Essays on Husserl's Theory of Signs.* Evanston: Northwestern University Press, 1973.

Emil L. Fackenheim, *Encounters Between Judaism and Modern Philosophy.* New York: Basic Book, 1973.

———*God's Presence in History: Jewish Affirmations, Philosophical Reflections.* New York: New York University Press, 1970.

———*The Jewish Return into History: Reflections in the Age of Auschwitz and a New Jerusalem.* New York: Schocken, 1978.

———*Metaphysics and Historicity.* Milwaukee: Marquette University Press, 1961.

———*Paths to Jewish Relief.* New York: Behrman, 1962.

———*Quest for Past and Future: Essays in Jewish Theology.* Bloomington: Indiana University Press, 1968.

———*To Mend the World: Foundations of Future Jewish Thought.* New York: Schocken, 1982.

Hillel Halkin, *Letters to an American Friend.* Philadelphia: Jewish Publication Society, 1977.

Emmanuel Levinas, *Autrement qu'etre ou au-dela de l'essence.* The

Hague: Martinus Nijhoff, 1974. Translated into English by A. Lingis as *Otherwise than Being or Beyond Essence.* The Hague: Martinus Nijhoff, 1981.

———*En decouvrant l'existence avec Husserl et Heidegger.* Paris: J. Vrin, 1967.

———*Theorie de L'intuition dans la phenomenologie de Husserl.* Paris: Librairie Philosophique, J. Vrin, 1963. Translated into English by Andre Orianne as *The Theory of Intuition in Husserl's Phenomenology.* Evanston: Northwestern University, 1973.

———*Totalite et infini, essai sur l'exterioriste.* The Hague: Martinus Nijhoff, 1968. Translated into English by A. Lingis as *Totality and Infinity.* The Hague: Martinus Nijhoff, 1979.

Norbert M. Samuelson (ed.), *Studies in Jewish Philosophy: Collected Essays of the Academy for Jewish Philosophy, 1980-1985.* Lanham: University Press of America, 1987.

Harold M. Schulweis, *Evil and the Morality of God.* Cincinnati: Hebrew Union College Press, 1984.

Jewish Philosophy: Secondary

Bernard Forthomme, *Une philosophie de la transcendance, La metaphysique d'Emmanuel Levinas.* Paris: La Pensee Universelle, 1979.

W. Krwietz, et al. (eds). *Argumentation und Hermeneutik in der Jurisprudenz, Rechtstheories.* Beiheft 1. Berlin: Duncker & Humbolt, 1979.

Thomas McCarthy, *The Critical Theory of J. Habermas.* Cambridge, MA.: M.I.T. Press, 1981.

Winfried Menninghaus, *W. Benjamins Theorie der Sprachmagie.* Frankfurt a.M: Suhrkamp, 1980.

Stephen Strasser, *Jenseits von Sein und Zeit, Eine Einfuehrung in Emmanuel Levinas' Philosophie.* The Hague: Martinus Nijhoff, 1978.

Jewish Theology: Primary

Eliezer Berkovits, *Major Themes in Modern Philosophies of Judaism.* New York: Ktav, 1974.

Eugene B. Borowitz, *How Can A Jew Speak of Faith Today?* Philadelphia: Westminster, 1969.

———*Liberal Judaism.* New York: Union of American Hebrew Congregations, 1984.

————The Mask Jews Wear: The Self-Deception of American Jewry. New York: Simon and Schuster, 1973.

————A New Jewish Theology in the Making. Philadelphia: Westminster, 1968.

Arthur A. Cohen, Natural and Supernatural Jew. New York: Pantheon, 1962.

Samuel H. Dresner, Between the Generations. Bridgeport, CT: Hartmore House, 1971.

————The Sabbath. New York: The Burning Bush Press, 1970.

Robert Gordis, Judaism for the Modern Age. New York: Farrar, Straus, and Cudahy, 1955.

————The Root and the Branch: Judaism and the Free Society. Chicago: University of Chicago Press, 1962.

Louis Jacobs, A Jewish Theology. New York: Behrman, 1973.

————Faith. New York: Basic Books, 1968.

————Jewish Thought Today. New York: Behrman, 1970.

————Principles of the Jewish Faith. New York: Basic Books, 1964.

Lawrence Kushner, The River of Light: Spirituality, Judaism, and the Evolution of Consciousness. Chappaqua, New York: Rossel Books, 1981.

Norman Lamm, Faith & Doubt: Studies in Traditional Jewish Thought. New York: Ktav, 1968.

Zalman I. Posner, Think Jewish: A Contemporary View of Judaism, a Jewish View of Today's World. Nashville: Kesher Press, 1978.

Zalman M. Schachter-Shalomi with Donald Gropman, The First Step: A Guide for the New Jewish Spirit. New York: Bantam Books, 1983.

Zalman M. Schachter, Fragments of a Future Scroll: Hassidism for the Aquarian Age. Edited by Philip Mandelkorn & Stephen Gerstman. Germantown, PA: Leaves of Grass Press, 1975.

————and Edward Hoffman, Sparks of Light: Spiritual Counselling in the Hasidic Tradition. New York: Shambala & Random House, 1983.

Joseph B. Soloveitchick, Halakhic Man. Philadelphia: Jewish Publication Society of America, 1984.

————On Repentance. Translated into English by Pinchas Peli. New York: Paulist Press. 1984.

————Shiurei Harav: A Conspectus of the Public Lectures of Rabbi Joseph B. Soloveitchik. New York: Hamevaser, 1974.

Moshe Halevi Spero, Judaism and Psychology: Halakhic Perspectives. New York: Ktav and Yeshiva University Press, 1980.

Arthur I. Waskow, God-Wrestling. New York: Schocken, 1978.

Arnold Jacob Wolf (ed.), *Rediscovering Judaism*. Chicago: Quadrangle, 1965.

Jewish Theology: Secondary

Abraham R. Besdin, *Reflections of the Rav: Lessons in Jewish Thought adapted by Lectures of Rabbi Joseph B. Soloveitchik*. New York: Department of Torah Education & Culture, World Zionist Organization, 1979.

Alter B.Z. Metzger, *Rabbi Kook's Philosophy of Repentance*. New York: Yeshiva University Press, 1968.

Holocaust Theology: Primary

Eliezer Berkovits, *Faith After the Holocaust*. New York: Ktav, 1973.

———*God, Man and History*. New York: Jonathan David, 1959.

———*Not in Heaven: The Nature and Function of Halakha*. New York: Ktav, 1983.

———*With God in Hell: Judaism in the Ghettos and Deathcamps*. New York: Sanhedrin Press, 1979.

Steven T. Katz, *Post-Holocaust Dialogues: Critical Studies in Modern Jewish Thought*. New York: New York University Press, 1983.

Richard L. Rubenstein, *After Auschwitz*. Indianapolis: Bobbs-Merrill, 1986.

———*The Age of Triage*. Boston: Beacon Press, 1984.

———*Morality & Eros*. New York: McGraw-Hill, 1970.

———*The Religious Imagination*. Indianapolis: Bobbs-Merrill, 1968.

Rosemary Ruether, *Faith and Fracticide*. New York: Seabury Press, 1974.

Elie Wiesel, *Dawn*. New York: Hill and Wang, 1961.

———*Night*. New York: Avon, 1960.

———*The Town Beyond the Wall*. Translated into English by Stephen Becker. New York: Avon, 1964.

Holocaust Theology: Secondary

Jack Riemer (ed.), *Jewish Reflections on Death*. New York: Schocken, 1975.

Alvin H. Rosenfeld, *A Double Dying: Reflections on Holocaust Literature*. Bloomington: Indiana University Press, 1975.

Alvin H. Rosenfeld and Irving Greenberg (eds.), *Confronting the Holocaust*. Bloomington: Indiana University Press, 1978.

Jewish Ethics: Primary

Jacob R. Agus, *The Vision and the Way: An Interpretation of Jewish Ethics.* New York: Frederick Ungar, 1966.

Gersion Appel, *A Philosophy of Mitzvot: The Religious-Ethical Concepts of Judaism, Their Roots in Biblical Law and the Oral Tradition.* New York: Ktav, 1975.

Simon Bernfeld, *The Foundations of Jewish Ethics.* New York: Ktav, 1968.

J. David Bleich, *Contemporary Halakhic Problems.* New York: Ktav, 1977.

Eugene B. Borowitz, *Choosing a Sex Ethic.* New York: Schocken, 1969.

Henry Cohen, *Justice, Justice: A Jewish View of the Negro Revolt.* New York: Union of American Hebrew Congregations, 1968.

Samuel H. Dresner, *God, Man and Atomic War.* New York: Living Books, 1966.

Marvin Fox (ed.), *Modern Jewish Ethics: Theory and Practice.* Columbus: Ohio State University Press, 1975.

Robert Gordis, *Great Moral Dilemmas.* New York: Harper, 1956.

Louis Jacobs, *Jewish Ethics, Philosophy and Mysticism.* New York: Behrman, 1969.

———*Jewish Law.* New York: Behrman, 1968.

———*Jewish Values.* London: Vallentine Mitchell, 1960.

Menachem Marc Kellner (ed.), *Contemporary Jewish Ethics.* New York: Sanhedrin Press, 1978.

David Novak, *Law and Theology in Judaism.* New York: Ktav, 1974.

Fred Rosner and J. David Bleich (eds.), *Jewish Bioethics.* New York: Sanhedrin Press, 1979.

Fred Rosner, *Modern Medicine and Jewish Law.* New York: Yeshiva University Press, 1972.

Daniel Jeremy Silver (ed.), *Judaism and Ethics.* New York: Ktav, 1970.

Arthur I. Waskow, *The Bush is Burning: Radical Judaism Faces the Pharaohs of the Modern Superstate.* New York: Macmillan, 1971.

The State of Israel

Yoella Har-Shefi, *Beyond the Gunsights: One Arab Family in the Promised Land.* New York: Houghton Mifflin, 1980.

David Polish, *Israel—Nation and People.* New York: Ktav, 1975.

Gideon Hausner, *Justice in Jerusalem.* New York: Harper & Row, 1966.

Judaism and Christianity

David Berger and Michael Wyschogrod, *Jews and 'Jewish Christianity'.* New York: Ktav, 1979.
Eugene B. Borowitz, *Contemporary Christologies: A Jewish Response.* New York: Paulist Press, 1980.
Arthur A. Cohen, *The Myth of the Judeo-Christian Tradition.* New York: Schocken, 1971.
A. Roy Eckardt, *Your People, My People: The Meeting of Jews and Christians.* New York: Antidefamation League, 1977.
Paul Van Buren, *The Burden of Freedom: Americans and the God of Israel.* New York: Seabury, 1976.
————*Discerning the Way: A Theology of the Jewish Christian Reality.* New York: Seabury, 1980.
Michael Wyschograd, *Body of Faith: Judaism as Corporeal Election.* New York: Seabury Press, 1983.

Additional General Readings in Contemporary Jewish Philosophy: Primary

Jacob B. Agus, *Jewish Quest: Essays on the Basic Concepts of Jewish Theology.* New York: Ktav, 1983.
————*Modern Philosophies of Judaism.* New York: Behrman, 1941.
Leo Baeck, *The Essence of Judaism.* New York: Schocken, 1948.
Will Herberg, *Judaism and Modern Man.* New York: Macmillan, 1951.
————*Protestant-Catholic-Jew: An Essay in American Religious Sociology.* Garden City, New York: Doubleday, 1960.
Abraham J. Heschel, *A Passion for Truth.* New York: Farrar, Straus and Giroux, 1973.
————*Between God and Man: An Interpretation of Judaism.* Edited by Fritz A. Rothschild. New York: The Free Press, 1976.
————*God in Search of Man: A Philosophy of Judaism.* New York: Harper and Row, 1955.
————*The Insecurity of Freedom: Essays in Applied Religion.* New York: Farrar, Straus and Giroux, 1965.
————*Israel: An Echo of Eternity.* New York: Farrar, Straus, and Giroux, 1969.
————*Man is Not Alone: A Philosophy of Religion.* New York: Harper and Row, 1951.

————*Man's Quest for God; Studies in Prayer and Symbolism.* New York: Scribner's, 1954

————*The Prophets.* Philadelphia: Jewish Publication Society of America, 1962.

————*The Sabbath.* New York: Farrar, Straus and Young, 1951.

————*Who Is Man?* Stanford: Stanford University Press, 1965.

Max Kadushin, *Worship and Ethics.* Evanston, IL: Northwestern University Press, 1964.

Henry Slonimsky, *Essays.* Chicago: Quadrangle, 1967.

Milton Steinberg, *The Making of the Modern Jew.* New York: Behrman, 1944.

The Condition of Jewish Belief, A Symposium Compiled by the Editors of Commentary Magazine. New York: Macmillan, 1969.

Additional General Readings in Contemporary Jewish Philosophy: Secondary

Leonard Baker, *Days of Sorrow and Pain: Leo Baeck and the Berlin Jews.* New York: Oxford University Press, 1978.

Eliezer Berkovitz, *Major Themes in Modern Philosophies of Judaism.* New York: Ktav, 1974.

Joseph L. Blau, *Judaism in America.* Chicago: University of Chicago Press, 1979.

Peter Gay, *Freud, Jews and Other Germans.* New York: Oxford University Press, 1978.

Nahum Glatzer (ed.), *On Judaism.* New York: Schocken, 1967.

Steven T. Katz, *Jewish Ideas and Concepts.* New York: Schocken, 1977.

————*Jewish Philosophers.* New York: Bloch, 1975.

William E. Kaufman, *Contemporary Jewish Philosophies.* New York: Reconstructionist Press & Behrman, 1976.

Bernard Martin (ed.), *Contemporary Reform Jewish Thought.* Chicago: Quadrangle Books, 1968.

Nathan Rotenstreich, *Tradition and Reality.* New York: Randon House, 1972.

————*Jewish Philosophy in Modern Times.* New York: Holt, Reinhart, and Winston, 1968.

Byron L. Sherwin, *Abraham Joshua Heschel: Makers of Contemporary Theology.* Atlanta: John Knox Press, 1979.

Name Index

Subject Index